It Isn't Difficult to Do It *if* You Know How to Do It

A Compendium of the Most Important Tips You Should Know to Succeed in High School, College and in Life

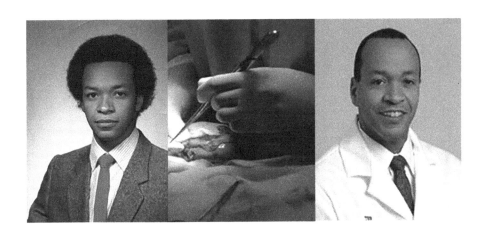

D1548207

Charles S. Modlin, MD, MBA

NEWMAN SPRINGS PUBLISHING
320 Broad Street
Red Bank, NJ 07701

First originally published by Newman Springs Publishing 2020

ISBN 978-1-64801-837-4 (Paperback)
ISBN 978-1-64801-838-1 (Digital)

Printed in the United States of America

To my late parents, Charles and Grace Modlin, to whom I am indebted. I thank God for bringing me into this world as their child. I am grateful for the love (necessary tough love in some instances) and life lessons they provided me. I am thankful for the countless sacrifices they made so that my sisters and I, as well as my nephews, cousins, church community, and others, might have a better life than afforded to them. Throughout this book, I recognize my parents' contributions to my growth, development, and successes.

Also to my siblings, Beverly Williams, Deborah Edmunds, Rebecca Modlin, and Pamela Modlin. We had wonderful times growing up together. Sisters, I cannot express or articulate how important you were to me growing up. The simple act of daydreaming with you, lying in our backyard among the dandelion cloud and stargazing, singing, riding bikes, swimming, going to "the Beach" (which was an historic black church in Carthage, Indiana, near where my mother grew up, not a real beach), and playing hopscotch, ghost-in-the-graveyard, four-square, monopoly, and countless other games as well as learning from how you each individually endured the challenges we faced instrumentally helped me grow and achieve the self-esteem necessary for me to persevere in my personal and professional pursuits.

I am indebted to my late grandmother, Clara Hampton, who lived to the ripe old age of 103 years old. I give credit to her in addition to my parents for making me realize and recognize at a very young age the importance of family and that I must always remember from whence I came, as well as helping me realize that I as a young black kid am special. I enjoyed her stories of the past and how she was raised on a farm. She was born in 1888 and stood six feet tall and was a strong woman who had endured and overcome many obstacles in life. It's amazing when I think about it, but she was already seventy-three years old when I was born, so much of what I recall of her in my impressionable years was when she was already well into her seventies and eighties. I recall fondly her sitting with us, cooking for us, and keeping us in line when we were sometimes unruly as young kids. As I reflect, for her to have been able to do this at her age was nothing less than remarkable. In spite of the many injustices she endured, she always saw the best in people and was always ready and willing to lend a helping hand to anyone whom she could help. I recall that whenever one of her neighbor friends on Twenty-Third Street were sick, she would worry immensely about them and take them food and sit with them. My grandmother also helped to develop my sense of empathy for others, which has guided me to this day to try and place the feelings of others ahead of my own. I am human and have not always succeeded at this task, but because of my grandmother Clara Hampton and my parents, I have tried and recognized the importance of doing so.

Grandmother Clara Hampton age one hundred years old

Grandmother Clara Hampton's hundredth-year birthday
party, New Castle, Indiana, February 2, 1988

I am indebted also to my aunt Mildred Faye, who in 2016 passed away on her ninetieth birthday. She was a schoolteacher, ahead of her time, in the Indianapolis Public Schools district. Her support, encouragement, and recognition of my accomplishments were additional confirmation that my family believed in me and held great expectations for my successfulness. I thank my departed aunt Sarah Virginia Hampton, Uncle Gerald "Buddy," Grandfather Wayman Modlin, Eva Ross, Terry Ross, Nancy Thompson, Ella Hill, and my cousins Gene Wilson, Kevin Varnado, Jeff, Jenny, Benita Kay, and Mitsy Basset and countless others for the contributions they made to me during my childhood and beyond. I thank the church community of Wiley United Methodist Church, of New Castle, Indiana, in which I was raised, as well as the many members of the Bethel AME Church of New Castle, Indiana.

To the thousands of people whom I have encountered during my lifetime and who contributed to my personal and professional development. I apologize that space limitations in this book do not allow me to individually list everyone I wish to, but I wish to specifically acknowledge my special friends, role models, and mentors who enriched my life tremendously and who helped keep me on track to achieve my set goals.

I am indebted to you all—Mr. Jeff Ayres, Mr. Ian Sheeler, Mr. David Hamilton, Mr. Henry Pak, Dr. John Shaird, John Herndon, Dr. David Eckman, David Zott, Dr. Robert Stevenson, Dr. Steven Yu, Dr. Yan Wolfson, Dr. Richard Maggio, Dr. Jeffrey Rosenblum, Dr. Subu Dubey, Dr. Paul Field, Dr. Paul Caldron, Dr. James Holland, Dr. Stuart Flechner, Dr. Craig Zippe, Mr. Robert Allen, and Carlumandarlo Zaramo, PhD, and Alan Clark, PhD, and Lateef Saffore, PhD.

Special thanks also go to my children, Charles "Trey" Modlin, Sarah Modlin, Hannah Modlin, and Meredith Modlin and Sheryl Fridie Modlin, MD, the mother of my four children, whom I met in 1983 in medical school and married in 1987.

Contents

A NOTE TO THE READERS OF THIS BOOK REGARDING THE USE OF THE WORD "PARENTS"

In recognition that not all students live in situations with or have access to their biological parents, and that many students have been and/or are currently being raised by other caregivers or providers, and in recognition that there are sensitivities held by some people regarding the use of the word *parents*, please note that in the imperative to publish this book so that it get into the hands of the students and other readers in a timely fashion so they can start to put these success tips into action in their own lives, the word *parents* (other than when I am referring to my own parents) is understood to be interchangeable and inclusive with the words *providers*, *guardians*, *caregivers*, and *caretakers*. This is also reflected in the title of chapter 14.

Thank you,
Charles Modlin, MD, MBA

Forward

Moral character and integrity are rare commodities these days. So when you find them in an individual it's a gift that you will want to give to yourself and others.

Dr. Charles S. Modlin, Jr., or as my younger brother I'll refer to him as Charlie, possesses those rare character traits that have given him the strength and courage to pursue his dream of being a physician. But he didn't stop there. Charlie is a rarity because he pursued a specialty that few in the Black Community of physicians have dared. Beyond that he has given back to his community in selfless ways including mentoring young people of color to pursue their dreams in the medical field as well. And if that weren't enough he and his wife have raised 4 brilliant children.

But Charlie knows he didn't do this alone. I believe he would want me to bestow credit upon our ancestors including our parents Charles S. Modlin, Sr. and Grace Hampton Modlin for their willingness to do whatever it took to raise their children with the values and morals to be grateful for what we have and to always give back to our communities.

Our father Charles S. Modlin, Sr. gave us this quote to live by, "Nothing in life is work; it's all exercise." He was a proud member of the US Navy during WWII. He was a father, husband, brother, uncle, multiple gold medal champion and record holder as a USA Senior Games participant in every event he entered (100m, 200m, 400m and long jump) for many years and proud role model and citizen of his community and of the world.

Our mother Grace Hampton Modlin was the first Black teacher in Henry County Indiana graduating from Ball State University with a Master's of Elementary Education degree while raising 5 children. She was a Brownie Leader, supporter of the downtrodden (taking in children from neighborhoods in Chicago, IL raised in poverty to live with us in our very small and modest home several summers while we were children). She was a mother, wife, sister, aunt and proud citizen of her community and of the world.

They were also healthy voices and role models during the civil rights movement, which gave Charlie and their other children a voice to accomplish many things.

Now that doesn't mean Charlie was or is perfect. Growing up he just seemed like my little brother doing little brother things with his friends. One notable memory is when he put a salamander in the bathtub that he and his friend found in our backyard. He knew very well I was going to take a bath and I bet you can guess my reaction. So, never once did I know he aspired to such greatness, but I wasn't surprised when I learned of his plans and never doubted he would succeed.

So this prose is meant to help the reader understand that a boy born to modest means because he stood on the shoulders of greatness was able to succeed in life and so can you. I hope you'll take the time to read it with intention because I guarantee you that is how it was written and that is a rare gift indeed!

Debbie Edmunds, MA, LPC-S, CART
H.O.P.E. Psychotherapy of Houston, PLLC
www.HopePsychotherapyOfHouston.com
281-373-5200

Charles Modlin, M.D., MBA

One of the signature benefits of involvement in any alumni association is the opportunity to meet and engage with alumni from different generations. So it was during my participation with the Northwestern University Feinberg School of Medicine (NUFSM) Alumni Association that I met Charles Modlin, MD, and became aware of his notable dedication to his profession, his community, students of all ages, and his Northwestern Alma Mater, having received both undergraduate and medical degrees. This commitment resulted in his leadership in the establishment, with his classmates, of their Medical School Class of 1987 Endowed Scholarship for Northwestern medical students in need. It was also during his two terms on the NUFSM Alumni Board that Charles was inducted as a member of the Alpha Omega Alpha Medical Honor Society. Because of his continued involvement with Northwestern and NUFSM in so many ways over the years, the university awarded him the coveted Northwestern Alumni Merit Award in recognition of all of his professional accomplishments. The readers of this motivational book will come to know of Charles's dedication to underserved communities with respect to his kidney transplant surgery and urology expertise. In addition, they will clearly realize the ultimate life benefits of commitment to scholarship, hard work, and concern for others. Finally, I am sure any student will feel duly mentored by this successful individual, Dr. Modlin, who overcame so many obstacles and challenges on his way to fulfilling his professional dream.

Andrew D. Bunta, MD
Associate Professor, Department of Orthopaedic Surgery, NUFSM
Northwestern University Feinberg School of Medicine, 1964, 1967
NUFSM Alumni Board President, 2001–2003

Mentorship is indispensable for any lifelong pursuit. After having been rejected from medical school in two separate application cycles, discouragement and frustration nearly set in but my relationship with Dr. Modlin gave me renewed hope. As a black male trying to navigate healthcare and the medical school application process, assisting Dr. Modlin in his work within the community to improve the health outcomes of minority men was both refreshing and awe-inspiring. I will never forget how one of the men Dr. Modlin served through the Minority Men's Health Fair at the Cleveland Clinic told me that had he not participated he did not think he would be alive today. Working with Dr. Modlin allowed me to realize precisely what I wanted to do as a future physician and for that I am thankful. If you are a student in pursuit of accomplishing a dream or succeeding in whatever you do, I strongly encourage you to read this book for valuable insights and understandings on how to achieve success in your life journey.

Marcus Wright | MD MBA Candidate
Tulane University School of Medicine | Class of 2024

Dr. Modlin has included in this book excellent topics that are especially valuable for all the kids we are working with in our Civic K-12 Education programs at Cleveland Clinic.

Nedra Starling, MA, MPH, DrPH/ABD
Program Manager for Youth Education
Community Health & Partnerships Department

I connected with Dr. Charles Modlin, as a college freshman. I had no family members in medicine but found in Dr. Modlin an invaluable role model and mentor. Dr. Modlin embodies the call to service. His dedication to meeting the needs of undeserved patient populations continues to serve as a source of inspiration. He has paved an extraordinary road—and remains committed to mentoring the next generation of health disparities leaders and innovators. I believe his stories and guidance will touch you, as they have touched my own life.

A Samba Northwestern University, College of Arts
& Sciences Religious Studies Graduate, 2017

The first time I met Dr. Modlin, he just wrapped up 14 hours of surgery, and trudged through two feet of snow to make our 9:00 a.m. Worldwide Classroom connected learning experience, where he dazzled over 800 students with a lecture and video educational session about kidney transplantation replacement surgery. He's tireless in his pursuit and passion for mentoring and educating youth, and that snowy day he truly proved it. He's done countless education and connected learning sessions with middle and high school students and has been a mentor to literally hundreds of interns. The middle and high school students that participate in Cleveland Clinic's Youth Programs light up when they come into Dr. Modlin's orbit. His enthusiasm for health education and mentoring is infectious and our students are drawn to him. I can't remember a time when he doesn't have an intern in tow, he's always willing to serve as a mentor, and always willing to participate as an educator when we run connected learning programs. He's tireless in his pursuit and passion for mentoring and educating youth and we're fortunate to have as our "go-to" caregiver for our youth programs.

Tom Miller
Manager, Connected Learning
Cleveland Clinic Youth Programs

"I still can recall the first time I met Dr. Modlin, it was during my first few weeks as a medical student. He took the initiative to introduce himself and encouraged me to reach out to him. It was this enthusiasm and commitment that has made Dr. Modlin one of my most valued mentors and role models throughout my journey in medicine and the field of urology. He truly embodies all of the characteristics of an effective mentor and I would advise all students to utilize this book as a guide to success.

Lamont Wilkins, MD
Urologic Surgery Resident
Johns Hopkins"

"In the Black community we often say that it takes a village to raise a child—well Dr. Modlin was definitely a part of my village. Growing up as friends with his daughter, I remember sleeping over at their house and being intrigued by his work in healthcare and all the community work he was involved in. Even with a demanding job he always made time to converse with me and would be at the majority of his children's events (…probably with some type of video camera lol). Even though I did not study healthcare at Hampton University, I quickly learned how powerful Black doctors are in our healthcare system. However, Dr. Modlin's passion for healthcare transcends into the community, which will always be a part of his legacy. Now as I am in the beginning of my career in Cleveland, I value the moments when we are in the same meetings and I can directly learn from him as a community leader. Dr. Modlin shows us that success is not about how much money you make but the legacy and impact you leave in your community. If you desire to not only be successful but also a change agent—I highly encourage you to read this book! Thank you, Dr. Modlin for being an example for Black change agents—Tiara Sargeant, Student Group on Race Relations Adviser

Gladys "Tiara" Sargeant
Hampton University '18
216-978-5981
tiarajeanae.com

I began working with Dr. Modlin early in my undergraduate career. During that time, my interest in medicine was the result of an interest in science combined with a goal of helping others. Through shadowing Dr. Modlin and his mentorship, my desire to become a physician become a concrete goal that I wanted with all my heart. Watching him practice and learning from him showed me the truth behind being a physician and I knew that I wanted nothing more. Luckily, through his continued encouragement and guidance, he showed me the path to accomplishing that goal. I am finally in the midst of starting my career and I couldn't be happier. I also know that I would not have made it to this point without Dr. Modlin's mentorship. I highly encourage all to read this book as a guide to your own road to success. Mentorship is an extremely important part of any career path and Dr. Modlin is truly an expert in the field.

Ashley Grimes
First Year Medical Student
Ohio State University College of Medicine

Dear Student,

I have had the pleasure of working with Dr. Charles Modlin over the past six years. Though I was only a sophomore in college when we first met, Dr. Modlin took the initiative to orient me to minority health disparities and engage me with clinical research in this area. In the years that followed, we were able to present this work on minority perspectives on organ donation at conferences and publish a paper in *The Journal of Racial and Ethnic Health Disparities*. I have learned how to be an inquisitive and culturally sensitive investigator under the guidance of Dr. Modlin, which ultimately motivated me to enter medical school. Dr. Modlin's work in the Cleveland Clinic Minority Men's Health Center, which he founded in 2003, is critically important, and should inspire others to address disparities in their communities. Please use this book as a roadmap as you consider your future and your ability to foster a more equitable society.

—Bryan Naelitz, MS

Working under Dr. Modlin has truly been a significant part of my educational career. Having the opportunity to work and learn under such a passionate physician has been invaluable, as the lessons he has taught me about medicine, life and mentorship has paved the way in my own role as a mentor. Moreover, Dr. Modlin inspired me because he constantly goes above and beyond to teach me new things even if it has nothing to do with medicine and I aspire to do the same for others in my career. Dr. Modlin is an amazing role model, mentor and friend and I owe a big part of my success to his care and support throughout the years.

This book truly outlines the dedication and care that is needed in the world today and I encourage all at any stage to read!

Thank you,
Taborah Zaramo B.S
The Ohio State University College of Medicine C/O 2023

During the summer of 2015, I was privileged to work with Dr. Charles Modlin. As his intern, Dr. Modlin was sure to teach me all he could about the technical aspects of his work—allowing me to watch his surgeries and help to develop his survey project surrounding health disparities. And the experience could have ended there. But Dr. Modlin went above and beyond to mentor me, investing his time and knowledge to help me grow and prepare for my future. He pushed me to work my hardest in school, and inspired me to explore healthcare for minorities, which led me to study psychology.

Dr. Modlin has achieved so much success in his life as a leader in his field as one of only a handful of African American kidney transplant surgeons in America. He showed me that it is possible to achieve greatness no matter one's background. He is an amazing mentor, teacher, and role model, and absolutely a resource to anyone who wants to discover how to reach their highest potential.

Dana Harris
Princeton University
Psychology, 2021

"Dr Modlin's own success makes him an authority on how to become successful. We served as Urological Surgery Residents together in a very demanding program at New York University Medical Center and Bellevue Hospital. He was always a hard worker as well as a team player who put the well-being of his patients first. His care and compassion was palpable."

Dr. Richard Maggio, Urological Surgeon

I have known Dr. Modlin for over 30 years. If there was anyone who knows the meaning of achievement and success, it would be Charles. I remember the gleam in his eyes when there was a goal to be attained, and the joy when we got there. To this day, he has always been my role model and my best friend. Always look ahead, there are higher highs to scale, and Charles will be leading the pack.

Dr. Steven Yu, Urological Surgeon

My name is Nathaniel H. Reese Jr., I am the District MAC (Minority Achieving) Scholars Coordinator and teacher in the Shaker Heights City School District. I would first like to commend Dr. Charles Modlin on writing a long overdue book which is dedicated to mentoring those who will be leaders in the not-so-distant future. I have been a mentor to our youth for more than thirty years. Throughout that journey, I met Dr. Modlin. I respected him from day one. He has been an inspiration to people of all ages and backgrounds. He has especially been an excellent mentor, role model, and teacher as it pertains to the medical field as well as life in general. The fact that he has written this book as a guide for high school and college students demonstrates his dedication to assisting others in their efforts to be successful.

Mr. Nat Reese: Teacher, Shaker Heights City Schools

"Dr. Charles Modlin is a paragon of what it takes to succeed despite adversity. Growing up in mostly rural white central Indiana, Dr. Modlin had to overcome racism, adverse economic conditions and a system that did not encourage young black students to succeed. Despite those disadvantages, Dr. Modlin was able to overcome these adversities to receive both a bachelor's degree and a medical degree from Northwestern University. We were undergraduate students together. After a residency at NYU, he went to the Cleveland Clinic where he became the first black urologist and first black transplant surgeon in the nearly 100-year history of Cleveland Clinic and one of the few black transplant surgeons in the country. Today, Dr. Modlin is Executive Director of Minority Health at Cleveland Clinic where he founded and runs the Minority Men's Health Initiative where he has achieved multiple awards and acclaim in his work in fighting minority health disparities."

Henry Pak, M.S., MBA Northwestern University,
Technological Engineering Graduate, 1984,
Northwestern University Kellogg-McCormick
Graduate School of Management, 1996

I have known Dr. Modlin (Charlie) since I was very young. I can honestly say that had it not been for his kindness and encouragement I would neither be the person I am nor would I have ever gone to college. Once I was in college he encouraged me to continue and never give up. He has been both a lifelong friend and an inspiration to me my whole life, and his advice is and always has been the most valuable insights I have ever experienced.

Ian Sheeler
Lecturer in Communications, Indiana University
Purdue University Indianapolis (IUPUI)

Serving as a mentee under Dr. Charles Modlin has been an eye-opening experience. He has taught me so much about the field of medicine, kidney transplant surgery, and urology. Mentors are an important resource to have especially if you are entering a field that is unfamiliar to you. Dr. Modlin is amongst one of my most influential mentors I have had and he has served as a source of encouragement throughout my medical school application process. I am grateful to have studied under him. As a result of his mentorship & guidance, I was motivated to start my own business, www.mdme404.com, to help mentor other low-income pre-medicine students interested in pursuing a career in medicine.

Shami-Iyabo Mitchell
B.S. Biology, Spelman College c/o 2019
M.S. Bioethics, Columbia University c/o 2020
Case Western University School of Medicine, Class of 2025

"Dr. Modlin served as my mentor beginning in 2014 during a Cleveland Clinic internship for high school students of color. He was instrumental in reinforcing my interest in medicine and stimulating an interest in healthcare disparities. His genuine interest in helping students navigate their pre-health interests and caring for those in his community are just two examples of the many reasons I recommend students use this book as a guide on their own pre-health journeys.

Lyndsi Powell, B.A.
University of Pennsylvania, 2019"

I was fortunate enough to have the opportunity to have Dr. Charles Modlin as my mentor for two years through the Cleveland Clinic Summer Internship Program. Dr. Modlin was a great mentor who helped me to develop my professional skills, assisted me in meeting and working with caretakers, and introduced me to shadowing opportunities in other departments. Dr. Modlin has been an invaluable mentor to me and countless other students. I encourage other students to read this book, and to use it as a helpful guide on your way to success.

Caitlin Spicer
Student, First Year, University of Dayton

"My experience with Dr.Modlin for the two years I worked with him is an irreplaceable one. He was a great mentor, role model, and teacher. This book will give students and others both a roadmap and a guide to use on their own journey to success."

Jannat Ali
John Carroll University, Premedical

Dr. Modlin is an upstanding figure and true role model. He mentored me and helped show me the importance of giving back to your community. He exemplifies how leaders also can have heart. I recommend his advice to anyone who is seeking to make a difference in the world.

Maggie Sawyer, teacher, University of
Pennsylvania '21, Haverford College '19.

Dr. Modlin played a very instrumental role in helping me find my path in medicine. He has provided me with valuable mentorship and he allowed me to shadow him in his clinicals and in surgery. I recommend all students to read this book and use this book as a guide during your own journey to success.

Layla Joseph
Stanford University, BA Human Biology
& Medical Humanities, 2020
Research Assistant, Feinberg School of Medicine
Department of Medical Social Sciences

While I was a pre-medical high school and college student, I shadowed Dr. Modlin in multiple medical settings, including outpatient visits, minor procedures, transplant surgeries, and post-surgical visits with hospitalized patients. Dr. Modlin has been a strong role model not just from the things he taught me directly, such as the health disparities that Black men experience with prostate cancer outcomes, but from the empathetic qualities that I observed in him when he interacted with patients and colleagues. He showed me how he put his goals into action, by connecting me with younger pre-medical students or inviting me to volunteer in the annual Minority Men's Health Fair that he organized. Dr. Modlin is down-to-earth and honest about the challenges he has faced, and I am grateful for his mentorship. While there are many unique paths to take in one's professional career, I encourage you to use this book as a guide as you seek out mentors and plan your own journey to success.

Spencer Seballos
Medical student, Cleveland Clinic Lerner
College of Medicine, Class of 2021

As a high school student, I had the opportunity to work with Dr. Modlin during a summer internship program at the Cleveland Clinic. Throughout the program, Dr. Modlin became an invaluable mentor who shaped how I approach my life to this day. As someone who has spent his career addressing health disparities in minority populations, Dr. Modlin taught me the importance of pursuing a career that can have a meaningful impact on people. While I ultimately went on to study electrical engineering at Harvard University, I continue to employ the lessons that Dr. Modlin taught me in my work today. I encourage any student looking for a role model to learn from the valuable wisdom Dr. Modlin has to offer.

Jordan Canedy
Product Manager at Google
Harvard University Graduate

Dr. Modlin was my research mentor for the Cleveland Clinic Internship program when I was a junior in high school. He was the best mentor I have ever had and is the reason why I decided to pursue my career in medicine. Whenever there were surgeries he would allow us to observe and explained everything he was doing so we would be able to understand him even though we do not have the vast amount of medical knowledge that he does. Dr. Modlin has an extremely busy work schedule, but he always makes time to help people and do as many volunteer projects as he can. By interning with Dr. Modlin

I was also able to learn all about the health disparities happening in society today and ways to combat them. Dr. Modlin helped me solidify my decision in becoming a physician and I am honored that I was able to have such a caring and respectable physician as my mentor.

Krithika Sundaram, Loyola University

"I have known Dr. Charles Modlin and his family for about 14 years and over that time I have had a chance to experience the many wonders he has been able to achieve throughout his professional career. Dr. Modlin is a leader in his field, a talented professional and most importantly he is a true champion of support for others. I look to Dr. Modlin for mentorship and advice often and understand that his guidance has motivated me and helped me to overcome challenges in my own life. I can recall walking the halls of the Cleveland Clinic alongside Dr. Modlin during shadowing opportunities, as he would then share words of wisdom and encouragement specifically speaking about navigating the hierarchies of an organization. Furthermore, as one of only a handful of black transplant surgeons in the United States, I am particularly intrigued by his interest in minority health and have watched his innovative thoughts grow into what is now a nationally recognized event in the Minority Men's Health Fair hosted by Dr. Modlin and the Minority Men's Health Center at the Cleveland Clinic. Dr. Charles Modlin has tremendous follow up and is always willing to step in and lend a hand whenever available. I am proud to support Dr. Charles Modlin and wish all the best in every area he pursues."

Aaron C. Kinney, Ohio State University

I was very fortunate to have the incredible opportunity to work with Dr. Modlin closely as my mentor beginning in my early ages of high school.

Throughout the years Dr. Modlin shared the external and internal pressures of creating a purposeful life—anxieties, quandaries, joys and accomplishments, big or small. Dr. Modlin's tenor is sincere, but yet his inquiry and feedback are constructive. He listens carefully and challenges you to strive for everything you are trying to accomplish. His ability to bring out the best in each of his students is truly remarkable. He encourages you to take risks, poses questions that really make you think, and most importantly provides an atmosphere of support.

I'll never forget him asking me, "whose shoulders do you stand on?" and then proceed with a presentation before his next kidney procurement. Where would I truly be without his teachings, lessons and resilience? I thank you for all your support and guidance. I would strongly encourage anyone still searching for mentorship with tangible results to read this book. Learn from this book. Study this book! You are the best, and now I see some of your reflections in myself.

—Mariah Howard, B.S. Molecular Genetics, Ohio State University, CEO & Founder of Made Marketing Agency Inc.

Preface

When my middle daughter, Hannah Grace, was just three years old, her nanny, Mrs. Carolyn Jackson, whom our kids affectionately called "C," was sitting in the living room watching Hannah play a video game. It was the *Crash Team Racing* video game, which required Hannah to use two hands to operate the video console to manipulate the fast-moving car in the game around multiple obstacles on the raceway. Mrs. Jackson was observing Hannah sitting in her little blue chair playing the game. Hannah didn't say a word but was immersed and focused on playing her video game so that she could score as many points as possible. C, after a while, said, "Hannah, that game looks very difficult to do. Is it difficult to do?" Hannah, even though she was immersed in playing the game, was obviously listening to C because she immediately, without taking her eyes off the video screen and while continuing to play to game, responded to the question by clearly and emphatically answering, "It isn't difficult to do it if you know how to do it." Hannah's statement led Mrs. Jackson and I to laugh followed by conversations as to just how profound of a statement that the three-year-old Hannah had made. Hannah's profound but true pronouncement has led me to much reflection and has since resulted in subject matter for commencement speeches that I have given at high schools and colleges as well as other occasions. It has become the genesis for me writing this book of success tips for those with ambition to succeed in life.

This resource is written specifically for ambitious students like you (along with your parents, guardians, and other loved ones) who are aiming for success in achieving your goals, whatever they may be. This book details for the reader what I consider to have been the

31

most important tips for success I have learned during my lifetime, before, during, and following my college years and that I continue to learn even today during my professional life. Starting in high school, my goal was to become a physician, and during my medical school clerkships, I more specifically set my goals in becoming a urologist. Later, during the fifth year of my six-year urological surgery residency at NYU, I decided to pursue a surgical fellowship at Cleveland Clinic to become a kidney transplant surgeon. I achieved my goals and am proud that I became a kidney transplant surgeon and that I have successfully performed kidney transplants on literally several hundreds of patients and thus improved and saved their lives. I am gratified to have helped cure thousands of patients of prostate, kidney, and bladder cancer and helped treat thousands of other patients afflicted with a variety of ailments. During the course of my journey, my objectives changed over time as I initially had no aspirations of specializing in either urological surgery or kidney transplant surgery. Instead, I initially desired to become a general practitioner first and perhaps a surgeon second, like Hawkeye Pierce, the fictional character in the show *M*A*S*H*, the 1970s–1980s long-running situational television comedy depicting the antics of a military trauma surgeon. The lead character, Hawkeye, espoused many of the characteristics of what I wanted to become, an extremely talented, dedicated, and respected physician and surgeon who always put his patients first but still knew how to have some fun at the same time. I also admired the persona of other dedicated television doctors such as Marcus Welby, Doc Adams of *Gunsmoke*, and *Trapper John, MD*, and the doctors of the 1980s hit television series drama *St. Elsewhere*.

No matter how I glamorized Hawkeye and other doctors in the fictional television programs, the reality is that I would not define or characterize my journey in becoming a physician and surgeon as easy or fun. In fact, I would characterize it as downright difficult and at times very painful. I still face many day-to-day challenges even now more than thirty years after graduating from Northwestern University Medical School. Considering that I admit my journey was a difficult one, why then would I entitle this book *It Isn't Difficult to Do It if You Know How to Do It*. In fact, is not this main title kind of nonsensical?

Is it not obvious that if you already know how to accomplish something, then it won't be as hard to succeed at it? If you have come to this conclusion, then good for you because this is the precise point of this book. The title *It Isn't Difficult to Do It if You Know How to Do It* is in fact *not* nonsensical, but rather the title of this book (what my daughter Hannah said), in fact, represents one of the most profound statements I have ever heard or read in my entire lifetime. It is a statement and in fact a pronouncement that I contend deserves to be recorded in the annals of history as one of the most insightful and deeply philosophical declarations of all time. Stop for a second and think about how profound this is, "It isn't difficult to do it if you know how to do it." I contend that college courses should be structured and taught around this statement. This statement is a brilliant assertion that ranks up there among the best truths ever espoused by the likes of timeless geniuses such as Socrates, Plato, Aristotle, and Albert Einstein, as well as quotes articulated by presidents Abraham Lincoln, Franklin Delano Roosevelt, John F. Kennedy, and others.

The title of this book directly implies that whatever we are trying to achieve in life, if we are armed, prepared, and positioned in advance of our journey with the right information, specific and detailed oriented education, preliminary training, insight, wisdom, knowledge, awareness, and practical tips, plus infused with a working knowledge about how we should attempt to achieve our goals, then doesn't it make sense that our journey, although still filled with unavoidable challenges, will be less difficult as opposed to had we not been prepared and well equipped? Classroom education is invaluable. However, based upon my life experiences, many of which I acquired as a result of failures, trials, and tribulations, I have concluded that most of what one needs to know about how to succeed in life is not "covered" in classroom lectures or within the syllabus prepared by teachers or professors. Rather, much of what you need to know to achieve and reach your goals will originate from your ongoing life experiences. But here's a success tip—you can take your own life experiences and exponentially leap decades ahead of your own physical years of life experiences by being willing, ready, and eager to learn from some of my life experiences, which I have detailed for you in this book, as well as from the lessons of those people around you and from the life experiences of those who preceded you. My father often told me and my siblings that "the best place to learn is by sitting down at the feet of an old person." That's the purpose of this book, for you to learn and benefit from the experiences of others. I hope you will enjoy this book and take advantage of the lessons contained within its pages. Learning and benefiting from the life lessons learned by others, "It isn't difficult to do it if you know how to do it." This book is going to tell you how to do it. So read on.

Acknowledgments

I would like to thank the following people for their love and support. Please forgive me as I know there are additional names of individuals whom I should have been included but mistakenly omitted:

- Charles and Grace Modlin
- Beverly Williams, Deborah Edmunds, Rebecca Modlin, Pamela Modlin
- Mrs. Clara Hampton
- Mrs. Mildred Faye Varnado
- Mrs. Twila Basset
- Ms. Sarah Virginia Hampton
- Mr. Wayman Modlin
- Mr. Gerald Modlin
- Sheryl Modlin, MD
- Mr. Trey (Charles III) Modlin
- Ms. Sarah Modlin
- Ms. Hannah Modlin
- Ms. Meredith Modlin
- Ms. Carolyn Jackson (nanny)
- Mrs. Genevieve Marshall (nanny)
- Ms. Carolyn Clifford (nanny)
- Mr. Ryan Williams and Mr. Richard Williams
- Mr. Jeff Ayres
- Mr. Ian Sheeler
- Mr. Henry Pak
- Mr. David Hamilton
- Louis Hamilton, RN

- The Keith Family
- Mr. Jeffery Rust
- Mr. Brian Hacker
- Mr. John Pitchford
- Mr. Jamie Miller
- Mr. Terri Miller
- Ms. Mary Cox
- Mr. Mark Orr
- Mr. Todd Reitz
- Mr. Brent Maze
- The Maze Family
- Mr. Aaron Bogue
- Mr. and Mrs. Joseph Bogue
- Mark Orr
- Kevin Orr
- Mr. Robert Allen
- Carlumandarlo Zaramo, PhD
- Lateef Saffore, PhD
- Stuart Flechner, MD
- Craig Zippe, MD
- Robert Fairchild, MD
- Robert Kay, MD
- Robert Stevenson, MD
- Roland Chen, MD
- Paul Blake, MD
- Brian Butler, MD
- Richard Grady, MD
- Kevin Banks, MD
- James Holland, MD
- Charles Berry, PhD
- Jack Snarr, PhD
- John T. Grayhack, MD
- Anthony Shaffer Sr., MD
- Paul Caldron, MD
- Paul Field, MD
- Allan Micco, MD

- David Eckman, MD
- John Shaird, MD
- Subu Dubey, MD
- Stephen Yu, MD
- Richard Maggio, MD
- Yan Wolfson, MD
- Jeffrey Rosenblum, MD
- Scott Niditch, MD
- Joseph Presti, MD
- Andrew Novick, MD
- Pablo Morales, MD
- Jordan Brown, MD
- Carl Eric Johannson, MD
- Salah Al-Askari
- Pablo Torre, MD
- Mr. Bill Hamilton
- David Zott, JD
- Mr. Martin Moon
- Mr. Thomas Bennett
- Mr. James Willis Jr.
- Mr. Sanford Weisman
- Mr. Edward Scina
- Mr. Meredith Boatwright
- Mrs. Gladys Boatwright
- Mrs. Eva Ross
- Mr. Terry Ross
- Mr. Kevin Varnado
- Mr. Gene Wilson
- Mr. Jeff
- Ms. Jenny Basset
- Mr. Ricky Cottman
- Ms. Sylvia Modlin
- Mr. Timothy Modlin
- Reverend Calvin T. Word
- Mr. Louis Poindexter
- Mrs. Nancy Thompson

- Mrs. Ella Hill
- Mrs. Inez Thompson
- Mr. Eugene Bailey
- Mrs. Thelma Bailey
- Mrs. Ola Mae Williams
- Mrs. Mary Thurman
- The Beach Church, Carthage, Indiana
- The Boatwright Family, Knightstown, Indiana
- Anderson, Indiana, cousins
- Mr. Ed Walker and Mrs. Barbara Walker
- Mr. Quinn Walker
- Ms. June, Mr. J. R., and Mrs. Betty Clark
- Mr. Maurice Bassett
- Mr. Satch Basset
- Panzy and her tulips
- The Socialites
- Weir Elementary School
- Riley Elementary School
- Northwestern University
- Northwestern University Feinberg School of Medicine
- Dr. Charles Berry, dean of Admissions, Northwestern University Medical School
- Dr. Fitzsimmons, Urology mentor, Northwestern University Medical School
- New York University Medical Center
- New York University, Dept. Urology
- Bellevue Hospital, NYC
- Manhattan Veterans Administration
- Cleveland Clinic
- Cleveland Clinic Kidney Transplant Center
- Cleveland Clinic Department of Urology
- Cleveland Clinic Minority Men's Health Fair volunteers
- Cleveland Clinic Board of Governors
- Ball State University
- Shaker Heights City Schools
- New Castle City Schools

- Chrysler High School, New Castle, Indiana
- Class of 1979, Chrysler High School and other classes
- New Castle Chrysler High School Band
- Kentucky Fried Chicken, New Castle, Indiana
- Famous Recipe Fried Chicken, New Castle, Indiana
- Becker Brothers Grocery Store, New Castle, Indiana
- Henry County Hospital, New Castle, Indiana
- Brooks Ketchup Factory, Mount Summit, Indiana
- Dana Corporation, New Castle, Indiana
- New Castle Little League Baseball, Tigers Baseball Team
- New Castle Babe Ruth Baseball, Phares Baseball Team
- New Castle Cub Scouts
- Coach Denny Bolden
- Coach Jim Hamm
- Coach Bob Lee
- Coach Lowell Lee
- Indiana All State High School Band, 1978–1979
- Mrs. Denise Vogel Wadsworth
- Mr. Wayne Vogel
- Mr. Deveraux Clifford
- Alan Clark, PhD
- Jeff Sedlack, MD
- Mr. Robert Leighton
- Ms. Sue Glatter
- Mary Leonard, MD
- Mr. Alton Taylor, elementary school principal
- Mr. Ray Pavey
- Mrs. Stamper, Teacher
- Mr. Robert Shauver, band teacher
- Mrs. Liz Shauver, math teacher
- Mr. William Pritchet, band teacher
- Mr. Larry Ash, band teacher
- Mr. Gary Wadman
- New Castle City Schools
- Ms. Gorenz, Latin teacher
- Dr. McGrath, Latin teacher

- Prof. Michael Tierstein
- Dr. Harold Zimmack
- Mr. Herbert Bunch, principal
- Mr. Paul Crouser, principal
- Mr. Miller, teacher
- Mrs. Dye, third-grade teacher
- Mr. Virgil Vaughn, teacher
- Dr. Roy Stricker and Dr. McKee
- Wiley United Methodist Church, New Castle, Indiana
- Bethel AME Church, New Castle, Indiana
- Church of the Saviour, Cleveland Heights, Ohio
- Rev. Dr. Charles Yoost
- Rev. Dr. Leonard Budd
- David Gratner of KFC
- Mr. Mark Medley
- Ms. Hilda Piercy
- Mr. Cecil Tague
- Mr. Kent Benson
- Ms. Maria Hernandez, secretary
- Ms. Theresa Martin, secretary
- Ms. Tanya Moore, secretary
- Mr. Jamal Gambrel, secretary
- Ms. Shannon Graham, secretary
- Black Professional Association Charitable Foundation
- The Oberdorfer Family Scholarship
- Mr. Alvin and Mrs. Annette Fridie
- Andrew Novick, MD
- Pablo Morales, MD
- Jordan Brown, MD
- Arthur Tessler, MD
- Carl Eric Johannson, MD
- Jeffrey Glasser, MD
- John Provet, MD
- James Drale, MD
- Mark Adelman, MD
- Mrs. Bebe Sheehan

- Judith Green, MD
- Edwardo Farcon, MD
- Andrew Bunta, MD
- Mark Adelman, MD
- Greg Kiray, MD
- Eric Winter, MD
- Bert Fichman, MD
- Mr. Robert Fellinger
- Mrs. Lynn Hutter
- Ms. Dolley Finney
- Mrs. Pat Frew
- Mr. Michael Joelson
- The Rosner family
- Mr. George and Mrs. Louis Vance
- Mrs. Beverly Suber
- Mrs. Ruth Matthews
- The Givens family
- Mr. Ron Kisner
- Rev. Dr. E. Theophilus Caviness
- Rev. Dr. Larry Macon Sr.
- Rev. Paul Sadler
- Pastor Jerome Hurst
- Pastor Marcus Gould
- United Pastors in Mission
- Cleveland City Councilman Kevin Conwell
- Ohio Governor John Kasich
- Ohio Governor Ted Strickland
- Ms. Cheryl Boyce
- Boyd Funeral Home
- Ms. Margo Copeland
- Delos Toby Cosgrove, MD
- Robert Kay, MD
- National Senior Games Association
- Cleveland NAACP
- Cleveland Black Professional Association Charitable Foundation

- *Cleveland Call and Post*
- *Cleveland Plain Dealer*
- Mr. Leon Bibb
- Moreen Bailey Frater
- Mr. Russ Mitchell
- Rev. Sam Tidmore
- Rev. Larry Harris
- Rev. Dr. R. A. Vernon
- Judge Gregory Clifford
- Mr. Gregory Lockhart
- Mr. George Fraser
- Mr. Harry Boomer
- Mrs. Margaret Daykin
- Ms. Carolyn Albright
- Mrs. Megan Begala
- Alberta (Bertie) Benedetto, RN
- Anna Marie Ottney, RN
- Mrs. Kathy Pieton
- Mr. Wilburt (Bill) Cobbs
- Omega Psi Phi and Kappa Alpha Psi fraternities
- Cleveland black sororities
- Christian Business League, Michael Shinn
- Tina Rice
- LaVerne Lynch
- Demeatrice Nance
- Barbara Cooper
- Congresswoman Stephanie Tubbs Jones
- Congressman Louis Stokes
- Cleveland Mayor Frank Jackson
- Honorable Judge Sarah Harper
- Ms. Connie Harper, *Cleveland Call and Post*
- Ms. Beverly Charles
- Cleveland City Councilwoman Mamie Mitchell
- Cleveland City Councilman Zach Reed
- Angela Townsend, *the Plain Dealer*
- Kimberly Fleming

- Mr. Michael Trivisonno, radio host
- Mr. Mansfield Frazier, radio host
- Mr. Ronnie Duncan, radio host
- Radio One
- Sam Sylk, radio host
- Mr. Jae Williams, *the Gospel Kid*, radio host
- Mr. Barry Mayo, radio producer
- Mr. Mark Ribbons, radio host
- Ms. Grace Roberts, radio host
- Ms. Sue Johnson, *Wake Up* radio host
- Mr. Jeff Wilson, Radio One manager
- Cleveland City councilman and radio host Bashir Jones
- *The Sports Brothers, Delvis Valentine*, radio show
- Cleveland Section, National Council of Negro Women
- Southern Christian Leadership Conference
- Mr. George Forbes, esq.
- Mr. Warren Anderson
- Rev. Hilton Smith
- Stanley Miller, NAACP
- Marsha Mockabee and the Greater Cleveland Urban League
- 100 Black Men of Greater Cleveland
- Michael Taylor and PNC
- Christian Business League (Mike Shinn, rest in peace)
- Cleveland Black Nurses
- Greater Cleveland Partnership
- National Technical Association
- Greater Cleveland Sports Commission
- Cleveland Cavaliers
- Cleveland Indians
- Ms. Sharon Reed, TV Broadcaster
- Mr. Wayne Dawson, TV Broadcaster
- Mrs. Sam Sylk, Radio Broadcaster
- Mr. Ronnie Duncan, Radio Broadcaster
- Mr. Bashir Jones, Radio Broadcaster
- Mr. Rev. Dr. Marvin McMickle

- Mr. Larry Kuhns, Northwestern
- Mr. Michael Lawson, MBA
- Mrs. Hope Buggy
- James Young, MD
- Nikki Williams
- Bridget Gorman, MBA
- Pam Pawlecki, MBA
- Mrs. Quintene Graham, secretary
- Mrs. Cynthia Haywood
- Mrs. Sabrina Spikes
- Keybank Foundation
- New Castle, Indiana Public Library
- YMCA, New Castle Indiana
- Boyd Funeral Home
- Main Frame Funeral Home, New Castle, Indiana
- Countless student mentees, many of whom have written testimonials and from whom I have learned a great deal. Thank you.
- *Who's Who in Black Cleveland*
- Thousands of patients who have entrusted me with their very lives
- Thousands of physicians and healthcare colleagues with whom I have worked
- Hundreds of teachers and professors
- And many, many other individuals and organizations who helped support my vision

Also, I thank other forms of wholesome influencers that helped mold my character at an early age, which are as follows:

- 1970s music
- Early 1980s music
- The Jackson 5
- Motown music
- Paul McCartney and Wings
- The Beatles

- Electric Light Orchestra (ELO)
- Alan Alda (Dr. Benjamin Franklin Pierce) and M*A*S*H
- *St. Elsewhere*
- *Good Times*
- *All in the Family*
- *The Jeffersons*
- *Diff'rent Strokes*
- *Roots*
- The Wild World of Sports
- *Sunday Night Mystery Series*
- *Marcus Welby, MD*
- *Emergency*
- *The Waltons*
- *Sesame Street*
- *The Electric Company*
- *Mr. Rodgers' Neighborhood*
- *The Brady Bunch*
- *The Partridge Family*
- *Sammy Terry Show*
- *Gilligan's Island*
- *I Dream of Jeanie*
- *Bewitched*
- Saturday-morning cartoons
- WNAP Indianapolis Radio
- WERK Radio
- Sue Berg, Chicago Radio
- NBC Nightly News with Tom Brokaw and John Chancellor
- And many other musicians and entertainers

And to the many places I frequented and loved growing up and still do, such as the following:

- The Cherrywood Drugstore
- Mount Lawn Lake
- Lake Michigan
- Warren Dunes State Park, Michigan

- Lake Erie
- Evanston, Illinois
- Chicago, the Windy City
- New York City, the Big Apple
- Central Park, New York City
- The East River
- The Twin Towers
- The Chicago Bulls
- The 1986 Chicago Bears
- NBA Basketball
- Michael Jordan, Scottie Pippen, Magic Johnson, James Worthy, Dr. J, Larry Bird, BJ Armstrong
- ABA Basketball
- 1970s and 1980s professional tennis
- The New Castle Courier Times
- The Castle, New Castle Theatre
- Memorial and Baker Park, New Castle
- Washington Square, Indianapolis
- Karma Records
- Muncie Mall
- Cleveland Museum of Natural History
- The City of Shaker Heights

Dr. Charles Modlin with father Charles Modlin Sr.
at Cleveland Clinic Minority Men's Health Fair

Introduction

It is advised that you read this book in its entirety ideally before you finish high school or before you complete college. Parents, it is even better if your student begins reading and digesting the success tips contained in this book while even in middle school (or even at an earlier age with your help and interpretation). At whatever stage you pick up this book, it will never be too late to benefit from the lessons contained within. The chapters in this book do not have to be read in chronological order, as each of the chapters is packed with extremely valuable information, which will augment, supplement, and facilitate you in achieving your goals, whatever they may be.

This book is written for students of all races, ethnicities, and nationalities. It is written not only for students but also for parents, guardians, and anyone who aspire to help a young man or woman achieve his or her life's dreams. This book is also useful for anyone who needs a refresher on the key principles that lead to success.

Certain sections in this book specifically address or reference the fact that I am an African American, and, as a result of this, detail how I faced unique challenges in life, which I contend were genuine and not imagined. In fact, to this day, I continue to face certain challenges as an African American. I include this perspective in this book in order to highlight that being African American or of any other minority group, persuasion should not be an excuse for you to not aspire to achieve great goals in your life. However, I do profess that, in reality, being of a particular minority group persuasion may, more precisely will, unfortunately force and necessitate you to work harder than the next person, as my parents taught me and as I have observed vividly over the years to be true. As a person of the African diaspora, I realize that often, we, though ambitious and bright, experience unfortunate situations that lead us to question whether achieving our goals is possible. Too often, discouragement or prejudice prevents people of color from even pursuing their dreams. Lack of support, lack of opportunities, poverty, and other social circumstances, such as experiences of racism and discrimination, account for some (many) of the attitudes that many African Americans, as well as others, have developed early in life. These experiences too often result in self-doubt coupled with a particularly toxic and pessimistic view about the future. Consequently, many give up and many never even try.

The same certainly holds true for other ethnicities besides African Americans. Therefore, this book will be beneficial for anyone desirous of success in life regardless of race, gender, ethnicity, sexual orientation, or age. Different readers will find specific segments of this book particularly advantageous. While some concepts will serve as reminders or refreshers, for many readers, these success tips will bring new awareness to the overall scheme of what is required to achieve success in this increasingly complex, interconnected, global, and complicated world in which we live.

"It's a jungle out there." I am sure that you've heard this phrase from a parent, loved one, friends, or in the media. I admit, in many ways, it is a jungle out there. The world is not always a friendly or hospitable place, and the people whom you will encounter may either intentionally or unintentionally make life difficult for you at times for a host of reasons. Many people may see you as the competition, which often causes people to be fearful and unkind. When you hear the phrase "every man for himself" from a loved one, it is often being said to help prepare you "for the real world" in which you need to be street savvy and possess survival skills and strategies to become successful. Your loved ones tell you these things because they care for you and don't want to see you hurt. The lessons in this book, whenever unpleasant, are not meant to scare you. I believe that the majority of people are good. But remember, the goal of this book is to help prepare you for the next phase of your life, whether as a student in college or trade school, a military recruit, intern, or a new employee entering the workforce. My goal is to strengthen and prepare you with the tools necessary for being on your own as a productive member of society, no longer protected by the sanctity of high school, home, or your parents' watchful and caring eyes.

As a surgeon and physician, I understand the hurdles that students, young or older, face in attempting to achieve their dreams of attending and graduating from college, trade school, etc., to pursue their chosen career objectives. I had to endure seventeen long, arduous years of formal education and training following my high school graduation to become a kidney transplant surgeon. I often speak to students about the four years of college, four years of medical school, six years of urological surgery residency, and three years of kidney transplant and renovascular surgery fellowship and transplant immunology research that I had to complete to become a kidney transplant surgeon. And as a practicing physician and surgeon, I am still required to undergo ongoing medical education and additional training to remain afoot of advances in the medical profession.

One of the questions students often ask of me is, "How did you do it?" "How did you become a kidney transplant surgeon, Dr. Modlin?" Of course, I cannot answer this question completely in a few sentences. However, I relay to students that through resiliency, planning, decision, drive, desire, devotion, dreaming and daring to think big, dedication, determination, and "doing," I became a kidney transplant surgeon. I endured and suffered many hardships, and sometimes many indignities, on my journey. I also learned a multitude of important lessons along the way that I readily share with the students whom I mentor and coach as well as with those students who come to me with questions and for advice. Only after being repeatedly questioned over the years by countless numbers of students, their parents, and others as to what my journey was like and inquiring of me how I achieved my goals to become an African American kidney transplant surgeon and urologist, one of approximately twenty or fewer African American transplant surgeons in the entire United States, did I begin reflecting back on my journey. I reflected on what it took for me to complete my college education and to get accepted to and complete medical school, residency, and fellowship and then to acquire a staff position as a kidney transplant surgeon and urologist at Cleveland Clinic and to go on to become a champion for the elimination of health disparities, which dispropor-tionately afflict minority communities.

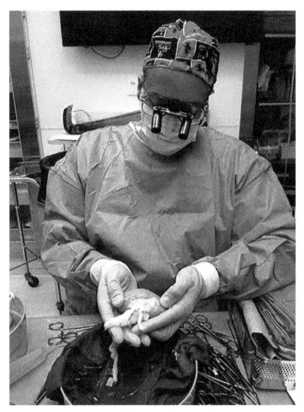

Dr. Charles Modlin, holding and preparing
a donor kidney for transplantation

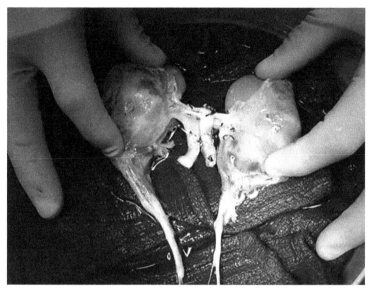

Dr. Charles Modlin holding and preparing small
pediatric donor kidneys for transplantation

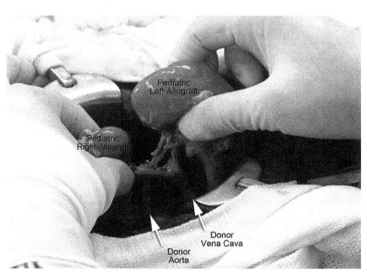

Dr. Charles Modlin holding successfully transplanted
and perfused pediatric donor kidneys

It was others, including my parents, family, friends, patients and their families, and members of the community and community organizations, who alerted me to the significance of my accomplishments through the many awards and recognitions bestowed upon me for my innovative minority health community outreach initiatives that I have become noted for establishing at Cleveland Clinic, in particular our Cleveland Clinic Minority Men's Health Fair and Minority Men's Health Center, which I, with the support of many volunteers and supporters, established to address the elimination of health disparities disproportionately afflicting minority and underserved men, along with establishing initiatives to help improve the health of their families and communities in which they live. During my long educational journey, I was fixated on achieving my goals and I always looked forward and projected myself living in the future I desired. This is a success tip. I did not take time to analyze as a whole the secrets of my success. I had never considered comprehensively reflecting upon my personal experiences and assembling a comprehensive guide as to what I consider to have been the "secrets" of and for my success so that others could benefit from some of these "secrets" (reasons) of success.

Not until sitting down to write this book did I remember being asked while I was in college to return to my hometown of New Castle, Indiana, to give a talk to the youth of Wiley United Methodist Church about advice I could give them regarding how they could achieve success in high school and prepare for entry into college. I recall not really wanting to give this presentation, because at that point in my life I assumed that anyone wanting to achieve academic success would know how to do it and also because I wasn't fond of public speaking. However, I recall my father's encouragement and insistence that I do so. I still to this day recount how proud he was sitting there watching me speak that morning in church. Likewise, a few years ago, when I was asked by the faculty director of the Shaker Heights Woodbury Elementary African American Scholars (a group of high-achieving fifth and sixth graders) to speak at their sixth-grade graduation ceremony, I responded that I might not be able to arrange my schedule to do so; and I advised that he should invite my son,

Trey, a recent graduate of Texas Tech University and a national chess master, to serve as their graduation keynote speaker rather than me. My son accepted the invitation and I was there sitting up in the balcony watching him deliver a very heartfelt, inspirational, and motivational speech to the young scholars, which was very well received. I was so very proud to see my son do this because he too was very reserved and doing so required that he get out of his comfort zone in order to impart his experiences and wisdom to benefit the young scholars. Success tip—be willing to get out of your comfort zone. I video-recorded my son's speech, which is online (please watch it now) and available for you to watch by googling "Trey Modlin Woodbury Scholars" or at the following link: https://youtu.be/2xrlPYw8jVw.

By the way, I also am quick to point out to students and others that I have not yet reached all of my goals (nor will I ever achieve all of my goals) because people who aspire to achieve always are striving to reach new goals. Nevertheless, after several years of reflection, I herein now have assembled into this book a collection of some of the most important life skills and lessons I have learned during my journey in becoming a physician and surgeon. Moreover, within this book, I have looked deep into my memory banks and inner soul to assemble for you, the reader, some of the lessons, practices, principles, and tenets that I believe undeniably have helped me achieve my academic and professional successes along with my personal and professional goals and dreams.

The tools and resources herein include guidance for developing personal, academic, and professional habits that will enhance and facilitate your success journey. From discussing the keys to building good relationships and social skills to reinforcing that you develop effective study habits to highlighting techniques to assist you in enveloping practices that will help you avoid, navigate around, and even prevent some of life's hurdles to helping you realize the multiple ways in which you will additionally transform yourself into a well-rounded individual who embraces lifelong learning, this book is written and formatted for students in high school as well as college or trade school and for their parents, guardians, and families who want to help them succeed. This book, in no way, is limited to or directed specifically toward students seeking to enter the medical profession. I have organized each tenet of success into a chapter according to a specific theme for easier understanding, organization, and reference; however, in practice and real-life situations, these tenets overlap and often build upon one another. Therefore, I strongly encourage the student to effectively adopt and utilize each tenet concurrently and fluidly as a part of their daily life. Every reader is different and unique and has differing past experiences to date and different goals in life. We each come from varied backgrounds and life experiences and each of us views the world from our own perspectives based on who we are and what we have experienced in life and according to our family and environmental and social circumstances. Nevertheless, my hope in writing this book is to provide you, no matter how sophisticated (academically, IQ, socially, street-smart, savvy, worldly, emotionally, or intuitively) you may or may not be at this stage (age) of your life, with an opportunity for self-reflection in combination with developing a deep appreciation for the details of what has already substantively contributed to your current level of success. I hope that by writing this book and reflecting back upon my own life and journey from my childhood to becoming a practicing urologist and kidney transplant surgeon that I will successfully disseminate to you much knowledge I have acquired over the years to ultimately make your journey in accomplishing your goals easier than mine. I know that by reading this book, you *will* find some pearls of wisdom at an earlier age than if you had not read it. Consequently, if reading this book has been at all helpful to you, I encourage you to please send me an e-mail to Contact@DrModlinMD.com and share your experiences with me.

For further guidance, I have included a list of suggested references, books, and other materials that I have found to be helpful and informative for me that you may choose to access. So with this being said, it is time for you to now read on, enjoy, and absorb like a sponge the information contained within the pages of this book; because by reading this book, you too will soon recognize and discover the profound wisdom, astuteness, and cleverness as to what my daughter Hannah, at the young age of three, was communicating when she proclaimed, "It isn't difficult to do it if you know how to do it."

CHAPTER 1

Mapping Your Success

Facing Your Fears Head-On

One of my first acts when interacting with, coaching, and mentoring students who have just graduated high school or are high school seniors is to remind them as I wish to remind you, the reader now, that your graduation represents not the end of your educational journey, but in reality only the beginning of a lifelong journey of learning for you.

The life lessons and education you have obtained up to this point have prepared you to face the many challenges awaiting you after high school. But there is much more for you to learn and the sooner, the better. Remember, my intent in this book is never to scare you or make you fear the future or make you fearful of going out into the world; so please, students and parents, never take anything I tell you in this book as a negative message. My messaging is all motivational, meant to empower you, and is 100 percent for your benefit and you should take it that way. So are you ready to get started? Good, I knew you would be ready. As such, let me be clear that challenges, hurdles, and obstacles do indeed await you. Sometimes the challenges will be expected or predictable, but often you may not see them coming or anticipate them at all. You may experience minor challenges, but some may be potentially life altering. There will be obstacles within your control and others beyond approach. There will also be challenges that you can avoid or lessen and some you can even prevent and avert completely, while other challenges will be an inevitable part of your future and life experiences.

I realize that challenges, obstacles, and problems, whether known or unknown, can be a source of great fear for all of us. However, I encourage you to not fear obstacles, but instead embrace and learn to thrive in spite of them. You have to face your fears head-on regardless of whatever challenges await you because obstacle will serve to only strengthen you as an individual. I know this to be true, because the experiences and challenges I have experienced, in both becoming a doctor and working as a transplant surgeon and urologist, have collectively and exponentially served to make me a better surgeon and even more importantly a much stronger person.

There are various methods you can utilize to approach, face, and conquer challenges and difficulties. There are direct, head-on approaches, and there are indirect and more strategic ways in which to overcome challenges and difficulties. Your approach(es) will vary according to the circumstances as well as your level of maturity, critical thinking, communication, crucial conversation and crucial confrontation skills, networking skills, knowledge, and education and importantly also the level of your self-confidence, self-assuredness, and willingness to get out of your comfort zone. These methods are contained and discussed throughout this book. Also, in reality, you will discover that, more often than not, there is *no one way* to overcome a given challenge. It's up to you to discover and make the best decisions for your particular situation. I have discovered over the years that there are times when we must learn as a result of trial, error, and *failure*. It's true. We can learn a great deal from failure. Therefore, take heart, analyze, ponder, reflect internally, and reanalyze the possible reasons for your failures, and remember to discern the lessons from your failures and experiences and keep moving forward and making forward progress.

I have also found that observing and learning from the experiences of others can make our life journeys a lot smoother in many instances. Learning not only from the experiences and successes of others but also from the mistakes of others is the major focus and message (success tip) of this book. Therefore, I will share some of my significant life experiences and how I negotiated and overcame various challenges to achieve my goals to become a physician and surgeon. In preparing this book, I self-reflected upon my many experiences and assembled what I consider to represent the major determinants of my success. In other words, I am condensing, for your benefit, into the pages of this book, fifty-seven years of my life lessons. One of the most important being my understanding that challenges are a normal part of life. Anyone who desires success must be persistent, must possess or acquire a strong sense of self-confidence and self-belief founded on the substance and work ethic contained with them, and must possess resiliency, determination and grit, and self-awareness and a willingness to self-reflect. I recommend that you read the book *Grit*, a book recently written by Dr. Angela Duckworth, written entirely on the subject and importance of grit. I contend that embracing challenges instead of fearing challenges will make your resolve for success even that much stronger. As you read and digest the contents of this book, continually self-reflect upon your life experiences and apply the tons of tips contained in this book in real time to the experiences, obstacles, and challenges you currently face. Ask yourself, "How might I apply Dr. Modlin's success tips and guidance to my current real-life situations to aid me in overcoming whatever challenges now facing me so that I can achieve my own personal short- and long-term goals?" Yes, this book contains tons of success tips, so read and reread this book carefully.

So, students, keep repeating to yourself the wise words of my daughter Hannah, "It isn't difficult to do it if you know how to do it," and take to heart the deep but straightforward meaning of her statement so that you realize that your journey will be made easier and the obstacles you now face will in fact be more easily overcome if you now take the steps detailed in this book to learn, discern, and discover just how you can overcome and conquer your obstacles.

Father Charles Modlin Sr., pictured with Hannah (left)
and Meredith Modlin (right) at the National Senior Games
Association competition, 2009, Palo Alto, California

So another determinant of success for you now to absorb is that it is imperative that you recognize and reflect upon the main reasons for the successes you have already achieved. My father routinely reminded me that a community of people helped contribute toward my achievements. Likewise, I am sure you can identify people who have significantly inspired and facilitated your creativity, work ethic, self-confidence, and successes.

The life lessons my parents taught me are the main reasons for my successes. Why don't you take out a piece of paper and jot down right now a list of the many life lessons taught to you by your parents and loved one? My parents' sacrifices provided me with opportunities they never had. I am the first male from my family lineage to graduate high school because my father, at the age of seventeen, had to leave school while in good standing to join the navy during World War II to defend his country. My mother graduated high school and received a one-year scholarship to attend Butler University in Indianapolis, but she could not financially afford to return to college after her first year. But her determination to complete her college education to become a schoolteacher never abated. At the age of thirty-eight, as a mother to four small children, she made the decision to return to night school college to become an elementary schoolteacher, earning her bachelor's and master's degree and then becoming the first main classroom black schoolteacher in the history of Henry County, Indiana—and (no surprise) with this came many challenges. Some parents objected to having their children in a black schoolteacher's classroom (imagine that). But she did not let negativity and hatred prevent her from living her dream of being a teacher as a way of providing a better quality of life for her family, because she believed in herself and she had substance within her character to substantiate her self-belief.

Not only did my parents place expectations upon me at an early age to perform in school to the best of my abilities, but also they expected me to show respect to everyone I encountered. And I admit that showing respect to people who deliberately attempted to interfere with me achieving my goals has been difficult at times. For instance, after I had become a urologist and transplant surgeon, the superintendent of my hometown school system extended to me the honor of returning to my hometown to deliver the keynote address at their annual retiring teacher's luncheon and for the high school student's academic achievement ceremony. As I took to the podium at the retiring teacher's luncheon, in the front row sat my high school guidance counselor, about eighty-five years old by then. Seeing her brought back memories, which had never escaped me, of how she, when I was a high school student, had attempted to derail me and could have derailed my self-confidence in pursuing a career in medicine altogether if my *reactions* to her actions toward me had allowed me to doubt my character, substance, and abilities. Success tip—don't let others control your reactions or emotions. Maintain control of your emotions at all times.

Despite ranking among the top of my high school class, always the top in my science classes, my high school counselor, when I told her of my aspirations of becoming a doctor, in spite of my academic achievements, quite obviously based upon her prejudice that she could not conceal, chuckled. And in a dismissive and degrading intimidating tone, her arms crossed, she articulated to me, a young black kid, vulnerable and alone with her in her office with no witnesses or advocates present for me (you see there was no transparency back then), that I did not possess the requisite credentials nor abilities to become a physician. She was in a position of power and authority, so she thought I would take the bait and believe her. And why wouldn't I believe her? After all, for example, there were no black role model physicians in New Castle from whom I could look to as examples or receive mentorship or coaching. As far as professionals in my family, I had my mother and my aunt Mildred Faye and a few cousins in Indianapolis and Knightstown who were college graduates, but no one in my family was in medicine, nor did I know of any black doctors, not even on TV. As a young impressionable student, I was naturally puzzled, startled, rattled, and disheartened (but only for a minute!) by her attempts to convince me and dissuade me from even contemplating a career in medicine.

But her strategy of discouragement and disbelief did not derail me. Why? Because I knew the following five critical things:

1. My older sisters and mother explained to me that this counselor had a reputation of being derogatory toward black students.
2. I believed in myself (I possessed a justified self-confidence).
3. I knew my parents, family, and friends believed in me (they had confidence in me).
4. I had substance within my character (I had appropriately prepared myself academically, and I possessed the requisite drive, determination, and work ethic) to substantiate my self-belief.
5. I wasn't raised to just give up.

I therefore used my guidance counselor's negativity as *fuel* to strengthen my own resolve to achieve my goals. Anyway, some twenty years after her attempts to derail me, during my keynote introductory remarks at the retiring teachers' luncheon, with my parents proudly in attendance, my elderly high school counselor seated in the front row, eyes and ears fixated upon me, I now, having achieved my goal of becoming a surgeon practicing at one of the nation's leading hospitals, literally stood in a position to either publicly or privately attempt retaliation by humiliating her for her behavior toward me in high school. But remembering my parents' admonition to show respect, I knew I could not bring myself to show her disrespect or admonish her, so I instead publicly thanked her for her service to the school district and for *empowering* me to become a physician. Likewise, I encourage you to use adversity and adversary as a tool to increase your strength and resolve for success and recognize how challenges serve to strengthen you.

Do not allow detractors or adverse situations to divert you from your goals. Maintain your belief in yourself, but I stress that just believing in yourself is not enough in and of itself alone; to the contrary, despite what you may have heard said, a person cannot become anything he or she wants to become just because they wish it. Instead, I believe it is first essential that you prepare, put in the work necessary, and possess substance to support (which will serve to justify) your self-belief so that you indeed position yourself to achieve your goals.

Picture of Charles Modlin's first day moving into
Northwestern University Medical School, September 1983

Northwestern University Medical School Graduation Day,
June 1987, pictured with parents Charles and Grace Modlin

Always Maintain Your Strong Work
Ethic and Don't Procrastinate

My parents molded my work ethic. After my father's military service, he labored for twenty-eight years in a factory that closed just two years before he could have retired with full benefits. To make ends meet, my sisters and I stepped up and went to work at early ages. When I was ten, I washed storefront windows, mowed lawns, and shoveled snow. In high school and college, I worked several jobs as a grocery store sack boy, and I excelled at washing dishes, mopping floors, and cooking chicken at Famous Recipe Chicken and Kentucky Fried Chicken restaurants. I labored in cornfields and scorching hot factories, getting my skin scalded from hot metal. I even labored so hard that I suffered heat exhaustion and was taken to the hospital. I worked as a hospital orderly giving enemas and emptying bedpans and urinals—maybe explaining why I decided to become a urologist to work with urine. LOL. I thank my friend's mother, Mrs. Louis Hamilton, RN, head nurse of the Henry County Memorial Hospital at the time, for getting me my orderly job that helped solidify my decision to become a physician. My many work experiences taught me how to take orders (commands), often under hostile circumstances, and work as a team player. Also, these taught me to not work according to whether others were working just as hard as I, but to work to do the best job I could do and prepared me for the challenges awaiting me. The lessons I learned from my early work experiences continue to serve me well today. In most places of employment I worked, it was usually customary for me to work harder than others around me. In fact, many people I worked with exerted much effort and energy to figure out ways for them to avoid working.

The lessons and examples my parents set for me, along with my work experiences, enabled me to develop both the physical and mental capacities to endure hardships such as having to go without meals for almost entire weekends in college when the food service was closed when I didn't have money to purchase food in restaurants. I often had to save up on apples and bananas from the college food service during the week so I would have something to eat. The lessons I learned about stamina, sacrifice, and delayed gratification enabled me during my surgical internship, residency, and fellowship to routinely endure working 140-hour weeks and staying up all night without sleep or food while putting my patients first by attending to their needs before my own. I remember as an intern at times jumping up out of bed in tears from leg cramps resulting from becoming dehydrated and potassium depleted as a result of my having to literally stand and be on my feet for days at a time. My father used to mail me boxes of beef jerky that I could easily carry around with me to chew on while at work because he knew I often didn't otherwise have an opportunity to eat. He helped me out a lot in many ways.

Deciding Which Is the Best College or University for You

I have mentioned that as you prepare to start out on your success journey and are in the early stages of your journey, you need to formulate your goals, write them out visually, and routinely review your goals and develop an action plan to reach your goals. (Of note, remember that you can reset your goals and plans at any time if you determine it is to your advantage.) One of the most important decisions up to this point in your life that you will make and need to make on a timeline, if you have not yet done so, is to make an informed, well-researched, well-thought-out decision as to where to attend college. For many people, this is a very stressful decision to make, and one's choices in many respects depends upon the decisions they have made up to this point. One's decisions have, in many but in not all cases, impacted upon their current level of success. It is beyond the scope of this book, but I completely recognize and understand that the social circumstances and external forces, including home structure and financial situations, that face many students do place some students at distinct disadvantages when it comes to the opportunities they may have had regarding their education up to this point compared to other students of their age. They may be just as bright, intelligent, and mature and they may have similar if not identical aspirations and work ethic as the next student; but due to many circumstances, not necessarily of their own doing or within their control, many students will not be in a position to compete to attend the same colleges or universities as are some of their peers. This is true and is another reason as to why I emphasize that those students who have been fortunate to have supportive parents and families who have provided them the foundation necessary to allow them to focus on their education and provided them with opportunities to take preparatory college entrance examination courses and attend fancy preparatory schools, etc., should maintain their humility at all times and be thankful that they have had such opportunities, because as I said, and repeat again, there are other students, equally bright, who did not have the same opportunities and consequently may not able to reach their full potential. I hope this resonates with you, because there is nothing more obnoxious than to see a spoiled high school or college kid boasting and "looking down" on other students because they themselves went to the best private prep school and they are attending the finest private exclusive college or university. Maintain your humility because "It isn't difficult to do it if you know how to do it." And knowing how to maintain your humility is a simple matter of possessing good manners, recognizing that no one is better than anyone else, and recognizing the importance of showing respect to everyone you meet.

This being said, in consideration of which college or university you wish to attend, there are many things to consider and much research that you, preferably along with your parents, must do. The subject of comparing colleges and universities to one another is beyond the scope of this book, and I refer you to a listing of excellent resource books in the appendix of this book. Keep in mind that the information on and comparisons of individual colleges and universities changes on a year-to-year basis, and keep in mind that there is much subjectivity that goes into ranking colleges on national ranking lists. Much information is contained online, and you can also order and purchase detailed updated books and magazines on the subject online or in bookstores. Discuss with your high school counselor, teachers, mentors, coaches, and parents your thoughts about which schools or types of school you wish to attend and get their advice as to which schools they believe would be a good fit for you. Remember, choosing a school to which to apply and attend is your decision, not theirs, and you personally must do your own research and homework on the subject.

Your advisors and others do however possess valuable information and insight into different schools, and you should definitely consult with them. However, do not let a high school advisor or counselor dissuade you from applying to a particular school if you feel in your heart you wish to pursue attending that school and you feel strongly that you have the credentials to do so. More than ever before, colleges and universities are taking into consideration for their admissions policies parameters more than just college entry examination SAT and/or ACT standardized scores, class rank, and grade point averages. In fact, some colleges are going away entirely from even accessing these test scores. Many high schools no longer even compute exact class rank, but rather compute and provide to college admissions committees the student's class percentile or decile. Many admissions committees seriously take into consideration the difficulty of the high school curriculum chosen by the student as well as their level of involvement in extracurricular activities and, of course, the quality and content of your college essays (and the remainder of your college application, including your grammar). Some colleges require that you submit to them only the essay from the common college application, whereas other colleges require that you write a specific essay as to why you wish to attend their college. Students, in submitting a special essay to a particular college (or even on the common application essay), take special care to not mistakenly include the name of a different college that you wish to attend in that essay. I have attended college admission information sessions with my kids and heard from admissions committees' account where this mistakenly and unfortunately does happen and is a reason some students are rejected from a particular college. This happens when students cut and paste the same essay into different college applications. Please do not let this happen to you. To see some example of essays previously written by other students, I refer you to consult with and review a number of books published on the subject matter. I don't need to remind you of the repercussions of plagiarizing college essays. Colleges and universities and even high schools now have sophisticated word processing programs that can detect if an essay is plagiarized.

Also, some colleges in making their admissions decisions do take into consideration the area of country from which the student hails, and some schools do take into consideration other demographics such as race, ethnicity, nationality, if the student is a first-generation college student, financial considerations, gender, and other factors, which they may or may not publicly acknowledge. Many admissions committees will also look to see if you took the time to visit their campus for a formal information session and tour. I've even heard an admissions officer from a local elite university say that they especially expect students who live locally and who apply to their university to have officially registered and attended one of their admissions information sessions and toured the campus to prove that they indeed are genuinely interested in attending their university. Many universities resort to tactics such as this because of the many thousands of applications they receive, and this is one way they use to eliminate many applicants from their pools. So if you have questions about the admissions requirements of a particular school, first take the initiative to thoroughly read the online materials provided by that university. Read the sections of commonly asked questions. Then and only then after having read the materials, if you still have questions, pick up the phone and call the admissions office to very politely ask your questions. Please note that some admissions offices will advise that you first e-mail them your questions, whereas some are more welcoming of phone calls. Remember to say please and thank you and yes, sir and no, sir, etc., during your phone call. Success tip—parents, you may and probably also will have questions to ask of colleges.

You should also take the time to read and study the college materials provided online. Parents, please note also that many colleges and universities are "funny" in that many of them much prefer that the student himself or herself call and/or e-mail them rather than the parents. However, most colleges and universities will welcome inquiries from parents. But, parents, use discretion when calling and allow your student to take the initiative to contact the schools. This demonstrates to the schools that your student is mature and genuinely interested in attending their school. If your student does not have much experience in contacting university admissions offices, and most do not, I would strongly advise that you as a parent help coach and prepare them and practice with your student in advance as to the questions they will ask and how they will ask their questions and coach them in the proper ways to communicate with professionals on the telephone and even in e-mail communiques. With modern-day texting and social media, students these days are often not as skilled as students were in the past in doing such things. Your student may sulk and think you are being silly in wishing to help them prepare for such things, but my best advice to you is that you do help ready them if they are not experienced in doing so. The reality is that some students are more prepared and naturally more gifted in communicating with admissions offices and professionals as others. They all need to learn how to do this, but there is nothing wrong with you helping them prep for this. It isn't difficult to do it if you know how to do it.

A Quick Word on College Interviews

Some colleges require an on-campus in-person interview, whereas other colleges consider interviews as optional. Also, many colleges will offer students who live a distance away from their campus an opportunity to interview locally in their home city with representatives from the college who either will periodically travel to that area or are in charge of student applications from your part of the country. Some of these local interviews may however be conducted by the college's alumni residing in your local area. Whether or not you elect to undergo an optional interview is totally up to you. But if you do decide to interview, please make sure you practice and prepare for the interview in advance. There are certain basic questions that many interviewers will ask of you that you should anticipate. Some typical questions include the basic question as to why you are considering their college to attend, what area of study you wish to pursue in college, what types of activities you like to do outside of school, what are some examples of your leadership experiences in high school, how you handle disappointment, give an example of a failure you had, and other questions. Read up on and learn about examples of behavioral-based interviewing, which is increasingly becoming more popularly used.

During your interview, you wish to appear relaxed and you want to come across as genuine and confident but not cocky, pompous, presumptuous, or entitled during your interview. Of course, pay attention to your dress attire and make sure it is appropriate for your interview. Show your parents what you will be wearing in advance and take a backup shirt and tie just in case. Also, don't forget to take along with you to the interview several copies of your resume, in nice but inexpensive presentation binders, printed on good-quality stock paper, that includes a list of your high school classes and extracurricular activities and even your college essay. Smile, get up out of your chair and stand up straight, speak clearly and confidently, and present yourself with a firm handshake upon meeting your interviewer. Practice techniques of public speaking so that you do not use fillers such as "uh" and "you know" in speaking with your interviewer. With practice and effort, you will be able to limit the habit of using fillers in your speech. You can practice in advance by video and/or audio recording yourself speaking and by listening to and watching the recording of you doing so. Do not be hypercritical of yourself and realize that with continued practice, you will improve. Practice speaking aloud in your room by yourself also to just get into the habit of speaking. Trust me on this that doing so makes a difference. For those of you who are more introverted by nature, I emphasize these points even more strongly. Practice interviewing with your friends, parents, teachers, and mentors and if you need to enlist the services of a professional to help you prepare for your interview, by all means do so. But start preparing way before the interviewing season, which usually starts the fall of your senior year in high school. Often it is wise to choose to have an optional interview, especially if you feel that your candidacy for a particular school is borderline, and you feel that an interview may propel you over the top toward being accepted. Please keep in mind, however, that interviews that go poorly may have the opposite effect by detracting from your candidacy for admission.

I believe if given a choice to have an interview with an admissions officer on campus versus an alumnus in the field back in your region, in my opinion, I recommend you chose the former, to interview on campus with the admissions officer, if you and your family can financially afford to do so. Depending upon how many colleges to which you apply, it may not be feasible or practical for you to even expect to interview at every college to which you applied. This is a judgment decision that you should make along with your parents and advisors. Decide carefully.

What now follows is a brief outline of things you as a student should consider in selecting which colleges to apply and ultimately which college to select to attend.

Some Factors to Consider when Deciding Which Colleges/Universities to Attend

- Many resources are available to help you decide such as online and printed materials, counselors, teachers, parents, mentors, coaches, current students attending particular schools, and college alumni.
- Visit the campus in person prior to deciding to attend there.
- Go online for a virtual campus visit also.
- Register formally your visit with the college office of admissions.
- Attend campus tours with your parents.
- Apply to several schools including safety schools (discuss candidly your credentials with advisors, teachers, and parents). What does the data say are your chances for entry into a particular school versus others?
- Do apply to stretch schools. If you don't apply, you can't get in.
- Make special note of and pay attention to and strictly adhere to college application deadlines.
- Approach your high school counselors and teachers several weeks to months before deadlines to request college recommendations to meet deadlines. Your counselors and teachers will need several weeks to prepare your recommendations.
- Approach teachers and others to write *strong* letters of recommendation on your behalf. Do not approach teachers whom you don't believe will or who decline to write you strong letters of support.
- Most high school counselors do advise that you waive your right to view college recommendation letters and most colleges prefer that you waive your right. It is up to you and your parents if you waive your rights or not. Most colleges are suspicious if you don't waive your right, fair or not. Many teachers will let you see their letters regardless.

- Let your high school counselor (or office administrators as required) know in advance to which colleges to send your official sealed mailed or officially e-mailed high school transcripts.
- Register and take (more than once if necessary) the SAT and/or ACT test. Determine if your schools of choice require the SAT subject tests and/or ACT either with or without the writing portion of the exams. Know the rules of taking both exams; for example, is guessing on questions beneficial or harmful? Know the rules of which tests to submit and when to submit to your schools. Submitting to over a certain number of colleges results in an additional small fee.
- For students just entering high school, with your parents and counselor, determine which academic tract you should pursue—AP, International Baccalaureate, AP, Honors, or College Prep. Know and understand the differences. Look to the future and aim high and challenge yourself and be willing to work harder than you ever have in school. Don't lowball or short-change yourself.
- Take time (but meet deadlines) in making your decision on which colleges and universities to which to apply. Have a candid discussion with your parents your family's financial situation and how this may influence to which college you can apply.
- Once admitted to colleges, take your time in finalizing which school to attend.
- Don't let your parents make the decision for you. This is your decision to make, no one else's.

The following are additional important things to consider:

- Do you, the student, feel, upon visiting the campus, that you will be happy there? Be honest with yourself. You may need to visit more than once.
- Strength of academic areas of your course of study.

- Do the students you see and meet on-campus look and say they are happy?
- School location (city, suburban, rural)
- Size of college (number of students)
- Student/professor/teacher ratio. Does professor teach courses or only teacher aids?
- Are professors available to students for questions?
- What is the school's reputation toward undergraduate education versus graduate student education?
- How are the dormitory rooms?
- How is the quality of the food service?
- College distance from/proximity to home
- Ease of travel to and from school. Is an airport, train, or bus station nearby?
- Safety and security of campus.
- Semester versus quarter system
- Graduation rates of their college students
- Ratings of quality of life of students attending that college
- Weather (climate) of college city
- Is on-campus housing available for all four years of college?
- Is it important to you that other students from your high school go there?
- Does the school provide the student with a free computer?
- College graduation rates
- Single gender versus coed college
- Single gender versus coed dormitory buildings/floors
- Process for selecting roommates (important: see chapters 12 and 13)
- Gender mix
- Racial mix
- Does the school have the Greek system of fraternities and sororities?
- Religious-based schools
- Proximity/availability or places of worship close to campus
- Proximity and quality of local hospitals (students with serious health conditions)

- Historically black colleges and universities (HBCUS)
- Does the college/university have its own professional schools also? If so, do the professional schools give acceptance priorities to their undergraduate students?
- Does the college offer accelerated programs of study?
- Can you design your own major of study?
- Research opportunities for undergraduates?
- Travel abroad opportunities?
- Extracurricular opportunities?
- Financial aid packages (need-based, merit-based, work-study, grants, or scholarships)
- Recruitment opportunities to play sports, debate, or chess
- National universities versus liberal arts colleges (know the differences)
- Which schools require or recommend an in-person on-campus interview versus a local interview with an alumnus or admissions officer versus an optional interview?
- Other considerations
- Some colleges have on-campus residential summer programs for high school students to attend to explore their college before the student applies.
- Certain companies in the springtime offer bus tours for students to visit multiple colleges.

Checklist for Items to Take and Not Take to College

Below is a list that my daughter Meredith was given regarding recommended items to bring with you to college along with what they recommend you not bring. Because colleges vary in what you are allowed to bring, check early with your school to see what they recommend you bring with you and what they recommend you don't bring.

The following are things to bring:

The basic necessities

- Extra-long twin bed sheets, pillows, pillowcases, and comforter
- Towels
- Toiletries
- USB flash drive
- Headphones
- Laundry bag/hamper, drying rack, detergent, and stain remover
- Raincoat and umbrella
- Shower sandals
- Cell phone charger
- Nonhalogen desk lamp or other bright light for reading
- Poster adhesive and removable hooks
- Portable fan (window or freestanding)
- Shower caddy
- Reed diffusers, deodorizers, and air fresheners
- Alarm clock
- Power strip electrical adapter
- Dry-erase board and markers
- Photo ID, driver's license, state ID card, and passport (If you plan to work on or off campus, you will need a Social Security Card, birth certificate, or US passport.)

Suggested health items to bring to campus

- Information such as insurance and pharmacy cards; physician's name, address, and telephone number; emergency telephone numbers; and prescription refills, including glasses prescription
- Current prescription medications, in their original containers

- Over-the-counter medicines for pain relief, allergies, colds, flu, etc.
- Glasses, contact lenses, cleaning solutions, extra lenses, and cases
- Skin care products such as soaps, lotions, sunblock, aloe, acne ointment, antibacterial/antibiotic ointment, and petroleum jelly
- Extra toothbrushes, toothpaste, and dental floss
- Band-Aids, gauze, adhesive tape, and "Ace" bandage
- Other personal hygiene items (deodorant, shampoo, conditioner, etc.)
- Ice pack/hot pack
- Thermometer (digital or electronic)
- Flashlight with extra batteries
- Shopping Green: We encourage you to make environmentally conscious choices when moving on campus.
- Mini-fridges, laptops, TVs, DVD players, and other electronics. Look for Energy Star products or EPEAT certification products. Before you buy new, see if you can share with roommates. Residential Services' preferred provider for mini-fridges is USS. Please visit their website for more information.
- Printer. No need to buy a printer; you can print at the library when necessary.[1]
- Lighting. Desk lighting is one of the most efficient ways to light your space when you're working. Consider an LED or CFL bulb for your desk lights. These last longer and are more energy efficient.[2]
- Irons. You would be surprised how many irons and ironing boards we find in the move-out donation boxes at the end

---

[1] Printer: I personally do recommend that you have your own printer in your room that you can use for situations when it is not convenient for you to go to the library or other location that has printers.

[2] I also recommend you bring a flashlight, book reading light, computer USB light, lighted pens, a strobe light/safety light for your bicycle or when jogging, a bright safety vest for use when bicycling/jogging, and a bicycle helmet.

of the year! Before purchasing these items, check if you can borrow them from your roommate(s) or friends.

- Sheets and towels. Consider organic cotton and other materials (e.g., bamboo fiber), which eliminate pesticides and herbicides, making it better for your health and the environment.
- Clothes drying rack. Save money, energy, and have your clothes last longer!
- Furniture. Higher-quality and durable furniture can be donated and reused; low-quality, particleboard-based furniture usually ends up in a landfill.
- Bottled water. Why waste $1.50 each time you're thirsty? Evanston has great tap water, so bring a reusable bottle or cup and fill from the tap or bring a water filter. Northwestern has bottle-filler fountains in all residential facilities and many campus buildings.
- Reusable items. Reusable water bottles, mugs, shopping bags, and food containers are a convenient and less wasteful option than single-use materials.

Items prohibited from residential facilities

- Microwaves (including microwave and refrigerator combination units)
- Heating or cooking appliances (hot pots, toaster ovens, coffee makers, etc.)
- Refrigerators with interiors larger than 3.1 cubic feet
- Cooking knives with blades longer than three inches
- Hanging blankets, tapestries, rugs, etc.
- Lighted candles, holiday lights, and incense
- Fireworks, explosives, incendiaries, firearms, and other similar items
- Air conditioning units
- Waterbeds
- Lofts or loft-like risers (Many of our beds are adjustable.)

- Cinder blocks, wooden platforms, and any other sort of "bed riser"
- Pets

Items prohibited from student rooms. The following items can be used in common spaces and/or bathrooms:

- Hair dryer
- Iron

CHAPTER 2

Developing New Skills

Identify Your Strengths and Weaknesses

To achieve success, you will need to develop new skills as well as hone those that you currently possess. The first step is to take an inventory to identify your strengths and weaknesses. This assessment will help you determine what new skills you require. Ambitious people are constantly trying to improve their performance because they want to remain successful. Students and adults alike often solely focus upon the areas in their lives in which they are weakest. This is a great avenue for addressing one's deficits. However, I contend that it is important that you not only identify your weaknesses but also become fully aware of your strengths. Building further upon your strengths will contribute to the successes you have already achieved. This plan allows you to focus on resolving your weaknesses, but not at the expense of failing to capitalize on the strengths that positioned you for the successes you have already achieved thus far.

I am by nature introverted. When younger, I never particularly enjoyed public speaking. But because of my work and mission to educate the entire nation and the world about the importance of undergoing preventive health screenings for the early detection of disease and elimination of health disparities, I have been required to get out of my comfort zone and embrace public speaking. And I have accomplished this endeavor quite successfully. I do still need to continually improve in the area of public speaking to more effectively achieve my goals. However, even though I have focused much effort on eliminating this area of weakness, I, at the same time, recognize that some of the major determinants of my successes are in my abilities to remain steadfast to my goals, anticipate roadblocks, and use my critical thinking skills to recognize and navigate roadblocks before me.

Dr. Charles Modlin at podium receiving 2015 Black Professional Association Award proudly wearing father's National Senior Games Association Gold Record Setting Medallions

Dr. Charles Modlin speaking at City Club of Cleveland

Dr. Charles Modlin on the television show
7 Minutes with Russ Mitchell

My other area of strength is a belief in myself, which helps keep me on course. I inherited physical and mental stamina from my parents, which has enabled me to endure hardships, setbacks, and roadblocks. It takes a concentrated and deliberate focus to be cognizant of both one's weaknesses and strengths. I admit that at a young age, I never really took the time to self-reflect upon my strengths. I credit my parents, family, and friends and their continued positive support that helped reinforce my strongest characteristics. You maybe haven't ever thought about it, but you too should sit down and reflect upon what are your strengths and get feedback from you family, friends, teachers, coaches, and mentors as to what they consider to be your strengths. One of my friends indicated to me that one of my strengths is my greatness. I laugh thinking about these words because in no way do I or have I or will I ever consider myself "great." But what he was trying to do by telling me this was to further inspire me to try to do great things to serve the community. By him telling me I was great, he (and later others) opened my eyes to comprehend that I was in fact using my education and leveraging my position as a physician to do great things in the community. Consequently, their recognition of my accomplishments in turn made me place even further expectations upon myself to do even more. Do you understand what I am saying?

Before my friends recognized and pointed out to me that work I was doing in the community and in helping students was important, I did not realize the magnitude to which the community and the students whom I was mentoring and coaching appreciated my efforts. This realization then motivated me and set expectations within me to even do more. One of the messages I want to stress in this book is that of the power of your friends and family and community. They all can inspire us forward on our march toward success, and likewise you can inspire others. Whenever friends, family, and others refer to any of my accomplishments as great, they serve to inspire me further to achieve more. You, in turn, possess the ability to empower your family and friends also. So focus on eliminating your weaknesses while concurrently recognizing the strengths that have contributed greatly to your present-day successes and undoubtedly will help ensure your future successes.

Tips for Verbal and Nonverbal Communications

No matter what your career objectives may be, it is imperative that you pay particular attention to developing both excellent speaking (proper English) and listening skills. In the previous chapter, I mentioned working hard at developing my public speaking skills. Some people naturally possess better speaking and listening skills than others. If you are someone who does not particularly speak well in public, then you will need to work harder at developing such skills. It will be to your advantage to improve your communication skills to advance further within whatever profession you choose, because having good communication skills will likely provide you with greater opportunities to be noticed, for example, by your boss or the CEO of your organization. For instance, if you want to become a businessperson, excellent communication skills are vital in order to promote your business and to communicate your vision and business plan to potential investors and clients. If your goal is to become a trial attorney, you will need both exceptional listening and speaking skills.

Regarding speaking up, whether it be one on one or in front of large gatherings, it is important that you have an opinion and that you learn how to effectively and clearly express your opinions publicly. Some people are much more adept than others in doing this, but with preparation and forethought in advance as to what you want to say and how you wish to say it, with practice, you will improve and grow more confident in speaking up to voice your opinions. Keep in mind that you do not have to feel compelled to always voice your opinions about everything, nor will you want to. But keep in mind also who is your audience and be careful and mindful to respect the diversity and sensitivities of your audience and to, for example, not tell any off-color jokes. Especially, when you are speaking in larger audiences rather than in confidential meetings, never say anything that you would not want to be rebroadcast for others to hear because you must and should assume these days that you are being audio and/or video recorded, even without your knowledge or permission.

I believe that we as individuals, oftentimes, both in social situations and in work environments, are more concerned with talking to others in order to perhaps express our ideas about a particular situation, while at the same time we fail at taking time to properly and attentively listen to those whom we have engaged in conversation. By not taking time to be an active listener during our interactions with others, we often are denying ourselves of valuable opportunities to learn from the information, knowledge, and experiences that others are willing to share with us. By perfecting your skills of actively listening, you will position yourself to discover the vast knowledge that others are willing to impact upon us, while at the same time, you will be showing the other party or parties with whom you are interacting that you do respect what they have to say in the discussions you are having with them. By stressing the importance of your active listening during conversations, I am not suggesting that you avoid verbally communicating in social or work environment interactions. To the contrary, you must, in order to show that you are actively engaged and that you are indeed intelligent and have something to contribute to the conversation, also actively verbally communicate and not simply listen. Nevertheless, I am emphasizing the fact that it is just as important that you develop active listening skills to enhance your overall communication abilities. I caution you, and I am sure you have already noticed this yourself by observing others, that many people often feel unnecessarily compelled to speak and even dominate conversations when in fact they have very little or even nothing of substance to say. Nobody in business meetings or social situations enjoys being around a person who speaks just to hear himself or herself talk. Do you understand the critically important points I am making here?

Communication skills not only include possessing good speaking and listening skills. It is important to be aware of how you project yourself to others through your unspoken communication or your body language. It has been evidenced that approximately 80 percent of how we communicate with others is neither through the spoken or written word, but through our body language. Each of us must become aware of what signals our body language is projecting to others so that we can communicate more precisely what messages we intend to convey. We don't want people to confuse our intentions because of the body language that we project. Yes, it is true that people for a variety of reasons may conclude unfair and biased assumptions, opinions, and stereotypes about us based upon our race, ethnicity, age, gender, the way we speak, the way we move, the color of and style of our hair, frame of our body, how we dress, and other personal characteristics. It is not possible for us to always be in control of how we are perceived. Nevertheless, it is important to be aware that your body language is a powerful tool in how you communicate to others around you as to who you are, how welcoming are you, your attitudes, friendliness, approachability, etc.

You have the power and ability to be in control of your body language through self-awareness. Watch and carefully study the body language of others around you, on television, and in the movies. Try to associate, for example, how the actors and actresses on television, film, or in the theater effectively convey their messages and play their roles through the deliberate use of their body language. Just like the actors and actresses, you too can control your body language to convey your true messages to others. But a word of warning, in many social and business situations, you may not want to openly express what is truly on your mind through your body language if doing so could negatively jeopardize or threaten an important opportunity for you, such as obtaining a job or a position. In other words, if conveying negative feelings toward a particular person whom it is important for you to impress, such as a boss, teacher, or business contact, will serve to harm or hinder your progress or ability to achieve your goals, then in those situations, it would be in your best interests to portray through your body language (and verbal communication of course) a more positive attitude, even though inside you might be feeling different about that person or the situation or conversation in which you are engaged. I learned long ago that in certain situations, it is in our own best interests to not show our true feelings (through our body language or spoken or written word) about a particular person or situation if doing so will have a negative impact upon our current or future situation or opportunities. Providing this warning does not contradict the importance of you acquiring and perfecting an ability to engage in crucial and critical conversations, often with people who do not necessarily appeal to you.

Another avenue to improving verbal communications is to actively expand your vocabulary. This will not occur overnight, but it is possible to learn new words over time. Reading books such as a thesaurus, encyclopedia, dictionary, and other educational materials and attending lectures are mechanisms for expanding your vocabulary. Also, practice adding new words to your written communications. Doing so will greatly enhance your abilities to incorporate new and powerful vocabulary words even into your verbal/speaking communications. "It isn't difficult to do it if you know how to do it."

My father was an expert at expanding his vocabulary, and I credit him with really stressing to me the importance of doing so. He would routinely read the dictionary, and both he and my mother peaked my interests in the importance of self-education when in 1970 they purchased a full set of *World Book Encyclopedias* (which I still own) so that my sisters and I would have additional educational opportunities. To this day, I remember the door-to-door salesman ringing our doorbell and meeting with my mother and me in the living room to display the encyclopedias that my mother purchased. Back then, there was no Internet; therefore, the only way for students to perform research involved a trip to the public or school library to access resource/reference books such as encyclopedias. I recall taking a vocabulary class my junior or senior year in high school, which I enjoyed very much. In the class, our charge was to incorporate new vocabulary words into our class written assignments and homework. I recall the teacher returning a paper to me with her comments written with a red marker indicating to not "show off" my vocabulary. To me, her comments were perplexing, considering that she was my teacher in a vocabulary class. At first, I took offense to her comment because she was accusing me of trying to show off when all I was doing was only incorporating into my written work a few newly acquired vocabulary words. But I soon realized that she was offering me valuable and important feedback by cautioning me and aiming to teach me to not saturate my paper with a collection of words that did not seem natural or that did not flow within the context of my assignment. While you should incorporate new vocabulary words into written and spoken communications, your work should still appear and sound natural and not appear as if you are reading from a dictionary or trying to impress someone with your verbal acrobats specifically. Does this make sense to you?

So what are additional ways in which you can substantively improve upon your public speaking communication abilities? Watch *TED Talks*. Per the website, TED is a nonprofit devoted to spreading ideas, usually in the form of short, powerful talks (eighteen minutes or less). TED began in 1984 as a conference where technology, entertainment, and design converged and today covers almost all topics, from science to business to global issues, in more than a hundred languages. You can consider writing and giving a *TED Talk*. Develop your elevator speech and read voraciously in preparation. You may also want to consider becoming involved in Toastmasters or Dale Carnegie speaking courses, both of which focus on providing you with guidance on perfecting your public speaking skills and incorporate another strategy and technique for you to improve on your effective communication skills, storytelling.

Investigate the important art of telling stories. Until recently I never really appreciated the importance of storytelling or incorporating stories into my speeches and everyday conversations. However, many authoritative books address the importance of storytelling as a strategy to deliver captivating and influential speeches or simply how to more effectively communicate better. I have listed in the appendix section some books on storytelling that I advise you read. I've heard many people tell stories, but their manner of delivery detracted from their message. For example, in some cases, the stories were too long, off topic, insensitive, or crude. So a word of advice to help you in your ability to pull up from your memory banks some of your important life experiences that you wish to convey that might be best communicated in the form of stories—keep a journal and document your journey so that you'll be able to reflect back on your own experiences and realize how far you've come. You can analyze how you have grown over the years and share lesson(s) learned with others in the form of impactful storytelling, especially by incorporation of your real-life personal experiences. In doing so, remember the good and proper tenets of writing and public speaking. Have a beginning, middle, and ending to your story. Also practice telling your story so that when you tell it, you will be fluid in doing so. But I also strongly advise that you practice telling your story in front of your mentors and trusted confidants prior to telling your story publicly in a speech, formal meeting, or informal gathering in order to vet your story for appropriateness, especially in this era of heightened sensitivities, and matters of tactfulness to make sure your story will not offend others. The same goes for the telling of jokes. Vet them with others (inclusive of all genders) and stay away from telling racial and ethnic jokes or other jokes that others may find offensive.

Dr. Charles Modlin giving TED Talk

As students, get and use a journal to capture your experiences, which with practice you will be increasingly able to develop into stories that you can pull up at a moment's notice out of your memory bank to use to bring home your points. Being an effective and capable storyteller will make your communications more memorable. I am not speaking of making up or fabricating stories to tell if they are not your own experiences. You at all times in your storytelling must remain genuine. Keep in mind that you can tell stories of others' experiences as long as you don't claim them to be your own. Recently, in the news, we have heard about news reporters and even politicians fabricating stories of experiences they had that were not really true. With practice and preparation, you'll be able to effectively add life, color, and excitement to your life experiences and bring out favorable and "flavorable" elements of your personality to others.

The Right Way to Write

The elements in the preceding section on how to improve your public speaking and listening skills will also help to enhance your written communication abilities and vice versa. I will demonstrate some examples as to why you must make it a priority to improve upon (strive to perfect) your writing skills. After all, there is a right way to write. Right? As a student, I know you have taken English composition courses and probably (hopefully) a course or courses in a foreign language. In your English composition courses, the teacher or professor stressed the importance that you use the proper punctuation, tense, conjugation, and syntax in your written reports. Your instructors were correct in insisting that you adhere to the rules of proper writing. When I was in high school and college, I excelled in Latin class. I loved Latin and tested out of an entire year as a freshman in college. My daughters Hannah and Meredith both took Latin in high school, and Meredith particularly loves studying Latin and is contemplating majoring in Latin at Northwestern University. I particularly loved the exercise and challenge of translating original Latin works into English. One unique aspect of Latin prose is that there is no set or correct word order needed in constructing sentences. Typically, in English, when writing sentences (and in speaking), the writer (and speaker) starts off the sentence with the subject preceding the verb, which precedes the object of verb of the sentence. This correct word order is not relevant in Latin. Still, I strongly recommend studying Latin. It exponentially facilitated my English composition abilities, and I can emphatically say that the study of Latin still to this day helps me in my writing abilities.

Maintaining excellent written communication abilities is critical to your future. Often the first contact you will have with an individual who is or may be a key to your success will be through your written words. This may take the form of your writing a college application or essay, a scholarship application, a correspondence letter, or nowadays more commonly an e-mail, rather than a letter, seeking a job or your written response to any communique for a variety of reasons. It is always important that you possess and demonstrate, in a non-ostentatious manner, proper writing skills so that you effectively put your best foot forward and make great first and lasting impressions. Why disadvantage yourself by giving people opportunities to doubt your level of education by exhibiting poor writing skills.

Remember, you are competing with some other students who in reality may be competing against you to gain entry into the same colleges and competing with you for the same sources of college scholarships or jobs. Pay attention to your syntax, punctuations, and tense of words. Also, always proofread your written work and reread it several times before submitting it as you will often find mistakes previously unnoticed. I also recommend that you seek a friend, sibling, tutor, mentor, coach, parent, guardian, or another student whom you trust to read your work and to give you input or suggestions. It is important to ask someone who is knowledgeable in proper writing and grammar skills to help proofread *with* you your writing for grammar. You can also always ask someone to review your work for content. But always remember to maintain integrity and don't allow someone else to do your writing and don't plagiarize the work of others. If writing and rules of grammar are areas in which you struggle, I would advise that you consider taking additional courses in English composition in college, in class or online, or at a community college while in high school and ideally before matriculating at your college or university. Remember, you can also access educational grammar resources online, at your public library, or your high school and you can also find tutors to assist you; for example, current or former teachers or other students are excellent resources.

There are many examples in modern society and culture where improperly spoken and written works are celebrated, sometimes as a matter of the artistic works by poets, musicians in rap music (no disparaging), or actors on television or in other venues. Often our friends and family members may not exhibit the most proper verbal or written communication skills. There is no need to be judgmental against anyone who might not be skillful in verbal or written communication skills. However, so that you achieve the successes in the life you seek to achieve, you emphatically do need to be concerned with remaining consistent in using proper verbal and written communication skills (and as mentioned body language skills). As my mother always told her children and her pupils whom she taught in and out of the classroom, there is no such word as ain't. It's funny, but correct, that the spellchecker in Microsoft Word does not recognize the word ain't. Double negatives are also a no. Occasionally you should review when to use the pronouns "I" versus "me" and "we" versus "us" and "who" versus "whom" and the correct use of singular or plural wording. It is easy to sometimes forget some of the grammatical rules, and we all do make mistakes. Continue to try to write and properly speak. Doing so will advantage you and make a positive difference in your chances to achieve your short-term and long-term goals. Again, of course, none of us are perfect, but the objective is to continuously strive to improve upon our abilities. Proper speaking and writing do require practice and attention to detail. But you can do it! "It isn't difficult to do it if you know how to do it."

Develop Name Recognition Skills

Lastly, along with what I have included in this chapter on developing good verbal and nonverbal communication skills and the importance of writing the right way, it is very important for you to develop techniques and skills in the area of improving upon your name recognition abilities. In college and in your professional as well as your social life, you will encounter and meet literally thousands of new people. You won't be able to remember or recall every person's name whom you meet (there are a small number of people who do possess total recall abilities), but there are people whom you will encounter whom it will be to your advantage to recall their names and the circumstances for which you met them. In many business situations, you will be introduced to people whom you may wish or need to recall their names for future business networking purposes, and in college, likewise you may need to recall the name of a student to ask them a question about a class they took or you may need to recall the name of an alumnus whom you met so that you will able to later contact them regarding a potential job or internship, for example. I, in no way, pretend to be an expert in name recognition.

When I was younger, even though name recognition came easier and more effortlessly for me, I didn't really pay much attention to it or put a special effort in perfecting name recognition. As I have matured in my professional career, I have a much keener understanding of the importance of name recognition for business networking and social purposes than I did when I was younger. For some people, name recognition and recall is effortless, but for others, it takes considerable effort. There are many books published on various techniques to improve your name recognition. Some people even pay to take seminars in memory and name recognition. One technique that is often helpful is to upon meeting someone repeat their name aloud back to them and also in your head as a way of reinforcing within your memory what is their name. It is not impolite to ask a person to spell their name for you if you have some difficulty understanding or hearing the pronunciation of their name. In professional and even in certain social networking situations, it is quite customary and acceptable (and even expected) also to exchange business cards with individuals you are meeting. As a way of helping remember their names, do glance at their business card when they give it to you and, in turn, always carry your business card to exchange with others, because, likewise, you want them to remember your name and who are you. That's right, even as a high school or college student, you should have a business card that you can give especially to individuals whom you consider key connections for you. Presenting to someone your own business card is not being gaudy or pretentious. Quite to the contrary. It is a way of telling the world that you are somebody who has credentials and that you have a plan and aspirations to succeed in life. It tells them that your name is important. I have listed some of these books in the appendix section.

It is absolutely, definitely, without question and undoubtedly worth your time and effort to develop techniques that work and are effective for you at improving upon your name recognition capabilities. When people sense that you remember their name and who they are, you give them the sense that you care about them, consider them to be important, and respect them; and consequently, people in turn tend to remember your name and who you are and tend to be more amicable in interacting with you and networking with you. Name recognition takes practice and is an important part of communicating effectively with others. As with the many other success tips contained in this book, with dedicated effort and practice, you will come to appreciate that name recognition "isn't difficult to do it if you know how to do it." You will learn more about the importance of networking in other sections of this book.

CHAPTER 3

Becoming an Emotionally Mature Adult

Remain Adaptable in an Ever-Changing World

Writing down and routinely visually reviewing your goals will serve to help you maintain your focus and direction. And let's not forget the importance of self-confidence and preparation in helping you achieve your goals and dreams. However, as I explain to the students whom I mentor and coach, and now share with you, it is to your advantage to remain adaptable, flexible, and willing to modify plans, when necessary. In life, circumstances change, and different opportunities arise. You, therefore, must remain flexible and adaptable to respond to these changing circumstances, because your goals may in fact change according to your experiences, growth, and evolution.

For example, you may plan to attend college with the hopes of becoming a surgeon. However, once you progress through college courses or medical school classes, it may become apparent that you become squeamish at the sight of blood. Or you may be adverse to the idea of standing for hours at a time at an operating room table. Students often hold a certain perception of a particular career and then through shadowing opportunities come to realize their original career trajectory does not interest them. Or you may find out that once in college, you are not excelling in a certain subject area as you did in high school. I am not at all suggesting that you give up on pursuing a particular career trajectory simply because you might be struggling in a particular class. As I have written and advised elsewhere in this book, I encourage you to remain focused and determined in your resolve to achieve your goals. However, it may become necessary during your journey and in your life when to your advantage to be introspective as to what path you ultimately want to pursue. In other words, sometimes things don't work out as we originally planned, and it is important that you realize there is no shame if you do decide to change your career goals. After all, it is your life, and it is imperative that you pursue a career in which you will find happiness and joy. Remember, you may be working in that career for an entire profession, which could be forty years or more in duration. Don't pursue a career just to please someone else. When I was in medical school, I encountered some students who seemingly had no real interests in pursuing a medical career, and in my professional life, I have also encountered students whom I have mentored and coached who seemingly were pursuing a particular career goal just to please their parents.

Remain flexible. Perhaps you set a goal to perform research during the summer following your freshman year in college but then discovered an opportunity to go on a medical mission trip instead. Writing down a plan does not justify automatically ignoring a great opportunity that may further enhance your career objectives and life experiences. You must constantly and actively be alert and aware of unique and time-sensitive educational and life-enhancing opportunities that may arise, often with little or no notice. Weigh your options, but don't discount alternatives because they were not in your original plans. In real life, changing your mind about pursuing a particular course of study or career according to your growth, development, and informed choices does not mean that you have failed or disappointed your supporters. The people who love and support you want nothing more than for you to be happy in life, and you owe it both to yourself and to them to seek whatever course of study and career that will make you happy. Importantly, please note that if you have made a commitment to someone, for example, to perform a certain job over the summer, it is your responsibility to speak to that person if you find out that there is an important different opportunity for you to pursue. In life, you must come to realize that there will be times when you have already committed to perform a certain job or duty to someone that you will need to honor that responsibility regardless of other opportunities that may arise after you already have committed to the prior obligation. But my important point to you here is that if you find yourself in such a quandary, the mature thing for you to do is to lose your timidity and have a crucial conversation with the person you have committed to. In many instances, they may support you pursuing your new opportunity. But above all, do not simply abdicate and abandon your responsibilities. To do so would be unprofessional and reflect poorly upon you.

My junior year photo at Northwestern University

Empathy Is Admirable and Makes You a Better Person

Be of assistance to others who may need your help. As I have noted in this book, sooner or later, no matter how smart you are, or the level of your IQ or your EQ (emotional intelligence), there will arise a situation(s) where you will need help from a parent, friend, family member, colleague, another student, or maybe someone you don't even yet know. We see examples of this situation often. I am a fan of the National Basketball Association. I especially enjoyed watching Michael Jordan play basketball. In my opinion, Michael Jordan is the best basketball player who has ever lived. Yes, that's a subjective statement, but I miss seeing him play. I mention Michael Jordan because even though he was a great basketball player, Michael could not have won a single game all by himself, let alone an NBA championship. He needed additional players on his team. People often point out that the Chicago Bulls with Michael Jordan did not win an NBA Championship until Scottie Pippen arrived on the scene and matured to the top of his game. Do you get my point?

Everyone, eventually, needs help at some juncture in their life. You might need assistance in a particular college course from your professor, a teacher's aide, a classmate, or a friend. Don't allow either your pride or your shyness to get in the way of seeking help when you need it. Often, friends can help us consider additional options for whatever problem we might be facing that we had not considered. The perspective of someone who is not too close to the situation at times helps. In tough circumstances, we might consider these people who rise to the occasion to come to help us as lifesavers. However, receiving help can be reciprocal. Don't you want to be one of those lifesavers to someone who needs your assistance? Wouldn't it make you feel good and worthwhile to lend such counsel or advice to someone? Isn't it our human nature to help others? You'll see that whenever you help someone else, you will derive a great sense of personal satisfaction and reward, and you will further mature and learn from the situation yourself.

As a kidney transplant surgeon, one of the best examples I can give of man serving man is in the case of living organ donation. Living kidney donation, split liver donation, and bone marrow donation represent the only examples (of which I am aware) of surgery performed on patients who themselves do not physically benefit from the operation. Blood donation also represents a nonsurgical act that has lifesaving benefits for one's fellow human beings. When a person who is a living organ donor undergoes the operation to give their organ to another person, the operation is being performed to physically, physiologically, and anatomically benefit the recipient of that organ, not the patient who is the organ donor. However, research surveys of living organ donors have revealed that, in actuality, the living donors indicate that they do indeed psychologically, spiritually, and emotionally derive significant "benefit" as a result of serving as a living organ donor for the given recipient.[3] They are giving of themselves to help another human being. Likewise, I contend that whenever you do, a favor for someone or offer assistance, no matter how large or small the act, you too receive a benefit in the personal satisfaction of knowing that you are helping another person. Being of service to someone else will reenergize and bring out the best in you. Additionally, when you help another individual with no hidden agenda or expectation of something in return, your act of kindness will come back to benefit you in immeasurable ways. Let me close by encouraging you to read the motto of my alma mater, Northwestern University, which in the Latin (derived from Philippians 4:8) reads, "*Quecumque sunt vera*," and means, "Whatsoever things are true, if there be any virtue, and if there be any praise, think on these things" (Philippians 4:8).

---

[3] James F. Childress and Catharyn T. Liverman, eds., "Chapter 9: Ethical Considerations in Living Donation," in *Organ Donation: Opportunities for Action* (Washington DC: The National Academies Press, 2006), 269.

University Hall, Northwestern University

Dr. Charles Modlin, proud Northwestern University alumnus

With Northwestern University president Morton Schapiro

With Willie the Wildcat, Northwestern University mascot

Pictured with Sigma Nu Fraternity, Gamma Beta
Chapter, Northwestern University, 1981

Dr. Charles Modlin, visiting professor lecturer at
Northwestern University Feinberg School of Medicine

Dr. Charles Modlin advising Northwestern University
Feinberg School of Medicine students during alumni event

Learn from Your (and Others') Mistakes

No one is perfect. It does not matter whether if you are the high school valedictorian or a Rhodes scholar or possess an IQ of 400 or whether you score an 8,000 on your SAT and a 95 on your ACT college entrance examinations (yes, I realize that these tests don't score that high, but hopefully you get my point, LOL); there will always be times when you make a mistake or miscalculation. Place yourself mentally in a position where you can learn from your mistakes as well as learn from the mistakes of others. I could write an entire book, or many volumes of books (LOL), about the many mistakes I have made during my lifetime. Overall, I feel that I have mostly made sound decisions in setting out my life's course; otherwise, I would not be writing this book. However, reflecting upon my life, I should have spent (and still should) more time working out, eating healthier, getting a good nights' sleep whenever possible, practicing my trumpet, keeping in contact with friends, maturing my network, attending more on- and off-campus special educational and artistic events, and reading more, among other things. As an important aside and word of advice to you, I implore that you do take time to smell the roses on your journey.

In Evanston while an undergraduate student at Northwestern, my college experience was that much more enriched because I did intentionally open my eyes to appreciate the lovely environment in which I was in; I did take the time to smell the roses along my journey. For example, while in college, I always intentionally made a special effort to recognize the beauty of the Northwestern campus, whereas many of my student colleagues as they professed to me did not. Every day, as I walked down Sheridan Road to and from my classes, I took note of the beautiful tree-lined Sheridan Road while marveling at the elegantly designed flower gardens and landscaping and the majestic architecture of the Northwestern University buildings. I would routinely walk out to and sit and read out on the big rocks on the Landfill while enjoying the majesty, sights, sounds, and smell of the mighty clear blue waters of Lake Michigan with the majestic and spectacular skyline of Chicago standing proudly in the distance. I always felt privileged to have been fortunate to have been able to study and live on such a wonderful and beautiful campus, which was so built and meticulously maintained specifically for the enjoyment of its students and all who took the time and opened their eyes to behold. I surely hope that my daughter Meredith takes time on a daily basis to enjoy the beautiful Northwestern campus. Likewise, I thoroughly marveled at the beauty of the colonial architecture and pristine landscaping of the campus of the College of William & Mary in Williamsburg, Virginia, from where my daughter Sarah received her undergraduate degree in biology. The campus of Texas Tech in Lubbock, Texas, from where my son, Trey, graduated was also quite appealing and inspiring as well as the campus of Miami University in Oxford, Ohio, to which my daughter Hannah matriculated. In contrast, a large number of students I encountered while at Northwestern admitted to me that they never really paid attention to or appreciated the beauty of the campus.

So back to my point about the importance of learning from one's mistakes and the mistakes of others, I do recognize that a large part of my success has been the result of my ability and willingness to learn from my mistakes and that I put forth great efforts not to repeat the same mistakes. This approach has not always worked for me, and nor will it always work for you, because, as human beings, we are all fallible; but it is important for us to attempt to learn from our mistakes and missteps.

Also, learn from the mistakes of others. In conversations with your family, friends, colleagues, and others, if you are observant, you should be able to discern that there is a great deal of knowledge you can gain and absorb from even the simplest of conversations. As a surgeon, I routinely learn from the experiences of the other surgeons, physicians, and colleagues. We have weekly continuing education conferences and monthly meetings as physicians called morbidity and mortality conferences to review the cases from our department that have involved recent complications including unforeseen deaths. Needless to say, when you are a surgeon taking care of sometimes critically ill patients, you will encounter cases where patients will have complications or even expire, no matter how much talent you possess and how well-trained and prepared you are. Even as doctors, many things involving patient's illnesses are out of our control, whether we wish to admit it or not. It is a doctor's sworn responsibility to learn from every one of these unfortunate events, and in fact, we doctors do learn and continue to learn over the course of our careers from our experiences and the experiences of others.

At this stage in your life, I don't expect that you will be reviewing cases regarding life and death. But you get my point. Learn from the mistakes that are made in everyday occurrences such as on your math exam or even in your daily social interactions. What mistakes did you make on the test and why? In interactions with your friends and professors, how might you have communicated better to others your thoughts, insights, and perceptions about a particular topic at hand? How will learn from your mistakes? In speaking with your friend, for example, perhaps there was a misunderstanding that developed. Why did it occur? What could you have done or said differently in speaking with your friend that might have helped avoid such a misunderstanding? Misunderstandings can also occur through written forms of communication, particularly in short texts, e-mail messages, and tweets. How might you better communicate with people and avoid misunderstandings? What can you do differently the next time to avoid such mistakes?

In learning from others' mistakes, we must become students of history. While I did enjoy very much my history class in high school, with my teacher Mr. Cecil Tague, I did not fully appreciate the importance of studying history while in high school. It was not until later in life that I realized how we, in the present time, can learn from the mistakes made by prior generations. In knowing our history, we become better equipped not to repeat the mistakes of people from the past generations. Many students, I included, used to think that studying history was just an exercise in memorization. But now as an adult, I appreciate the value in reading biographies, autobiographies, and other historical references as a very valuable way to harness the wisdom of others for my own benefit. Learn to take advantage of history.

Make time to read books beyond your academic studies. If you were like me when I was your age, I was busy focusing my efforts on my academic, scientific coursework, reading chapters and doing homework problems. I did not feel there was time for pleasure reading. The purpose of this book is for you to learn from my experiences, including actions that I would change if given an opportunity to go back in time. Devoting more time to reading outside of my area of study, including history books, biographies, autobiographies, self-help books, books on leadership and philosophy, and novels, would have been of great benefit to me. I cannot go back in time but because I now understand the importance of reading such materials I as an adult have seized opportunities to now do so, still not as often as I would like due to work and family obligations. Please note that I cannot emphasize to you strongly enough that there is an infinite amount of wisdom in books. Absorb as much of it as you can. You'll be the better for it.

If I had a time machine, perhaps you will be the person to someday invent one, I would do again most of what I did on my journey to become a surgeon. However, there are definite things that continue to live and burn within my memory banks as to what I would have done and should have done differently. Have you ever seen the movie starring actor comedian Bill Murray called *Groundhog Day*? It's funny but is about a man who every day relives the previous day and he has an opportunity to changes things he did that previous day. All of us can think of situations that if we had the chance to do over, we would do differently. But our goal should be to do as many impactful things as we can now so that when looking back on our lives, we would be proud we did and how we did them and have as few regrets as possible that we seized important opportunities.

Learning from history is not limited to reading books about people from the distant past. History is among us everywhere we look. My father always told us, "The best teacher is at the foot of an old person." He meant that our elders possess much knowledge that can benefit the young greatly. Our elders are often eager and quite flattered for young adults to seek their advice and wisdom. However, too often, those from a younger generation either don't take the time to consult an "older person," as my father often referred to the elders of the community, or may not believe older people can provide them with any valuable advice or worse that older people don't know anything or have forgotten everything. This is very faulty and unwise to believe this. Keep in mind that just because people from an older generation may not be up to date on the latest in social media or technology does not mean that they are not an invaluable resource. In many instances, and this is by no way being disrespectful to the youth of today, it is true that older people have often forgotten more than younger people now know. Just look within your own family and community and think about an older person whom you might be able to approach for advice about a particular situation, problem, or goal. Ask them, and watch a smile appear on their face. Be bold and be direct. Inquire about any mistakes they made in life and what they would have done differently if given a chance. Ask how they handled different situations and get their perspectives on a current issue you are facing.

You can also stop and examine your mistakes thus far to read-just your current situation if you feel you are headed down the wrong path. Sometimes we need just to slow down and reflect upon our daily lives to analyze just how we are doing and progressing. "It isn't difficult to do it if you know how to do it," and how to do it is to just sit quietly, close your eyes, open your memory banks, and think. Of course, one must always look to the future, but it is imperative for you also to reflect upon your past so that you will be able to see where you are in relation to where you wish to be. Determine if any of your actions are pulling you off course. Sometimes pausing, stopping, taking a deep breath, thinking, and analyzing the situation will allow you to push the reset button and chart a new and better course. Remember, even though the shortest route between two points is a straight line, it is, however, in life, very rare to be able to maintain a straight course in all of our endeavors. Previously in this book, I discussed the importance of recognizing that you will invariably be confronted with obstacles, and I speak of the importance of positioning yourself to navigate such roadblocks. While we cannot anticipate every obstacle that lies in our way, this book will better position you to conquer whatever challenges await you, and trust me, there will be challenges awaiting you.

There is a personal assessment tool that professionals use called a 360-degree evaluation. This survey tool is distributed to various people in one's life, typically their workplace, to enlist them to answer questions about how they perceive the character, characteristics, and other important qualities of the participant, usually one of their coworkers, leaders, or manager. The 360-degree survey is answered anonymously; the individual responses are not linked to the names of those responding. The responses are compiled by an independent source and presented to that person (the participant), allowing a clear assessment of various aspects of others' perceptions of them. Completing a 360-degree evaluation is an invaluable tool to allow us to reflect on how we are progressing in our professional lives and can be invaluable in determining if any course resets are needed. I have been the participant subject of a 360-degree evaluation. One does not have to take every comment or opinion that is presented on the 360-degree evaluation as the absolute truth, but the evaluation offers a general idea of how one is perceived by others whom they interact. In trying to improve upon your communication skills, a 360-degree evaluation can be exceedingly valuable in shedding light on whether you might be giving off unintended body language signals or other communication signals that could be interfering with your progress. You can learn from such unintended projections and make modifications on your course. Of note, the 360-degree survey is not a perfect tool, and the independent reviewer/facilitator who compiles and helps interpret the findings should possess elements of cultural sensitivity and cultural competency and training in psychology and the social sciences.

Developing Meaningful Friendships and Associations

People such as parents, caregivers, teachers, coaches, advisors, mentors, role models, family, and friends have helped contribute to your successes and are enthusiastically willing to continue to do so in the future. In high school and even in middle and grade school, you likely gravitated toward developing friendships with students who were similar to you in that they took school seriously, they were studious, and they cared that their teachers thought of them as being good students. In fact, it was your parents and caregivers who likely were the ones who helped or at least reinforced and help strengthen your friendships with other successful students, even if you were not aware that they were doing this. They were doing this by interacting with the parents of other kids who seems to be on the same page as you in school and encouraging and facilitating activities with you and other kids. Your parents did a lot of the behind-the-scenes things to help you that you never even noticed, and still do. When you were younger, your parents may have invited those other good students to your house or to join you for a playdate. Teachers may have suggested to your parents which kids would be good play friends. In middle and high school, you may have formed study circles with other students because you realized the value in networking with other studious schoolmates. You certainly did not want to team up with students whom you thought would not carry their weight in group projects, and in fact, you probably avoided them whenever possible. As in your earlier school years, it is important that you continue to surround yourself with friends and associates in college and beyond who are likeminded and also focused and strive for success and who are not distractors of your focus. Friends can often give you different perspectives on circumstances, and they can serve to reenergize you when you need support.

Embrace Diversity

Embrace diversity in your friendships and associations. People from diverse cultures and backgrounds can open your eyes to the opportunities of the world, which you otherwise might have overlooked or not been evident to you. I was born in a small town in Henry County, Indiana—New Castle, population, 18,000. There was one high school. Most people in the area maintained their way of life by working either as farmers or in factories, foundries, or the local hospital or school system. The composition of the town was mainly

Caucasians with only about 1 percent being African Americans and probably not even that many. From what I recall and in looking back at my high school yearbook, I was one of only less than ten African Americans who graduated from my high school class of approximately a total graduating class of about 350 students. In the middle of fifth grade, my family moved to the "good side of town," and my sister Pam in third grade and I became the first African Americans to ever attend Riley Elementary School. The next year, when I was in sixth grade, my sister and I had the fortune of traveling to Washington DC on a class trip with my mother who volunteered to serve as a trip chaperone for the class. She was great at doing this. Of note, my mother, Grace Hampton Modlin, at that time was an elementary schoolteacher at another New Castle school (becoming the first black main classroom teacher in the history of Henry County, Indiana).

Traveling to Washington DC was an amazing trip, which made a lifelong impression upon me. In school and on television, I, of course, had read about and seen pictures depicting Washington DC and sights such as the Washington Monument, the Lincoln Memorial, the White House, the Capitol Building, the Tomb of the Unknown Soldier, and the Smithsonian Museum. And there we were, visiting those places in person. It was also the first time I, my sister, and my mother had ever flown on an airplane; and I laugh now because on the airplane, we were served a free and full hot meal, which typically airlines don't serve nowadays. Going on that trip opened my eyes to the reality that these places I had only read about or seen on television actually existed. But equally important, I realized that had our family not moved so that I was able to attend Riley School and had I instead remained at Weir Elementary School (which by the way was located in the predominantly black side and poorer side of town), I would have never been able to go on that trip. In other words, moving to this new elementary school opened my eyes to the fact that inequities existed in the experiences and opportunities that were available between schools in our town that were only three miles apart. It opened my eyes further that I wanted to have the opportunities in life that the *white* people had. I never did—nor did my parents or family ever teach me to—disparage or resent white people.

However, as I matured, I did start to realize from my own observations that in New Castle, many disparities existed in large part based upon people's skin color.

Moving to Riley Elementary School and that neighborhood also gave me the opportunity to meet Jeffrey Ayres and Ian Sheeler, who both, to this day, remain my lifelong best friends. Jeff and Ian and their families are by the way Caucasian. Being the first and only black students at that time to be attending Riley School, my sister and I did feel out of place at first especially when many of the kids would stare at us and want to touch our hair to see what it felt like. I recall my mother telling me that the kids at Riley School had been prepped ahead of time that my sister and I were transferring to Riley. In retrospect, I suppose this was definitely a good thing that the teachers at Riley did this as they were trying to make our transition into the new school less traumatic for us. We had team teachers, two teachers for each grade; and I vividly remember one of my male fifth-grade teachers making me race the two fastest boys in fifth grade, Jeff Ayres and David Phenniger because I could tell he wanted to see if the stereotype held true, if I could run fast because I was a black boy. I can laugh about it now, but at the time, it was traumatic and degrading to me. Well, both Jeff and David beat me in the foot race, which I never wanted to run in the first place, and this gave me an immediate sense of inadequacy as if I had disappointed my teacher and had not lived up to the stereotype. Strange that I would care about disappointing the teacher. Why I cared, I don't know, but at that young age and at that moment in my life, I did care. I am now, almost fifty years after this occurred, for the first time revealing this occurrence to anyone. But in the end, Jeff and another boy, Alan Broyles (and neither did most of the kids for that matter), did not see me for the color of my skin, but for the content of my character. Where have we heard these words before? I will always, always remain grateful and indebted to Jeff, Alan, Ian, David Hamilton, Kathy Bland, Brent Maze, and others for their genuine friendship and for helping me maintain my sense of worth and my self-esteem in an environment that did not always make it so easy for a black kid to maintain. There are other kids (they are adults now) who welcomed me with open arms to Riley School who I should thank, but sorry, I am getting older and don't have a Riley yearbook in front of me right now. LOL.

I remember the class trip well. Washington DC was about five hundred miles from New Castle. The furthest I had ever traveled until then was a trip to Chicago at around the age of eight with my mother's Brownie Girl Scout Troupe on a bus. I was never exposed to diverse cultures while growing up.

When I matriculated at Northwestern University in Evanston as an undergraduate and later while also in medical school in Chicago, I was exposed to a diverse group of students from not only all parts of the nation but also all parts of the world. It was not until I attended Northwestern that I had my first taste of Chinese food and Indian food in Evanston (when my friends Vivek and Chris took me out to eat—I need to look them up and reconnect with them). I had an opportunity to meet and become friends with people from the East Coast and the West Coast and from different nations. Many of these students and I became good friends, and although I did not get to know all of them closely, I still learned by observing and interacting with them whenever I could. To this day, as a physician, I embrace and take the opportunity to interact with individuals from different cultures, many of whom are my patients and entrust their health and very lives to me and many of whom are professional colleagues and Cleveland Clinic employees with whom I work and interact on a daily basis.

Learn and expand your awareness and knowledge of cultures other than your own. In college and the real world, especially in major metropolitan cities, you will invariably encounter fellow students who hail from different countries or come from different ethnic and cultural backgrounds than you. Be prepared to benefit from these experiences in school and after you graduate. As time marches forward, we are witnessing the diversification and globalization of the world, and an opportunity for you to share in the growing global community is enormous and immense. Take advantage of the diverse populations surrounding you. This being said, have you considered learning some foreign languages? Spanish, Chinese, Arabic, or others? Learning foreign languages is easier when you are younger. But no matter how old you are, you can get started. So should I.

Most colleges nowadays offer students opportunities to spend a portion of their undergraduate experience in study abroad. Unfortunately, during my day, I personally did not have the fortune to pursue study abroad opportunities. My nephew Ryan Williams who attend Earlham College spent six weeks in England. In most circumstances, study abroad opportunities nowadays are covered under the same tuition the student has to pay while on their home college campus. Of course, there are added expenses associated with traveling to different countries, obtaining passports and/or visas, or getting travel immunizations if necessary. Keep your eyes open and become aware of opportunities you may have to study abroad, the benefit of which is that study abroad, depending upon where you go, will expose you to different cultures and expand the scope of your vision about the world and expand your diverse ways of thinking about different countries and societies—and let's not forget people.

Make friends with those who don't all look like you and who come from different states, nationalities, cultures, ethnicities, races, and religions. There may be opportunities for you to be invited to far-off plays around the world to visit your friends. Even if your friends live in your own country, state, or city, if they grew up with different cultural experiences, the opportunity to share in their experiences will expand your mind and benefit you now and in the future. My senior year roommate, David Zott, one weekend took me up to his home in Lincolnshire, on the North Shore of Chicago; and the experience was outstanding and left a lasting impression upon me as to the beauty and splendor of the North Shore of Chicago, but more importantly of how kind David's family was to me. They could have never known about how heartwarming and special their hospitality was to me. Of course, it is important that you provide reciprocal opportunities for friends whom you meet from different ethnicities, races, cultures, and nations.

Going to Northwestern exposed me to
cultures previously unknown to me.

As a word of caution, when considering international travel, there are places in this wonderful world where travel is simply not safe to visit even if you are accompanied by a host friend. Search the State Department Web site, the Internet, and other resources to educate yourself about particular travel advisories that might be in effect at your desired destination. Traveling to an unsafe country or even a particularly unsafe area of a city within your own country is not wise. If your friend invites you to travel with them or offers to host you in what you consider to be an unsafe destination, it is best to put safety first and very respectfully decline their offer. In deciding upon how much to share regarding the reason(s) for your declination, your friend(s) should be able to understand how you feel. Of course, discuss such situations with your parents or guardians. They may have additional advice or knowledge as to the accuracy of your fears or insecurities of traveling to certain locations or they may alert to the fact that a certain place is unsafe in which to travel in contradistinction to what you thought. To err on the side of caution is best. In many, if not most, situations, taking up your friend's offer to visit them will hopefully be safe, educational, and fun and even provide you with wonderful lifelong memories.

Avoid Distractions and Remain Focused

The reasons for the many successes you have had up to this point are multifactorial. Your past, current, and future levels of success have been, are now, and will continue to be a result of your abilities to focus on your school work, projects, and goals and avoid distractions. Maintaining focus and avoiding the many distractions that come before you on a daily basis are not always easy, as I am sure you have discovered by now. Increasingly, the number of opportunities to become distracted and thrown off our course has become magnified, especially in many cases as a result of increased exposure to a multitude of media sources, especially social media. When I was in college, there were no cell phones or texting and the Internet was not available to us, nor was cable TV, Twitter, Instagram, Snapchat, YouTube, or Facebook. We didn't even have Google or Amazon, Lyft, Uber, or Uber Eats. LOL. It is easy to see how distracted people are now by their smart cell phones. Everyone is seemingly multitasking, and our smart devices may not be making us smart at all because our ability to concentrate is being affected due to continuous distractions. Do you agree? We are often watching television or a movie while at the same time talking on our cell phone, texting, or sending tweets out to let people know what we are doing and amazingly often texting people who are literally sitting in the same room with us. It gets even worse because many people text and drive. Numerous automobile accidents and even deaths[4] are the results of people texting and driving. Data in 2017 indicated that eleven teens die every

---

[4]   https://www.edgarsnyder.com/car-accident/cause-of-accident/cell-phone/cell-phone-statistics.html., accessed February 11, 2018.

day as a result of texting while driving (Edgarsnyder.com). Pedestrian deaths increased by 10 percent in one year as reported by Horn in *USA Today* (2016) in which it was believed to be attributable as a result of people walking and texting and not paying attention when crossing the street or walking into dangerous situations.[5] Are you one of these people who is having trouble concentrating on one task at a time because of your social media and technology gadgetry? Be honest with yourself. Reexamine your habits if the answer is yes.

Finally, if you are going to start college soon or have just matriculated into college, it is true that you are about to experience your most freedom and independence ever. No one will be around to tell you when to go to class, what to eat, and when to go to bed. It is up to you to maintain the discipline, focus, and work ethic that got you to college. Avoiding distractions and maintaining your focus I must say can be difficult at times to do, but by being honest with yourself and alert and aware as to what potential distractions are out there, which you know may present greater risks for which you are more likely to succumb, you will significantly lessen your chances of becoming a victim to or casualty of. For example, if you need to study for an important examination that is coming up and you know that once you turn on the television to watch the ball game, knowing this to be a major weakness, you will want to avoid turning on the television in the first place.

Don't Get Ahead of Yourself: Pay Attention to Present-Day Details and Responsibilities

My advice regarding your remaining focused and avoiding getting ahead of yourself and continuing to pay attention to your present-day details and responsibilities, I could have placed in multiple locations of this book because these are critically important success

---

5   Walking while texting can be deadly, study shows. Marissa Horn, USA TODAY, published 3:33 p.m. ET, March 8, 2016. Updated 7:42 p.m. ET, March 8, 2016. https://www.usatoday.com/story/news/2018/02/11/heres-biggest-news-you-missed-weekend/326691002/, accessed February 12, 2018.

tips. I have discussed with you the importance of making plans, writing out your goals, and reviewing them regularly as a way to help keep you on track. I have highlighted how important it is for you to project and imagine yourself working in your chosen profession and living in your future. These are all important things for you to do. Nevertheless, I must caution you and remind you that in order to reach your goals, whatever they may be, you must first excel at what it is in which you are now engaged. For example, your focus now is to do well in your high school or college classes so that you will be competitive when it comes to applying to medical, physical therapy, rocket science, or law school or whatever is your goal. In contrast, if your goal is to become a surgeon, even though it is important that you shadow a surgeon to get an inside look at the profession, when you are in high school or college, it is not critically important that you divert your course study time into learning how to tie sutures. You can and will learn this at a later time. Does this make sense? Case in point, I have encountered many young students, as young as third graders, who have told me that they wish to become surgeons (which is great and I encourage this); yet they haven't necessarily shown evidence of or initiative in excelling in their science classes; and their parents, even though taking the initiative to have them shadow me, haven't take steps, for example, to provide them with supplemental math or reading materials to strengthen their academic performance. Don't get ahead of yourself. Plan, prepare, and project yourself into your future; but don't get too far ahead of yourself to the point that you are ignoring your present-day obligations and responsibilities, which include sitting down to study for your classroom examinations. I hope you understand the importance and magnitude of what I am saying here. Concentrating on your current day-to-day responsibilities, "It isn't difficult to do it if you know how to do it."

CHAPTER 4

Manage Your Time: Don't Let Time Manage You

Improve Your Study and Note-Taking Techniques

You have achieved much academic success in high school, and much of that success was dependent upon your resolve and discipline in your study techniques, including the abilities that you have developed in your note-taking. I recall how my kid's teachers as early as in kindergarten instilled within them the importance of them keeping planners on a daily basis. In fact, the school even provided them with the planners up until they entered high school. Thank you, Shaker Schools.

Early on, when my kids were in kindergarten or first or second grade, we often wondered why the teachers gave the kids assignments that they obviously required that the parents assist their kids (and often required the parents to "go get things") and required that the parents sign off on countless forms verifying that the kids' assignments had been completed. The kids, being so young, could not possibly complete on their own many of these assignments. It was almost as if we as parents were back in school and were being given homework assignments! Some parents were genuinely angry about this, but I realized right away what the teachers were up to and as to why they were doing this. It was a deliberate strategy on the part of the teachers, without them saying so, to get the parents actively engaged in all aspects of their child's education at their early ages. And it was a strategy that worked. As parents, the teachers had recruited and gotten into the minds of the parents that we the parents were responsible for seeing that our kids had their assignments completed on time and that their work was quality work and that they had at home the necessary supplementary materials, markers, crayons, pencils, books, etc. Of course, most parents naturally would have done this, but not all parents would have understood their intimate roles in their child's education, and this included teaching their kids the responsibility of maintaining planners. The teachers in Shaker Heights, and I am sure in your schools also, would have made the parents feel guilty and shammed if their kid did not have their assignments or projects turned in on time and also if the parents were not present for the school art and music show to see their child's artwork and musical performance. Good for you teachers for doing what is necessary to get the parents to understand their role when their children are young. Not all school systems do this, and getting parents intimately involved in their child's education and progress and helping see to it that their child hands in quality work does without question ultimately make a big difference in determining which children are successful and which are not.

Similarly, as our kids advanced in school, I was impressed as to how my kid's teachers instilled within the students the importance of recording in their notes the most important points from their lessons for them to recall and learn. One thing we always tried to do was to establish a routine for our kids when they arrived home, which first involved them getting something to eat and then to sit down at the dining room or kitchen table to complete their homework before doing anything else. (When they were younger, they had their own cute little genuine official school desk and chair at home, complete with a top that lifted up, just like they had at school, which I purchased from an antique store.) But there were oftentimes when the kids just needed to unwind a bit by playing outside and/or discussing with us (and their nannies Mrs. Marshall and later Mrs. Jackson) what they did at school that day and show us, for example, some of the artwork they made at school. As they got older, they, of course, had various afterschool activities, such as baseball practice, band practice, gymnastics, self-defense, ballet and hip-hop dance classes, art classes, soccer, lacrose, vollyball, swimming, music lessons, fencing, chess club, sign language, study sections, and tutoring sessions; and if that's not enough, some other activities that I can't even remember.

So, students, the main point I am trying to make simply is that even though you are in now in college (or even if you are still in high school), whether you are living on campus or living at home, you need to remember how you achieved the successes that got you to where you now are; and that includes your abilities to manage your time effectively, responsibly, and efficiently and your attention to detail. Don't let others control your time. Time is such a precious commodity, and with a heavy class load, you will soon discover if you have not already that to complete your homework and class assignments including reading countless amounts of book chapters and writing loads of college essays, you won't have the luxury of wasting your time. So remember and refine you class note-taking abilities and be meticulous in keeping your planner so that you don't miss important class assignment deadlines or even scholarship application deadline.

It's funny in a way, but occasionally some thirty-five years after graduating from college, I occasionally still wake up from a bad dream panicked that I missed turning in a class assignment or that I slept in late and forgot to attend a certain class. This doesn't of course happen to me often, but sometimes it literally takes me a few seconds after I wake up to even realizc that I am no longer taking that class and that I am not even in college anymore. LOL. I do realize that with modern-day smartphones, it is now common for people to enter all their important meeting and assignment due dates into the calendar on their smartphone. I am also aware that there are apps and that the cloud and other sources such as Google give you the ability to access your calendar from anywhere. I have adopted some of this same modern technology such as Microsoft Outlook to help me keep track of my meeting schedules, for example; however, I still find it exceedingly helpful to continue to keep a hard copy calendar book where I can write down important meeting dates and to-do lists in such a format where I can see the big picture detailing my obligations a week at a time right before my eyes. Do what works for you, but my point to you is that you must be even more meticulous in college about meeting and adhering to your class schedule and deadlines. Trust me, the earlier in life you learn essential, reliable, and efficient time management techniques, especially when you are tasked with multitasking and meeting the demands of a rigorous college and work schedule, the better off you will be.

When it comes to taking notes, I also recommend that not only out of habit you take notes but also you set aside time on a routine basis to go back to review your notes often. I have visited some college classes over the past few years, and I observed that some students use small notebook computers during classes to record their classroom notes rather than write down their notes. Do what works best for you. I have also observed that many college professors and even high school teachers do provide important class notes even prior to lectures. It is to your advantage to read those online classroom notes in advance and after class, but this does not replace also taking some of your own notes and highlighting the most important and salient educational points of the lessons being taught. College professors too often speak very quickly in class and go through lots of information quickly, so make sure you are listening intently in class and not being distracted taking notes instead of listening and watching and hearing what is being said. It is a fine balancing act that the better you will be when you learn to do. Remember, different professors have different teaching styles, so pay attention to learn what teaching style your professors exhibit and pattern your note-taking, listening, and watching according to their differing styles. Again, to keep up with the fast pace of your college classes, it is important that you also plan out your study schedule and that you proactively read ahead of what your professor will be lecturing about on any given day. Having read the material ahead of time before the actual lecture will better prepare you to be able to focus on particular areas of the subject matter during the lecture that you may have questions or difficulty understanding. In other words, if you read ahead, then you've had a chance to have seen the materials ahead of the actual professorial lecture, and you will be more familiar, for example, with certain keywords and main points for which you will be responsible for knowing on your exams and quizzes. Does this make sense to you?

In addition to the practice and habit of reading course assignments ahead of time to optimally position yourself for successes in your classes, I recommend that you also obtain your class books or required reading materials and even reading assignments whenever possible ahead of time. Often, in fact usually, the required reading list or class syllabus is posted online even before the official start of classes; and even if, for example, you may not know the exact books or articles you will be assigned, there is no reason as to why you cannot simply start reading other materials ahead of time on the subject matter you will be studying. When my kids were in school, from elementary school through high school, I would take them down to the school after the last day of classes for the year and give the school a security deposit check that allowed me to check out the books for the classes they would be taking following their summer vacation. This came to be a ritual I did with my kids that they each looked forward to and the school administrators in charge of the textbooks anticipated our arrival every year. I recall one year being a week or more later in getting down to the school with my kids to pick up their books in advance and the administrator said she was wondering where we were and why we had not yet been down to see her to get the books. LOL. Student and parents, I know what you might be thinking. No, I did not deprive my kids of having all the fun they could during the summer, but it was nice that they had their books ahead of time to start leisurely looking at the materials ahead of time. There was a situation that one of my daughters in college had when she showed upon on the first day of the college school year only to learn that a book she needed for a particular college course had already been sold out. The college didn't order enough books. It then took her over a week to get the book, and by that time, she was already behind in her reading assignments. I'll admit—I'm sure that she won't admit it—that I advised her to get the book prior to going to college, but she didn't listen. Students, remember that your parents still do know some things. Don't allow this to happen to you. Learn from the mistakes of others and at least try to get your books early and start reading ahead of your class lectures and class assignments. After all, "It isn't difficult to do it if you know how to do it."

There are multiple ways these days to acquire books ahead of time, including going to your college bookstores in person or going online to the Amazon, Barnes & Noble, and the Web sites of your college bookstores among other outlets and sources. At times, and often, you can acquire used books from students who previously took the courses you will be taking. Keep in mind that new volumes of college and even high school textbooks do often change, so in some situations, getting books from other students may result in your getting the wrong books. However, as you know, many basic subjects (I am not referring to the research side of subjects) such as the hard sciences (not frequently) and the classics don't change, and even getting prior editions of books may serve to be beneficial to you.

Punctuality, Promptness, and Meeting Deadlines

I am sure that your parents and your teachers in high school stressed the importance that you be punctual to appointments, your job, and your classes. In high school, your teachers, principals, and administrators were very strict about you getting into the classroom and in your seat before the bell rang. In college, I reiterate that you will have the freedoms of which you have never before experienced, which emphasizes even more just how important it is that you are disciplined and practice punctuality and promptness in arriving at your classes and appointments with your professors and others and at your place of work. In fact, it will be to your advantage if you make it a habit of arriving early to your classes and appointments whenever possible.

In planning out your class schedules, you may wish to try to avoid scheduling classes that are back-to-back and across campus from each other. In such situations, it would be almost impossible for you to finish one class and travel all the way across campus to arrive on time to your next class, not to mention that this would make it next to impossible for you to stay after class even for a few moments to ask your professor important questions or to address problems or concerns you may have about the class materials. It is conceivable that upon entering late to your second class, you would be noticed by your professor that you are routinely entering late. You might be disturbing the class and also missing important announcements and information given to the class by the professor at the start of the class. Your professor might get the wrong impression that you are perpetually tardy out of disinterests in his or her class. Even though this may not be the case and there is a legitimate and logistical reason as to why you can't get there on time; unfairly but true, the fact is that often one person's perceptions of you, even if inaccurate, are their reality.

One of my former *bosses* at work, whose name I will not state here, told me face-to-face that "perceptions are reality" even when based upon false assumptions and conclusions, and he told me that once he reaches a conclusion about something, there was often nothing that the person could do to change his perceptions. So your attention to promptness and punctuality in arriving at meetings and meeting deadlines will serve you well in all aspects of your life even beyond your college days. Another important point to consider in planning out your class schedule is to make sure you give yourself enough time to grab lunch or a healthy snack. In certain situations, you may have to plan ahead on certain days in your schedule and pack your lunch if your schedule won't allow you to go to the dining hall to sit down for a leisurely lunch. As your parents and teachers always told you, try to also eat a healthy breakfast, as breakfast is the most important meal of the day. I know that many college kids don't eat breakfast, but remember what helped get you to where you are today. Okay?

Here is a critically advanced point that you should become aware and maybe considered part of what is called office politics (which I discuss later in this book)—that substantive so-called office small talk, socializing, strategizing, and office networking that can lead to job promotion opportunities for those present often commence and transpire before the "official" stated planned and agreed upon formal meeting start times. In addition, early in the agenda of the formal meeting, it is also common that important information is often discussed and disseminated in the meeting, all reasons necessitating as to why it is ideal and so important for you to establish the habit of arriving early to meetings and classes (whenever possible preferably before the official starting time of meetings) and be ready and prepared to participate actively. Similarly, promptness in turning in your assignments and finishing projects is a quality that is well-respected in professional and business circles.

CHAPTER 5

Become an Even Greater Student

Respect

A great lesson to learn early in life is the importance of being respectful to all whom you encounter, not only toward your teachers and bosses but also toward everyone. Of course, you will come upon students, teachers, and others whom you do not respect or even like and maybe for good reasons. Perhaps they have disrespected or been unfair to you. The best avenue, when you can, is to avoid interacting with these types of people. In certain situations, this will not be possible. In these situations, it is best to minimize your exposure to such individuals, again to the extent that you can. I detailed elsewhere in this book about the importance of speaking up and losing your timidity. Before reading on, can you stop and think of an important situation when you felt too timid to speak up, but now, in retrospect, you wish you had because, maybe, just maybe the outcome might have been different? Don't get me wrong, there are many situations in life when it is not the best approach or strategy to speak up, but when you decide to speak up, remember you should have a purpose for so doing. The same approach should apply here. Do you believe that there are serious issues with your instructor being biased against you? If so, go to your college advisor and speak up regarding your concerns or consider a transfer to a different professor's class. Of course, in doing so, to enhance your credibility with your advisor, you must be able to communicate effectively and factually your concerns to your advisor so that they will be able to understand your genuine concerns. You never know, perhaps your advisor has received similar complaints or concerns from other students currently or formally enrolled in that same professor's class. In addition, it is to your advantage to not wait until the last minute to go to your college advisor if you feel your professor is treating you unfairly or is biased against you. Unfortunately, as a last result, this may necessitate dropping a class and changing your schedule, but that decision is dependent upon the ramifications of remaining in that professor's classroom.

Remember that you are not alone. You have friends, fellow students, family, professors, advisors, and other people whom you can consult to help you determine the best course of action for you. Nevertheless, even regarding that difficult professor or instructor, always maintain professionalism in interactions with them and also show them respect. Being disrespectful is not an option because you never know whom they can influence, and you want to avoid providing additional incentives for anyone to derail you with other staff.

One final but important note regarding registering for classes in general—it is wise before registering for a particular professor's class to ask around to elicit feedback from other students who have already taken that professor's class just to get their input regarding the class and the quality and personality of the professor. I am not saying that you should go through college or life attempting to avoid difficult course and classes or professors; nevertheless, do some homework ahead of time to try to determine which professors best match your style of learning and your personality. This being said, just realize that it is not always going to be possible to avoid a certain class or professor and remember that some of the most tough and difficult professors, just as some of the most difficult bosses and supervisors you will encounter later in life, in retrospect, will turn out to be some of the best teachers and people from whom you will learn, even if it is unintentional on their part.

As I said before in the opening chapter about how I used the negativity of my high school guidance counselor as fuel to future invigorate my resolve to succeed, you too can use difficult people and situations as sources of energy that serve to further motivate, stimulate, and empower you. Without naming names, I have used the technique of using haters as fuel to enhance my abilities and resolve not only as a student but also throughout my professional career. Your ability to be able to utilize these techniques will improve over time and requires foresight, strategy, mental fortitude, grit, and critical thinking skills and very often requires that you have a strong support system. So just keep this in mind. My best advice again is to consult with your college advisor, your parents, friends, mentor(s), and coach(es) as early as possible when you encounter situations and difficult people whom you feel might be intentionally or unintentionally attempting to derail your progress. Speak up and lose your timidity. Remember, whenever possible, practice in your mind as well as out loud what you are going to say and how you will say it before approaching others in critical conversations. And anticipate how the course of the conversation may go as this will help you be prepared with the necessary facts that are important for you to highlight during your conversation; but during your crucial conversation, listen carefully and intently to the person with whom you are engaged in conversation. But in doing so, always—I remind you to always, a-l-w-a-y-s—show respect and professionalism in interacting with people, even the most difficult of people; and in doing so, always maintain your composure, dignity, and cool. Do not resort to shouting or using foul language. Remember, sometimes people try to intentionally try to get you to lose your composure, and many times they or someone else may be recording you without your knowledge or permission, and they may use such recordings as evidence against you that you are "an out of control and unstable person." Be smarter than they are and don't let this happen to you.

First Impressions, Dress for Success, and Rules of Etiquette

First impressions do matter in college as well as in other areas of your life in which you interact with others. The manner of your dress attire contributes to the first impressions others have of you. This I admit is not always fair, but it is what it is. Moreover, as a college student, it is most likely that you do not possess an extensive and expensive wardrobe, and you don't have to, nor should you break the bank in order to do so. I certainly didn't possess an extensive wardrobe in college, but many students around me did, along with the fancy accoutrements. Nevertheless, I always made a special effort to dress as respectfully and professionally as I could, even as a college student. Of course, I would commonly wear jeans and T-shirts as every college student does. However, I made sure that my clothes were clean and that my shirts were pressed. Yes, I had an iron and ironed my clothes in my dormitory room, and I hung my clothes up in my closet. I laugh about it now, but at the time, I was not always amused by the fact that one of my roommates, of whom I have fond memories, would routinely pile his unwashed clothes on the floor and run out of clean clothes to wear and therefore on many occasions resort to wearing my clothes. I remember seeing my roommate on more than one occasion walking down Sheridan Road wearing my shirt. I never confronted him about it because I wasn't bothered by it.

Now please allow me to say a serious word or two, which goes beyond a simple discussion of creating favorable first impressions based upon one's choice of fashion or your desire to be dapper on the college campus, but instead has implications of *respect*. I would never wear a shirt or clothing that was disrespectful such as a shirt laced with profanity or that had a controversial political statement on it, regardless of where your politics lie. Not so much during the period in which I was in college, but nowadays I am shocked at some of the clothing I now see college students wearing. As far as donning shirts, hats, or headgear laced with controversial offensive politically charged statements, one can never necessarily know where on the political spectrum one's professor's beliefs lie; so why unnecessarily should you, whether knowing or unwittingly, instigate ill feelings between yourself and your professor or other students or others? I know and appreciate that especially on college campuses one should be encouraged to express oneself, but I believe that there is a proper place, time, and manner even on a college campus in which to do this; and the proper time or place I bet is not necessarily in the middle of your chemistry class or probably does not involve you blocking entry to other students into a campus building or involve the campus police being called to arrest you. Perhaps a philosophy or political science or debate class might be more appropriate for you to advertise your political or even your antiestablishment views if that's what you have, but for your own sake, trust me you will want to remain strategic concerning how, when, and to whom you do so. This is how I feel about this subject. Looking now at things from the perspective of being thirty-five years removed from my undergraduate days and aware as to how many potential employers "judge" prospective employees (including doing checks as to whether you have been arrested in the past), I am just giving you my best advice. And yes, I, of course, am aware of the many contributions that college students and others have made during my lifetime to advance civil liberties of society through "peaceful" protests, including sit-ins on college campuses. You may feel differently about this, and I respect your right to feel differently. My main point here is that pick your battles on campus very wisely, and if you are going to protest, please know precisely what you are protesting and why and consider the consequences and ramifications of doing so. Don't go protest if you don't feel passionately about the cause or to go just because you friend is going.

So, with the above being said, it is true that in college and during your professional career, you will be thrust into some social and business situations for which you should have a basic understanding of the rules of etiquette. I never had the benefit of attending charm school, and I am certainly no expert in any stretch of the imagination when it comes to the rules of the Queen's etiquette. Nevertheless, the point of this book is to highlight for you a variety of life lessons that I have learned are important, even lessons I did not necessarily appreciate at a young age. Therefore, I believe that the first rule of thumb for you to follow is simply to remember some of the lessons that your parents or guardians taught you—to present yourself with a smile and firm handshake, to look people in the eyes, to maintain the proper distance from people in social situations (i.e., to not invade their space), to not be in public intoxicated (for that matter, I personally don't think you should ever be intoxicated in private or public), to say please and thank you, and to mind your table manners. I will not attempt to write within the confines of this book an entire treatise on the rules of etiquette. Rather, I have included in the appendix of this book some credible references on etiquette that you may wish to consult. In addition, the Internet is replete with loads of readily available information on etiquette. So read away.

There are extensive rules of etiquette that you may wish to familiarize yourself with, some of the rules of which you will need to know in the event you are invited to a state dinner with the president of the United States or the Queen of England. But quite seriously, you will find yourself in some important social situations, including black-tie dinners and receptions, and the more you know now about the rules of etiquette, the more comfortable you will be interacting with others in these social situations. Knowing how to interact in important formal settings, "It isn't difficult to do it if you know how to do it." Smile.

One quick last piece of advice here—men, make sure you take to college with you at least three or four ties and please learn how to tie a tie. There are different acceptable ways in which to tie a tie. I have included in the appendix a list of books on how to tie a tie. Such information is also available on the Internet in the form of YouTube videos. Check them out.

Men and women, please learn how to shine your shoes and keep some shoe polish on hand with a cloth to polish your shoes in your dorm room. Men and women, have in your dorm closet business appropriate attire; men, that means you need to take to college a suit and a couple of dress shirts while women, a business suit or business appropriate dress. Have dress socks and dress shoes on hand as well. Keep some cologne (men) or perfume (women) in your room; it doesn't have to be expensive and break your bank account. Maintain a neat hairstyle, and this is facilitated by locating on-campus or off-campus a barber shop or beauty salon (i.e., located in a safe location if off-campus). Some students manage to cut their hair or style their hair themselves, and this is acceptable if you know how to do it. I give you this grooming advice because, as a college student, you never know when you might be invited to attend a special event at the bequest of the president of the university or attend an important alumni event or special event at the invitation of your dean or one of your professors to perhaps give you an award to recognize some important research you have been performing, or perhaps your roommate's parents might invite you and your roommate out to a nice dinner or to go see a nice orchestra concert. You need to have in your room at all times for you to use some business appropriate attire. Female students, whether this means having on hand whatever makeup you prefer to use is of course your choice, as I do understand that many women chose to not wear makeup. Men, always wear a white T-shirt under a white dress shirt. And, men, yes, in most business situations, a plain white dress shirt is preferred over colored or patterned dress shirts, although this is not an absolute rule. I have myself as have others worn plain nonwhite dress shirts at business meetings, and this is okay. However, the most traditional color of a dress shirt remains to be plain white. Men, know also how to put on and wear a tuxedo. This includes knowing how to place studs and cuff links on tuxedo shirts and how to either tie bowties or put on a tuxedo tie with a latch. As my father always taught me, also be mindful that the color of your belt and shoes matches that of your suit and pants.

Regarding sporting the multiple exotic hair colors that many college students sport these days (like Dennis Rodman was known for), I don't want to get into any trouble with anyone reading this book, so I will just say think carefully before you decide to sport multiple hair colors (green, purple, or blue hair) when you are going on job interviews, interviewing for college, or interviewing for professional school, not because I have anything against students sporting multiple exotic hair colors, but because many of the people who will be interviewing you for jobs or for professional school admissions may unfairly yet truly judge you negatively about having multiple exotic hair colors. I am the messenger here—please don't shoot me. I am just giving you something to think about. Please forgive me again, but the same consideration and thoughts you should ponder when you are contemplating getting excessive amounts of body tattoos and body art that are visible (i.e., arms, neck, and face) as well as multiple ear and nose piercing. If you are applying for a job in the entertainment industry, perhaps (perhaps) sporting exotic colored hair, excessive body art, and/or multiple ear/nose piercings may not be of the same potential concerns; but again, I am just bringing to light that you consider the ramifications of doing so before you do it. This not about trying to make you conform; however, remember that many of the people on the admissions committees as well as many employers are of older generations than your own, and they may have differing opinions as to what is appropriate for their employees or their professional students.

Expect, Accept, and Embrace Competition

You may have graduated at or near the top of your class and been perennially listed on your school's academic honor roll, which is an outstanding accomplishment. Your schoolwork and classes may even have come easy for you. Or perhaps you had to work hard at getting good grades in high school. Regardless of where you fall on this spectrum, during your college years, anticipate and expect a level of competition exponentially greater than what you may have experienced in high school. I am not implying that you are not optimally prepared to excel in your college coursework or that you won't excel in college or that some college coursework won't come easy for you. However, there will be many other students who also excelled in their high school classes and are also, just like you maybe, academic over-achievers willing to do whatever it takes to compete with every student to get the best scores and grades in the class. Additionally, many college professors grade on a bell curve, meaning that they utilize a scale that does not allow all students to earn an A. As a student, I never thought this was a fair or ethical approach to grading, but rather a system designed to weed out and give poorer grades to some students. Concerning testing, I believe the better, more fair, and ethical approach is for professors to test students and grade and gauge them according to the percentage of correct answers they score on exams on the material that the professor deems is important that they learn from their class, rather than on a bell curve system that simply compares them to how well other students perform. Additionally, I believe students should be gauged according to their level of preparedness, contribution, and performance in classroom discussions. Many professors, depending upon the class, do grade students upon their participation in the class, which emphasizes, even more, my assertion that it is in your best interests and to your advantage that you lose your timidity and always strive to improve upon your many forms of communication skills and to actually attend your classes and to be on time to your classes and show respect to your professors and everyone you encounter and to lend a hand to be of assistance to others.

So, in short, anticipate and expect more competition from your peers in college than you have heretofore experienced—adapt to it and embrace it. Let this competition serve to fuel your competitive spirit rather than discourage you. Accept competition in ways that will be advantageous to you. Some students will be better than you are in a particular subject and you may be stronger in a different subject than other students. Befriend and network with those students who might be stronger than you in certain classes or laboratory settings, and learn from them. You may be in a position to return the favor by tutoring them in areas for which they are weak or in other matters unrelated to classes such as in the social scene. Perhaps you are a member of a college club, sorority, or fraternity and can assist students in the facilitation of a social life while in college. Don't forget how important it is to just also be a friend to someone else who may be looking for a friend like you.

A Word about Academic Integrity

At this stage of the game, I am sure you understand the importance of maintaining academic integrity at all times with respect to your homework and testing, no matter if you are in grade school, middle school, high school, college, or professional school. You are only hurting yourself if you resort to plagiarizing work or taking credit for school work that you did not do. Please be aware that with advancements in technology, teachers and professors have computer program tools and Internet tools to check for any evidence of plagiarism, so take special note to cite and appropriately reference the sources of any materials or quotes you include in your assignments. This includes not plagiarizing college application essays. College admissions committees can and will easily detect student candidate essays that have been plagiarized. Please familiarize yourself with what constitutes plagiarism; you can access many books and articles on this topic online. Don't become a victim to it, and in turn, don't allow other students to plagiarize you. For example, a professor who receives two assignments handed in from two different students won't know which student was guilty of plagiarism. Don't let this happen to you. Severe academic consequences, including expulsion, can and does occur to students who are caught plagiarizing schoolwork and cheating on examinations.

Expanding Your Personal, Intellectual, and Mental Growth

You are in college working hard in your major discipline of study. You are maintaining your discipline in trying to learn everything you can so that you can ace that midterm or final exam. You have written out your goals, reviewed them routinely, and even visualized yourself living your dream future. You are staying focused on your present-day tasks and responsibilities now before you. You are paying attention to present-day details. You believe in your abilities, remember your roots, and appreciate the many reasons for your successes thus far. If this is true, you are on the right path. Good for you.

Beyond working hard at your academic studies, it is imperative that you take some time on a routine basis to replenish your abilities to perform at high mental capacity. This will require that you find ways in which to enhance and stimulate your personal, intellectual, and mental growth and fortitude. There are deliberate ways in which you can accomplish this, and this means you have to intentionally give your mind a much needed rest. I can't stress enough how important it is for you to occasionally give your mind a diversion away from your major area of study. Entirely focusing on one specific discipline deprives your potential to experience the full breadth of obtaining a complete college education.

In college, one of your important goals should be to acquire a broad-based education. For example, if you are a science major, sign up for a course in literature or the arts. As a college student, or even later in life after you have entered into your professional position, it is important that you attend seminars, workshops, and lectures focused on topics unrelated to your major area of study. Doing so will allow you to broaden your education and connect with people from all sectors of society who have different interests and life experiences than you. Reading and participating in activities outside your major will additionally serve to stimulate and strengthen areas of your brain not normally roused because of a restriction to studying just one discipline. You will remain sharp and vital. These diverse studies serve to improve upon the additional skill sets that are so important to your ultimate success, such as refinement of your public speaking abilities, improving listening skills, and enhancing critical and strategic thinking skills.

Do you like music? It is scientifically proven that music is an excellent stimulus for your brain. Research has shown that exercise stimulates brain activity and listening to music has been shown to improve memory functioning, increase rates of healing, and improve your exercise performances and more.[6] Participation in activities such as chess, crossword puzzles, word searches, Rubik's Cube, and other brainteasers is an important way in which to help you keep your brain active and healthy.

There are other avenues as well that do not involve brainteasers but can have a stimulating effect on your body. I find particular joy in listening to music, going to concerts, visiting the Natural History Museum, taking walks on the beach, hikes in the park, and reading self-help and inspirational books. Yes, I enjoy working in my cho-

---

[6] Danielle M. Baker, "The Scientific Benefits of Music," https://webcache. googleusercontent.com/search?q=cache:mJq-hS19-FIJ:https://www.scienceofpeople.com/scientific-benefits-music/+&cd=1&hl=en&ct=clnk&gl=us.

sen profession of performing kidney transplants and other urological operations, procedures, and assessments to help my patients; yet I also look forward to engaging in many activities that are independent of my job as a surgeon as a means to help not only strengthen but also rest, replenish, and recharge my brain, mind, body, and spirit.

Read and Build Your Library

It is vital that you, throughout your life, learn to love and actively engage and immerse yourself in reading, for example, books, magazine articles, newspapers, and even articles on the Web in broad categories. Doing so will broaden your mind and help give you a break from the academic grind of your collegiate major. You may enjoy mystery, history, or even self-help books. The main point is to continue to enjoy reading for the sake of reading. The more you read, the sharper your mind becomes. Reading allows you to acquire new vocabulary. Fiction books permit your mind to delve into creative and imaginative places. By reading books, you may discover and develop a new hobby or passion or think differently about finding solutions to problems and even become further inspired. Additionally, reading books exposes you to the collective wisdom of literally millions of other people and cultures past and present. So further develop a voracious love of reading books and tap into the wisdom of others. I am proud that my youngest daughter Meredith, even more than my other three children, developed a voracious love of reading, with the encouragement of both her parents, her nanny Mrs. Carolyn Jackson, her preschool teachers, and others at a very young age; and she routinely incorporates reading for pleasure into her routine activities even now as she prepares to matriculate to Northwestern University.

As you choose books to explore, begin creating a library of excellent, helpful, and insightful books. The library can consist of books you intend to read as well as ones completed. For me, after reading a good book, I for various reasons often like to have that book within my reach to look at it again to perhaps refresh myself with some of the important content. It is quite common that when preparing a speech, blog, or Twitter message, I reexamine an important book from which to use a quote or a concept. Additionally, I often purchase books that I intend to read later. They remain in my library as a visual reminder of the need to find time to read them. I have included in the appendix a list of books that I recommend you read—books that encompass the subject matter of self-help, public speaking, leadership, and critical thinking, to name a few. Remember not to forget to make time to read novels and other fun books, if only for a few minutes per day, and other materials to allow your mind to refresh and escape away from just your major area of study. You never know, just perhaps you may want to even start writing your own novel, autobiography, or book to inspire or educate others.

The Delicate Art of Requesting College Letters of Recommendation and Seeking Scholarships and College Funding

Colleges and universities are in many cases extremely expensive. The costs to attend college are more than just the tuition expenses. You must consider the cost of food, housing, books, a personal laptop or desktop computer, clothing, travel to and from your home to your college campus, registration fees, cell phone costs, any medications you may need, personal grooming expenses, locker fees, and other miscellaneous expenses that all add up. Whether you are in high school or already a college student, I strongly encourage you to seek a variety of college scholarships, both merit (academic) and income based, depending upon your circumstances. Some colleges will deduct external scholarship money from your financial aid program. However, some schools allow you to keep additional money obtained through scholarships external to their offer. Check with your college's financial aid office to get the specific details of how much external scholarship money they will allow you to acquire. Most colleges encourage their students to seek as much external funding as they can. Additionally, indicating that you are a scholarship recipient on your resume will be impressive and to your advantage when you apply to undergraduate and graduate schools or when you are seeking internships and employment following graduation.

When I got accepted into Northwestern University, the tuition costs for the year were $5280.00, which at that time was exorbitant. My father at that time was earning only $18,000.00 per year from a full-time job, two to three additional part-time jobs, and odd jobs such as yard work and washing windows. I remember receiving my acceptance letter to Northwestern and showing it to my parents. They were so proud of me but unsure if I would be able to attend due to our family's financial constraints. My sister Rebecca was in college and my younger sister Pamela would be going to college soon also, and they also needed tuition money. It was not until a week later that the financial aid benefits package arrived in the mail and detailed how I could conceivably attend Northwestern. During my senior year in high school, I was also proud, honored, and fortunate to have received the prestigious four-year Oberdorfer Scholarship provided by benefactors to academically talented students.

Even still, despite my financial aid package, while on campus in Evanston, Illinois, at Northwestern, far from home, I suffered from major struggles to financially survive. On many occasions during my sophomore year, I did not eat meals (and relied on collecting a few snacks here and there) for thirty-six hours at a time because of a lack of funding to purchase food on weekends when the school's food service was closed. The school cafeteria was closed after lunch service on Saturdays and did not reopen until breakfast time on Monday morning. Of course, modern-day students at Northwestern have access to food services nowadays unlike when I attended. I could have contacted my parents and asked them to send me some more money, but they had already made extreme sacrifices for me so that I might have opportunities in life that they had not been afforded. They would have sacrificed further to do without so that I would have some extra food money, but I did not want them or my siblings to have to sacrifice further for me. I especially did not want to worry my parents about my not having money to buy food, so I just dealt with the situation. I did not complain then, nor am I complaining now. I will add that during the winter quarter of my sophomore year, I was living in the dormitory at Northwestern called Courtyard Hall (which no longer exists) that was about a mile off campus. My roommate, on the weekends in the dead cold of the winter, had a car, and he regularly would drive out (without offering for me to go with him) and bring food back from McDonald's to our dorm room and sloppily gorge himself on multiple Big Macs and Quarter Pounders and French fries right in front of me. He would not offer me one tidbit of a French fry, knowing that I had nothing to eat. I would often just leave the room and go to the study lounge while he did this. My junior year at Northwestern, I pledged and joined a fraternity, part of the reason for my doing so was not only because they served dinner in the fraternity house on Sunday nights but also because the fraternity provided me with some additional scholarship money that I desperately needed and greatly appreciated and for which I am grateful to this day.

Students, the Internet is an outstanding resource for searching for scholarship and grant opportunities. Also, your high school administrators and counselors and your college financial aid advisors and even college counselors possess a wealth of knowledge also regarding potential scholarship and grant opportunities. Visit them to discuss their recommendations for scholarships and grants for which you might seek. Search Web sites and social media sites, and also make phone calls and send e-mails and letters to various funding sources. Do not limit yourself to the advice of your counselor or advisor, because they may not be aware of all the opportunities that are available or they may be saving information about some of the funding for other students. Unfortunately, this is not necessarily fair but is a fact of life, as I discussed in an opening chapter detailing some of my experiences in high school.

This being said, in general, your guidance counselors and advisors are your advocates, as has been the experience with my children's high school counselor, Mr. David Peterjohn, of Shaker Heights High School. We owe a debt of gratitude to Mr. Peterjohn and his colleagues. Also, I encourage you to proactively speak to students (and their parents) who have graduated from high school about the types of scholarships and grants they acquired. Many churches offer scholarships to those students who have faithfully attended their churches for several years. Fraternities, sororities, and civic organizations are great funding sources as are individual philanthropists. Remember, many of the scholarships and grants are often directed toward students who are pursuing a particular area of study, so if you know what your major discipline of study will be, then you can include organizations offering scholarships and grants to students pursuing that area of study. Organizations also offer scholarships to students who have demonstrated activities in volunteerism and community service projects, while certain organizations limit scholarship funding to students based solely upon their financial need and even zip code of residence.

When selecting a college or university to attend, I am aware that the amount of financial aid that a particular school is offering you can be the final deciding factor in your choosing one school over others. In this scenario, it is critical to have a frank conversation with your parents about the financial feasibility for you to attend a particular college or university if one is providing significantly more aid than the other. Remember, your parents or guardians may have already made sacrifices, and it is a family decision as to what additional sacrifices your family can afford to make for you to attend a particular school. Remember, you can attain in equal measure as much of an excellent, well-rounded education at a state college or university as you can by attending an elite private college or university. Ultimately, your ability to acquire a quality education is not limited to which college you attend; rather, it is all about how hard you are willing to work and how aggressive you are at taking advantage of the opportunities both inside and outside the classroom. Whether or not you attend a state school versus a private university or you begin your educational journey at a community college with plans to transfer to a bachelor's degree-granting college, with focus, determination, and careful planning, you will be able to earn your four-year college bachelor's degree eventually.

In high school, in addition to having received a few scholarships as well as grants, part of my financial aid package required me to work in college in work-study jobs. I held jobs as a residence hall monitor and chemistry lab technician, and even in medical school, I worked in the Northwestern University undergraduate student health service. Each of these work-study job experiences, to this day, I consider to have been valuable learning experiences for me; and each of these jobs served to only add to my growth and maturity, helped me improve upon my time management skills, and enhanced my resume when I applied to medical school by highlighting evidence of my ability to multitask and responsibly maintain a job and provided me with valuable work references.

Because sources of scholarship funding change year to year and vary greatly according to your intended area of study, your place of residence, school of destination, and your family's financial situation, I advise you to perform a comprehensive search for such resources starting as early as you can during your high school years and even while in college. The scholarship search should involve your parents, guardians, or anyone else who is willing to assist you. However, by you personally actively being involved in this process, you will learn a great deal about seeking and securing funding for your own education. Become very much cognizant at all times of the deadlines posted for particular scholarship and grant applications. Read the directions very carefully and strictly adhere to the requirements and deadlines. Most scholarship applications require that you submit one or more recommendation letters as well as official copies of your high school or college transcripts, which take time to acquire. Be prepared well in advance by proactively approaching your high school and college teachers, professors, advisors, and counselors to notify them that you will be requesting scholarship recommendations. These individuals may be the same people from whom you have already solicited your college application recommendations. They should be familiar with you as a student, your academic credentials, and your career aspirations (if you have already formulated your particular career goals) so that they will be in the position to prepare the best letter of recommendation to increase your chances of being awarded a college scholarship.

Now, here's a strict word of advice and caution regarding the process of approaching individuals to write on your behalf letters for your college applications and/or scholarships. In deciding which teachers to approach to write on your behalf your college application letters of recommendation and/or scholarship letters, take care to only consider teachers, counselors, mentors, coaches, and others who you feel can and will provide you with a strong letter of recommendation. Importantly, do this by first specifically inquiring of them if they are willing to write for you a strong letter of support. If they indicate or give you the impression that they are not capable of providing you with a *strong* recommendation, then back off from them and seriously consider asking someone else to prepare your recommendation letter. In helping you determine if they will provide you with their highest level of support, please be sure not only to observe their verbal response regarding their willingness but also take a special effort to observe their body language in their response to your asking for a support letter.

Again, in approaching and requesting a letter of support, you should specifically, respectfully, inquire of them if they will be willing and able to submit a *strong* letter of support and within the time frame for which it is due. Before you approach someone to ask them for a letter of support, practice, in advance, what you will say and how you will respectfully and humbly ask them. In most situations, you will have a very good idea as to whom you can trust to do this. Important note—you may wish to select different teachers or mentors to write letters to specific schools or scholarships versus others. For example, if a particular teacher is an alumnus of one of the colleges to which you are applying but another teacher is an alumnus of another school to which you are applying, then you might wish to request that the alumni write to the respective school of which they graduated. This may not always be necessary, but this is just something else for you to consider. Remember, as always, to write an official thank-you card or letter to them, thanking them for their support. A thoughtful letter or thank-you card including your handwritten comments of gratitude I do believe is a more greatly appreciated expression of gratitude than you're simply sending a thank-you by way of e-mail to them. One more piece of advice I have is that you should make an attempt to remain in touch with those who wrote your letters of support. They will appreciate you sending them a brief note, card, or e-mail updating them of your progress in school and upon graduation. What would be even more meaningful for you to do is to personally pay them a short visit back at your high school when you are home on break from college. Is this really that hard to do? Don't make excuses that you don't have the time to do this. Imagine how honored and thrilled they will feel knowing that you still remembered them and how they helped you on your journey to success. So *do it*. It isn't difficult to do it if you know how to do it.

Obtaining Required Computer Equipment for College and Embracing Virtual, Remote and Distance Learning Technology and Practice

I realize that student's preferences and learning styles different in that some students are more visual learners, some thrive in in-classroom settings and/or group or team-based settings, while other students prefer learning and studying alone. With social distancing requirements necessitated by the Covid-19 Pandemic, the educational system as well as the nation as a whole has more than ever now embraced virtual, distance and remote internet-based technological platforms for our school educational instruction, work and social meetings. If you are a student who has trouble in virtual remote learning situations, I advise and encourage you to take steps to adapt to this form of learning environment because even after this Covid-19 Pandemic, I anticipate that many college classes, social and work meetings will continue to be conducted virtually. If you need assistance in adapting to embracing or coping with virtual learning, social and work environments, alert your school advisor and parents and by all means do not hesitate to seek counselling with a professional psychologist—seeking professional counselling for such matters is not a sign of weakness, it is a sign of maturity.

If you are not already familiar in using Internet-based technologies and Smartphone APPs such as Zoom, WebEx, Microsoft Teams, etc. I do strongly encourage you to quickly become familiar and proficient in using such technologies. I also encourage you to adhere to understanding certain video and audio privacy settings while using such virtual platforms. You should also ensure that your computer's antivirus and security software is up-to-date. Consult with an IT specialist if you need advice, guidance or assistance in installing or updating your computer systems. Also learn about what is the ideal computer camera and microphone hardware that will be necessary for you to have installed on your computer to allow you to login and attend your virtual classes.

Consult with an IT computer specialist regarding recommendations for the amount of computer memory, RAM speed and additional features that are recommended for your computer. Consult with your school regarding the antivirus software they recommend you to have and other computer software programs they suggest or require you to have installed on your computer, i.e. Microsoft Word, Power Point, Excel or corresponding Macintosh software if you are a Mac user. Speak with your parents to discuss what is your budget for your computer and software and anticipate early if you will need to seek financial assistance in acquiring the required computer equipment. I strongly recommend that students have access to a portable laptop and a laptop carrying case to protect your laptop as opposed to only having access to a desktop computer. I also recommend that you purchased a warranty for your computer and please store your warranty information in safe place for future reference should you need it. Speak with your college advisor and/or college IT department because in many situations most colleges do offer students discounted laptop computers and discounted computer software for purchase or lease. Some colleges even provide students free laptops as part of their tuition benefits.

CHAPTER 6

Becoming a Better Version of You

Overcoming Peer Pressure

Don't be afraid to be different. Maintain your uniqueness and maintain your sense of who you are. I have indicated in this book the importance for you to grow and evolve as a person. If you are an introvert, for example, it will be important for you to make attempts to get out of your shell and become more commutative and get out of your comfort zone to explore new and exciting opportunities and to meet more people that remaining introverted or reclusive in many instances may not allow you to experience. This is not to say that, if you are introverted, your goal should be to become the life of the party. I am in no way saying that you need to transform your entire personality. I am not saying that at all. I am by nature introverted, and over the years, I learned that it was in my best interests to get out of my comfort zone and become less introverted for some personal and professional reasons. By all means, it is important for you to be comfortable in your own skin and not to try to become a completely different person in an attempt to please or be appealing to your peers or for anyone for that matter. But not succumbing to peer pressure also includes avoiding alcohol, steering clear of drugs, and even not succumbing to underachieving out of fear of alienating others. As a physician and surgeon, I have witnessed tragedies in young people that have occurred at the hands of drug and alcohol abuse. As a transplant surgeon, I have sadly seen countless cases of young college and high school kids who have tragically died as a result of drugs and alcohol, and I have harvested and transplanted their kidneys.

It is hard to believe that students would intentionally under-achieve in an attempt to "fit in" and remain cool with their peers, but yes, this does occur in all races and ethnicities. From my work in minority communities, though, I have seen that this very commonly is seen in African American youth. This happens often in situations and environments where some kids who are not academically tal-ented or who don't themselves have aspirations for academic success actively attempt to thwart the progress and opportunities for those youth around them who do aspire to achieve academic successes in school. Avoid falling into these traps and actively seek to form associ-ations and friendships with students who like you are good students in school and have high aspirations for success. It's not cool to be an underachiever. So maintain the utmost respect for yourself and respect the people who helped you achieve success and your mission.

Maintain Your Spirituality

Depending on personal beliefs, your spirituality and religion may also be of importance to you. I encourage you to continue living a life based on your beliefs even while you are away in college. My oldest daughter Sarah has been deeply committed for as long as I remember to her United Methodist Christian faith and to her church family, and I am proud that she has demonstrated such a strong and active com-mitment to the church and to her faith. I am also proud that even while away in college at the College of William & Mary, Sarah was involved in the life of the church in Williamsburg. During one of my visits to Williamsburg, Virgina, to hear Sarah play clarinet in the William & Mary Wind Ensemble, and without Sarah knowing that I was going to visit the United Methodist Church at Williamsburg on Sunday morn-ing following her concert, upon ariving at the church, it made my heart sing to see Sarah already seated in the pews of the church.

In other chapters in this book, I stress the importance of not being afraid to be yourself. However, I understand that owning your uniqueness and not succumbing to peer pressure can often be easier said than done. For example, there seems to be a tendency from my observations that there are professors on some or many college campuses who do actively attempt to negatively influence students by trying to push their agnostic beliefs or worse upon students of faith. Do not allow other students or professors to negatively influence your desire or commitment to continue your religious or spiritual activities while in college. You don't have to change your innermost views and spirituality just to please them or others. Likewise, whatever your beliefs are, neither should you pressure nor try to force your religious or spiritual beliefs upon other students. At college, you may be experiencing more diversity in people around you than you've ever experienced in your life. Appreciate this diversity and grow stronger as a result of it.

Maintaining your beliefs may make some people around you uncomfortable, and as I will emphasize again, there may be attempts to discourage you in maintaining your own beliefs. As long as your beliefs or religious practices do not physically interfere with the functioning of other people around you (interfering with people's movement or a roommate's sleep, endangering the lives of students, or preventing civil liberties), then you should not let others interfere with your desire to maintain your spirituality. In fact, at most colleges and universities, you will find religious student groups or associations that you can join. Many Christian and secular campuses have very active campus ministry programs.

Let me leave you with this thought. In June 1890, the trustees of Northwestern University adopted the Latin motto "*Quaecumque sunt vera*" from Philippians 4:8, which means "Whatsoever things are true." I have a plaque of this motto hanging in my home library as a reminder of the fact that your college experience should not represent a situation where you limit your thinking; but rather, in college, your environment should encourage you to grow and develop as a human being, expand your critical thinking abilities, and even deepen your spirituality for the benefit of the world. The complete passage from Philippians 4:8 reads, "Whatever is true, whatever is noble, whatever is right, whatever is pure, whatever is lovely, whatever is admirable— if anything is excellent or praiseworthy—think about such things."

This was one of my father's favorite passages from the Bible. Don't you agree that this passage encompasses what is the true purpose and essence of acquiring a well-rounded college education?

Stay in the Know

During high school, college, and beyond, it is important that you stay abreast of modern culture and current events that pertain to a cross section of generations. I often encounter students who are knowledgeable only on current events pertaining to people of their age. Many young people (and also many older people are guilty of this too) do not stay abreast of national or worldly current news events and are only aware as to what is going on with pop culture. There are students whom I have met who don't even know who is the current vice president of the United States or the name of the governor of the state in which they live. Of course, I wouldn't expect a younger person to be knowledgeable about all the nuances of generations that proceeded them. But I must stress the fact that an honest effort to develop even a basic appreciation and awareness of some of which was and is important to older generations and to become knowledgeable of at least the major current worldly events happening is appropriate and smart to acquire. Expanding your knowledge base will give you broader subject matters from which to speak and plan out your pathways toward success. You will also become more relatable and interesting to those beyond your generation. Why is this important? The benefit of doing so is the wider networks you will establish of influence makers, movers, and shakers and friends and colleagues, as well as a broader exposure to a plethora of opportunities perhaps unavailable to other students your age. The current US population is aging and increasing; there are going to be more people who are older than you rather than younger than you. So rather than being exclusively knowledgeable in the latest trends and current events involving people of your age, why not open yourself up to an entire world of opportunities by simply becoming more knowledgeable about and appreciative of an older generation's ideas, experiences, and values?

I have a love for listening to '70s music and watching movies from the '70s, '80s, and '90s. To me, there is nothing that even comes close to the genius of musicians and singers of the '70s. LOL. Often, in interacting with my kids as well as my young student mentees, I will reference music, musicians, movies, or sports stars from the '70s, '80s, or '90s. I am sometimes surprised they are not aware of, for example, the Beatles, Bee Gees, Frank Sinatra, Elton John, ELO, or the Stylistics, to name only a few. Many students have never even seen or heard of such movies as *the Shining, Casablanca*, or *the Wizard of Oz* or actors such as John Belushi, John Candy, Dan Aykroyd, Chevy Chase, the Three Stooges, or even John Wayne, Bela Lugosi, Shirley Temple, or Judy Garland. I know many of you were not born when these musicians, actors and actresses, and movies were popular, but taking time to know about pop culture outside of your own generation will go a long way in imprinting positive impressions of who you are into the memory banks of older individuals. Many of these entertainers I mention above were before my time as well, but I took time to at least be aware of who they were because these were people who were important to generations before mine. Nevertheless, it may be those who are only a few years older than you or one or more generations older than you who may greatly assist you one day along your journey. For those students who may not know about the culture from my generation but who exhibit an interest in learning, it helps me establish a more fun, working relationship with them. I routinely have fun introducing some of my mentees to music from '70s. Some like it and some don't, and that's perfectly fine with me. So my advice to you is to be genuine in your interest in learning something about the culture of people outside your own generation and see the results. After all, "it is not difficult to do if you know how to do it."

Become Innovative and Creative: Conduct Research and Volunteer

Those who are innovative and creative both in school and in the workplace (and in life in general) are those who are most rewarded. Again, the purpose of your college experience is not for you to become simply programmed to rote memorization of facts from textbooks. The goal in college is for you to acquire knowledge and to assimilate it into creative and innovative thinking about ways in which to view the world and ways in which to solve problems experienced in your areas of study as well as problems of society and the world. Big task? It sure is, but that's the goal of attaining your college education and in life. Not everyone will become or is expected to become a Nobel Prize or Pulitzer Prize winner or discover a cure for cancer. But when we look at many of the world's scientific or technical discoveries, for example, in reality, such discoveries were only made possible by the cumulative mass of knowledge and wisdom that has been amassed as a result of the contributions and collective labor, work, vision, sacrifices, trial and error, and courage to think, inquire, and dream of previous eons of generations of people who have performed formal and informal research to further scientific and human discovery. It is true that each generation adds to the collective wisdom and knowledge of prior generations, societies, and civilizations. This being said, I implore and encourage you to become involved in research projects with professors during college.

Keep in mind that research can be conducted in any areas of study, not just in the hard or laboratory sciences. You must understand that participating in research projects with professors does take dedicated time, and remember that your major priority will be in the successful completion of your coursework academic requirements. Nevertheless, there will be countless opportunities for you to get involved in research projects during your academic school year or during summers. You need to be prudent and wise concerning what you can do in the amount of time you have to do it.

My daughter Sarah attended the College of William & Mary in Williamsburg, Virginia. In the summers following her freshman, sophomore, and junior years, she spent her entire summers at college conducting paid research for her biology professor and dean of Biology of the university, and one of the added benefits to her was that the college provided her additional scholarships to allow her to take courses during the summers. Please note that not all research projects will allow you to get paid for your contributions. Nonetheless, perhaps now more than ever, graduate schools and professional schools such as medical, dental, and physical therapy schools and others do expect that the student applying for acceptance has some research experience at the undergraduate level. In addition to performing research, depending upon your career trajectory, it is important for some students, over the summer, and in some cases during the academic years, to also have worked in internships or externships in their areas of study. Equally important is the fact that it is critically important that students also actively get involved in some volunteerism during their high school and college years as doing so represents an expression of one's commitment to helping others and helping improve the world.

One does not have to be an intern or volunteer in the White House or on Capitol Hill, but it is important that you do your part in some small way to serve as a volunteer for an important cause. It is very easy to find volunteer opportunities that abound in your very locale. Plan and research the vast opportunities that exist and then select what interests you the most. Again, some of the research positions, internships, and even volunteer opportunities may require that you seek a letter or letters of reference that speak to your work ethic and character. So, again, this is another example of how your actions in life are on display. Without you even being aware, many people are observing at all times your character and work ethic, and such assessments have the ability to help further propel you toward success or, to the contrary, hamper your progress toward your goals if you have not previously demonstrated a proper work ethic or respect for those whom you have encountered and continue to encounter on a daily basis. So let expand your mind and participate in research and innovative, creative projects. "It isn't difficult to do if you know how to do it."

Speak up and Ask Questions: Lose Your Timidity

Regardless of intelligence level, everyone eventually has questions and needs assistance. Be *politely* assertive in seeking assistance—being *politely* assertive is an important life skill to acquire, and I do emphasize the word *politely*. I am a very quiet person by nature. I am more of an introvert than an extrovert. However, my father always stressed to me the importance that I not be afraid to open my mouth and to lose my fear of speaking. He equally taught me that someone who speaks should have something to say and not just talk to hear the sound of their own voice. In school, I was never afraid or timid to raise my hand and speak in class because I usually felt confident enough that I knew the correct answer the teacher was asking. I was proud to be the student in the class who could answer the question, and of course, I did not always have the correct answer; but after all, I prepared and worked hard to be able to know the answers in many situations. I stayed up late studying, often read ahead of the class, and stayed after school to ask the teacher questions. I was proud of my preparedness. But I also was not quick to try to show off in class or try to beat other students to raising their hands and answering questions. I was very reserved, modest, and humble. Rather than me raising my hand more often than not, the teacher called upon me to give the answer when no other students in the class volunteered to do so.

Some forty years after graduating high school, I still remember raising my hand to answer questions posed by my high school Latin teacher, Ms. Gorenz. The question she asked the class was, "Who invented the alphabet?" "The Phoenicians," I said. Again, as I stated, I quite often intentionally did not volunteer in class to answer questions if not called upon because I was aware of the peer pressure of not giving the impression to my classmates that I was trying to show off. Yes, as an adolescent, I too from time to time caved into the peer pressure during my high school days. But at times during college, I was intimidated and timid to approach professors for help or to ask questions because even though some professors appeared more approachable than others, there were a few who were unfriendly, pompous, and arrogant and put off clear signals that they didn't want to be bothered. It was their job to "be bothered," and I didn't always stand up for my rights to approach them to ask questions.

If I knew then what I know now, I would have understood that these same professors worked at the university to serve me as a student. (And these professors did not represent the majority of my professors or instructors.) In other words, my tuition payments helped pay for their salaries; therefore, they had an obligation to at least make themselves available to me. I should not have felt intimidated by them out of fear that they would try and make me feel inferior if I did not understand a particular concept. The same situation should apply to you to learn from the mistakes I made in this situation and speak up, lose your timidity, and ask questions. In reality, asking questions represents an example of you taking the self-motivation to advance your education.

Speak up and lose whatever timidity you may possess not only in speaking with your college professors and/or instructors but also with other students in your classes who may be able to assist you in difficult areas of the class concepts or materials. In this situation, you may reap the rewards of networking as well as developing friendships and respect from other students, as outlined in a previous chapter. As you may have heard someone say before, and it is true, the journey of a thousand miles starts with the first step. Likewise, lose your timidity and start speaking up to ask questions and to demonstrate respectfully and politely that you are inquisitive and intelligent and that you can contribute substantively to discussions and conversations both in and out of the classroom and in the workplace and beyond. Prepare in advance what it is you want to say and how you wish to say it and how you wish to project yourself and how you wish you wish to be perceived. Go over it many times again and again in your mind and practice saying it outloud to yourself. Depending upon the situation, as I have indicated in a previous chapter, there may be situations where it may be wise for you to vet your remarks to a friend, coach, or mentor prior to publicly making your comments. In other words, think carefully before you speak, and when you do speak up, have something to say. Afterall, with practice and careful thought and preparation, "It isn't difficult to do if you know how to do it." If speaking up is something with which you do not have much experience, then start with baby steps, but get started now.

CHAPTER 7

Becoming a Whole Person

Expand Your Learning Base and Broaden Your Experiences

Work hard on a daily basis, but at the same time, enjoy your journey and expand your learning base. In reality, your college days and high school days will be brief, and you can't regain them, so try to appreciate your college and high school experiences each and every day. When I say enjoy your college experience, I mean "savor your college experience." Your number one priority in attending college is for you to attain the best well-rounded education possible. Your primary objective is to focus on excelling in your area of academic concentration. However, attaining a quality college education also entails being a sponge and receptive to absorbing as much knowledge as possible even in areas outside your major. If you are a science major, do not simply focus on excelling in your science classes but also expose yourself to courses in the liberal arts and humanities and vice versa. However, a well-rounded education does not simply mean acquiring an education inside the classroom. Keep your eyes, ears, and mind open to take advantage of the plethora of educational opportunities surrounding you outside the classrooms on your college campus as well as in the communities that surround your college or high school, whichever the case may be.

Northwestern University offered many cultural events on its campus throughout the school year, and the magnificent city of Chicago, just south of the Evanston campus, as you can imagine, was filled with all kinds of activities. Due to both time and perhaps some financial considerations, as a student, you likely will not be able to attend as many cultural events on or off campus that you would like or as often as you would desire. However, keep abreast of activities and opportunities and actively attempt to plan ahead so that you will be in a position whenever possible to take advantage of opportunities that are on the horizon. Most college campuses and universities host interesting and thought-provoking guest speakers on campus, with most of these events offering free or reduced price admissions to students who present a student identification card. Research a noteworthy speaker who may be well-known in your area of interests or perhaps someone speaking on a topic that is completely outside of your concentration that you want to hear. When I was in school, the best way for us to learn about such events was by reading our student newspaper *the Daily Northwestern*, noticing signs posted throughout campus on trees and taped on the sidewalks, and frequenting the libraries and the student center to glance at the poster boards and of course by word of mouth from other students and professors. We did not have the benefit of social media, texting, apps, or even the Internet. None of that existed at the time. Now, the Internet is a great source for you to stay up to date with on- and off-campus activities. Try setting Google Alerts to alert you about various topics, subjects, and even individuals who may be appearing on or near campus. Also, take advantage of the wealth of knowledge from your fellow college students and professors who surround you on a daily basis. Inquire about what type of activities they are involved in or attending out of the classroom. Consider asking a fellow student if you might attend an event with them.

Your college experience is not limited to attending lectures or events but also participating in extracurricular activities. Two of my favorite out-of-class activities while at Northwestern was taking sailing classes on Lake Michigan on Saturday mornings as well as going to see Northwestern students perform in the Waa-Mu Musical theatrical production. Of note, several of those students from Northwestern have gone on to become famous TV and/or movie actors and actresses as well as producers, late-night television hosts, sportscasters, and recently, at the time of the writing of this book, during the spring of 2018, even a princess of a prince in line to perhaps become the king of England. I also found a great deal of satisfaction as well as inspiration by simply walking through the campus of Northwestern, especially on the Lakefill, to watch and listen to the waves of Lake Michigan crash into the rocks and roll onto the Northwestern north and south beaches. I enjoyed watching Evanston families taking strolls and observing townspeople play catch with their dogs. I especially derived a great deal of inspiration and energy also by looking way up into the sky on late afternoons after class to gaze at the seemingly countless numbers of airplanes flying in from the east as they lined up over Lake Michigan preparing to descend and land at O'Hare Airport.

As a student from a small town in Indiana, I found it spectacular to look out from the Northwestern campus to marvel at the beautiful, majestic, and powerful skyline of Chicago and the sparkling waters of Lake Michigan (one of the largest bodies of fresh water in the world) and jet airliners flying into one of the busiest airports on earth. I recall being very curious as to where the jet planes were coming and who might be on those airplanes. Remember, in college, up to that point in my life, I had only been on an airplane once in my life and that was when I was in sixth grade on our school trip to Washington DC. Watching those jetliners float into view inspired me even further as I envisioned that someday myself I would also be flying to far-off places in the country and world. I also derived a great deal of enjoyment (and sometimes amusement) by simply observing my fellow NU students, how they walked, how they carried themselves, what they wore, etc. Thinking about what my fellow Northwestern University students wore and how they were adorned even now still at times brings smiles to my face as I recall some good memories and conversations that my friend Henry and I shared regarding this.

In the Northwestern University Library, every evening at nine o'clock, most students who were studying in the main library would take a twenty-minute study break to rush to the vending machines there in the library. But more on the agenda than just an opportunity to grab a quick snack, it was, in particular, an opportunity for the "preppy" and posh students to show off their fashions and accoutrements. Some of my friends and I referred to the study break as the NU fashion show. Sometimes I even tried to "fashion up" for the study break, but unfortunately, I didn't have the extensive preppy and expensive wardrobe or accouterments necessary to impress or attract anyone's attention. LOL. You may be asking yourself, What does the nine-o'clock study break have to do with educational opportunities or taking advantage of educational or entertainment opportunities around you? Well, quite simply, the nine-o'clock study break represented an opportunity for me to both educate myself and even, at no financial expenditure to me, entertain myself about certain aspects of human nature right in front of me. I am sure these occurrences way back when I was in college were happening on college campuses across the nation, and maybe to this day, this sort of thing still happens. In addition, when I was living in New York City completing my surgery internship and residency program, due to both time and financial limitations and constraints, I would often, if even only for a few minutes, make a conscious effort to walk over to Central Park to people watch and observe entertainers and skaters boogie down to the music of their boom boxes at the time, or I would simply just walk down the crowded avenues or take a walk or run alongside the East River and watch the luxurious yachts, tugboats, and helicopters go to and fro. Again, doing these things served as forms of entertainment, education, and inspiration for me. Likewise, when you are in college, you should take advantage of the endless opportunities that surround you that you will recognize if you open your eyes and take the opportunities to observe and take in your surroundings. And trust me, my observations were and even now in no way represent any disrespect to those people whom I was observing and from whom I was deriving education and entertainment. Much to the contrary, I admired the courage and inventiveness that many of my fellow students and others whom I was observing. And guess what, they were probably also looking back at me and observing and being entertained by me. I'll never know. LOL.

So what's my point? My point here is to strongly encourage you to expand your learning base, environment, landscape, and canvas to become more aware of both in-the-classroom and out-of-classroom educational and entertainment opportunities that abound and that you don't cost you any money but will energize and reinvigorate you and make you laugh, often at times when you are in most need to a laugh to help offset the pressures of your day. One fond memory I still have, even though I was a chemistry major, was when as a college senior, I took a government class taught by the then senator and former US presidential candidate George McGovern, of whom I also had the opportunity to meet with and of whom I had the opportunity both in class and after class ask questions. Become proactive about seeking out such experiences while you are in college.

In more recent years, I have been fortunate to have had the opportunity to meet US presidents Bill Clinton, George W. Bush, and Barack Obama. I promise you that taking time to explore educational opportunities that are outside your major area of study will vastly enrich your college life, and you will be thankful for decades to come that you took advantage of such opportunities. If you are not proactive and inquisitive in seeking out educational and entertainment opportunities that will enrich your mind, you may very well also likely for years to come look back with some regrets in retrospect for not taking full advantage of certain opportunities while in college. Don't let this happen to you. There are experiences that you will cherish from the totality of your college years. The education that you acquire outside of the classroom will help you grow into the confident, well-rounded person that you will need to be to succeed in your profession.

As I look back at my years at Northwestern University, I should have taken advantage of more on-campus and off-campus educational and entertainment opportunities than I actually did. Learn from my mistakes and missed opportunities, and I implore you, don't make the same mistake. Let me tell you one funny story that one of my best friends, Henry Pak, whom I met at Northwestern, and I still laugh about today. In the winter of 1981, on a frigid Saturday night with wind chills at record lows of literally minus 110 degrees (as I recall), the famed coach Bobby Knight and the Indiana Hoosiers basketball team, which was ranked number one in the nation at the time, came to Evanston to play the NU Wildcats. My friend Henry, who lived across the hall in our dorm, then called the Northwestern Apartments on Orrington Avenue and came to my room begging me to go to the game with him. However, because I was busy studying, but mostly because I didn't want to venture out into the elements to go to the arena, which was two miles away, I refused to accompany Henry to the game. So Henry went to the game without me, and wouldn't you know it, the underdog Northwestern team beat Indiana, the number one team in the nation, and Coach Bobby Knight was livid at his star player Isiah Thomas and the rest of the team and kicked a chair. Yes, years later, I regret a little bit (even a lot) not going to the game, but at the time because it was way too cold, I felt I made the right decision. Do you think I should have gone? What would you have done?

Regarding expanding your experiences, please also refer to the section in this book in chapter 3 discussing opportunities to study abroad.

CHAPTER 8

Physical Health and Wellness and Proper Nutrition

Eat a Healthy Diet

One of the main keys to your success in school and in life will be for you to take active steps with respect to maintaining and even improving on your overall health. For excellent references and up-to-date information on heart health and eating a heart healthy diet, I refer you to Cleveland Clinic's Heart Healthy Diet Web site. Prior to matriculating to your college or university, you should have a general health assessment and physical examinations by your physician. Maintaining your health while in college in large part rests in your maintaining (or establishing if you have not already done so) healthy eating habits. I am sure you have learned about basic nutrition in your high school health class and about the Food Guide Pyramid, which details for you the recommended guide to your daily food choices. In order to remain healthy, you should follow the recommendations set forth by the Food Guide Pyramid, which now also includes the recommendation to drink water. Do not ignore eating healthy fruits and vegetables while you are away at school. I recommend that you consult the Food Pyramid from time to time to remind yourself regarding recommendations for the number of daily food services and portion sizes you should eat. Also, physicians and nutritionists recommend that you do eat breakfast each morning because eating a good breakfast will provide you with energy that you will need to function well in your classes. For those of you who are vegan or vegetarian, my advice to you is to be very clear and knowledgeable about how on such a diet you will get all of your recommended daily allowances of protein, vitamins, and minerals. Also, check with your school prior to matriculating to your school to make sure that your college food service will have the food that you need to stay healthy on your vegan or vegetarian diet. For those of you who are not vegan or vegetarian but are wanting to convert to become either vegan or vegetarian, it is my recommendation that if you are going to, in fact, convert to become vegan or vegetarian, you do so prior to matriculating to college; and I do not advise that you convert during the school year as doing so may disrupt your ability to concentrate on your studies; you may suffer from side effects, and your overall physical and mental health may dangerously deteriorate. Speak with your physician and nutritionist prior to converting, and make sure that you are well-read on the subject of what foods to eat and vitamin supplements to take.

Regarding nutrition, please avoid or greatly minimize the amount of soda pop that you consume and don't eat at or greatly minimize the amount of fast food you consume because of the high fat content often found in fast foods. I refer you to view the 2014 very educational film documentary produced by Stephanie Soechtig called *Fed Up*, which features Dr. Mark Heyman who is a noted expert on the subject matter of the obesity crisis in America related to unhealthy eating habits.

A Word on Taking Vitamins and Mineral Supplements and Using Sunscreen and Mosquito Repellant

A quick word about taking vitamins. Most physicians and nutritionists do recommend that you should consume the majority of your daily recommended amounts of vitamins in the food that you eat each day. However, because college can be very stressful and because college students don't always eat right, I do recommend that you do take a daily multivitamin and that you also routinely take a vitamin C supplement. Vitamin C is known to enhance one's immune system and may even reduce the incidence of one acquiring the common cold and help prevent a cold or flu from progressing to pneumonia. Research has shown that taking Vitamin C prior to the onset of a cold can prevent the duration of the cold. There are a few over-the-counter products such as Cold-EEZE® (which are zinc-laden lozenges) and Theraflu® (for cold or the flu) that many physicians recommend taking at the onset of earliest signs of one's developing a cold or flu to shorten the duration of the cold or flu. Consult with your personal physician and a pharmacist who is aware of all the medications you are taking regarding taking over-the-counter or prescription medications so that you will avoid unintended side effects.

Physicians normally also do recommend that women especially take a multivitamin with iron, due to fact that women are oftentimes anemic due to their menstruation. I also recommend that you (and every student), *proactively* request your physician to order a blood test to check your vitamin D level. Vitamin D helps regulate your body's calcium levels, and low vitamin D levels can lead to disease and symptoms of poor bone health (Rickets and osteomalacia), bone pain, muscle weakness, hypertension, heart disease, depression, and dementia, among other symptoms. Research also has shown that low vitamin D levels can contribute to the development of various types of cancer. Vitamin D is found in food such as cheese, eggs, and fatty fish like tuna, mackerel, and salmon and food fortified with vitamin D such as dairy products, orange juice, and soy milk but is also synthesized when your skin is exposed to sunlight. African Americans and those of Mediterranean descent are very often found to have low vitamin D levels because in those with darker skin, the increased skin pigmentation interferes with vitamin D production in the skin. Generally, it is recommended that most people get 600 IU (international units) of vitamin D daily. Sun exposure and oral supplements are generally effective in increasing vitamin D levels in those who are deficient. Remember to maintain your skin health and wear sunblock and apply skin lotion and in areas, and situations where you will be exposed to mosquitoes, make sure to wear an insect repellant with DEET.

These are general guidelines I am providing you as a physician. However, each of you should consult with your own physician regarding your personal medical situation and recommendations for you to take vitamin supplements. Above all, when taking vitamins and mineral supplements and over-the-counter or prescription medications under, no circumstance should you ingest these supplements in excessive amount that are beyond the recommended daily amounts or amounts prescribed to you by your physician. If you have questions, always ask your physician and/or pharmacist.

Make Exercise an Essential Part of Your Everyday Routine

In the competitive and often stressful college environment for which you will find yourself, you will need to find time to incorporate physical exercise into your routine, and this is in addition to the exercise and steps you will likely amass by walking or even riding your bicycle to and from your classes, obviously depending upon the size of your campus and location of your classes. It is to your advantage to work both aerobic exercise that increases your heart rate and low-weight strength training into your routine on a daily basis. I am in no way even remotely suggesting that you start living in the gym and skipping classes and diverting attention away from your studies. Routine exercise will in fact serve to help provide your body with the much-needed energy and stamina you will need to remain competitive, meet deadlines, and fulfill responsibilities.

I advise that you register to become a member of your college's recreation facility. Find out the operating hours of the facility, the hours the pool and when exercise rooms are open, and the schedule of formal exercise classes, such as yoga and spinning classes. Consult with a fitness professional at your school's recreation facility to help you design a physical fitness exercise routine tailored specifically to accommodate your current state of physical conditioning and to help you meet your fitness goals. As any doctor will tell you, if you have been sedentary or have any preexisting medical conditions, please consult with your physician prior to undertaking a strenuous regimen of exercise activities. Preferably consult with your primary care provider or physician who is familiar with your medical history prior to matriculating to your college campus.

It is to your advantage also to start on your journey to physical fitness as early in your life as you can and dedicate time and effort to sustain this throughout your lifetime. This is easier said than done, and stressful situations in school and at work have a tendency to creep in between you and the time you have to dedicate to your physical health. Knowing and anticipating school assignments, tests dates, and other conflicts within your schedule will hopefully allow you an opportunity to figure out alternative times to commit to your exercise routine. I am proud that my son Trey—who at the writing of this book is a doctorate student of physical therapy and who was a baseball star in high school and who continued to play baseball well into his twenties—make time daily to exercise that helps maintain not only his physical health but also his mental acuity, which he needs to complete his physical therapy studies and to compete in competitive chess; he is a national chess master also. Of note, my father, Charles Modlin Sr., was a National Senior Games Association track and record holder. To date, he currently holds track and field records for men over the age of eighty years in the 100-, 200-, and 400-meter runs as well as in the long jump. Please take a minute to Google his name and read about and watch videos posted online about his remarkable and awe-inspiring story and accomplishments. I have also dedicated chapter 14 in this book to both my parents detailing their many accomplishments, which also highlight what an amazing and inspiring people they were.

Get into the Habit of Drinking Plenty of Water to Remain Hydrated, Avoid Energy Drinks, and Don't Become Addicted to Coffee or Caffeine

In addition to plotting out and sticking to a regular exercise routine, develop a habit of drinking water and become educated regarding your general health. Of note, medical research has recently shown limited value and even and unhealthy side effects of consuming popular energy drinks. Many of the energy drinks and energy supplements are filled full of caffeine and stimulants. As an aside, I strongly advise you against taking stimulants to stay awake to pull an all-nighter to cram for that exam coming up. Stimulants can be very addictive and harmful or even fatal to your health. I also recommend that you not become addicted to coffee. I hope this is not already the case. I've seen many high school and college students, let alone people at work, who quite literally cannot start their day with first consuming one, two, three, or more cups of coffee in the morning and then more throughout the day. This is a bad habit to form, not to mention a very expensive habit considering the costs of coffee especially at the popular coffee shops.

Now, back to the subject of exercising, most doctors recommend that you prior to, during, and after exercise hydrate with water. If you do have a particular medical condition such as heart or kidney disease, you may be on a restricted daily volume of fluid intake. If this is the case, you of course need to consult with your doctor regarding how much fluid to drink. But unless you have a particular medical condition, then you should make sure your body remains hydrated with fresh water. The general rule is to drink to fulfill your thirst "plus a little bit more." If while exercising you feel faint, dizzy, lethargic, confused, pass out, black out, see stars before your eyes, have chest pain or arm pain, slurred speech, or just don't feel well, then immediately stop and seek immediate medical attention. For simple light-headedness, you may need to just sit down or lie down and rest. But some of these other symptoms, you never know, may be serious signs of serious medical problems and be emblematic of serious life-threatening dehydration or other serious medical conditions, such as heart disease, stroke, hypoglycemia (dangerously low blood sugar), or other conditions. It never hurts and is most wise if you experience such symptoms to get immediate medical attention. If this does happen to you, you should not resume physical exercise until cleared by a physician. Make it a habit to routinely weigh yourself perhaps weekly or a few times a month. It will help to prevent what is known as the "15" or the fifteen pounds that freshmen supposedly gain during their first year at college.

Signs and Symptoms of Dehydration

So more about dehydration, because this is not uncommonly seen in college and high school kids, athletes, and nonathletes. One of the earliest signs of dehydration is unintentional weight loss, clammy and sometimes blanched or skin paler than your normal complexion, dizziness, less than your normal amount of urine output, and in more extreme cases weakness, fever, lethargy, confusion, altered sensorium, and other symptoms. If you are experiencing signs and symptoms of dehydration, go to your college medical facility, local hospital, or urgent care center immediately. Ask a friend to accompany you and call 911 if necessary (and if you witness this happening to another person, call 911 for them or help them get medical assistance). In addition, students, you should always notify your parents and family of any medical situations you may be encountering. They care about you and can contribute in many instances important medical information that will help the doctors take better care of you. Yes, you are a college student, and yes, you don't have to disclose to your parents what is happening to you medically. But common sense, remembering your roots along with the love of your family or caregivers who contributed to your success should give you some appreciation of your ethical responsibility to inform them. Additionally, you may still be on your parents' health insurance. Do not act blindly or succumb to peer pressure by not letting your family know about any significant medical problems you are experiencing at school. You owe it to them to inform them.

Personal Health Monitoring Devices and Personal Medical Identification Tags

I also advise you to gain access to and wear personal health monitoring devices that are commonly available for you to self-monitor your heart rate (pulse) and even your blood pressure while exercising. If you are diabetic or prediabetic, then you should also be aware of the importance of monitoring your blood sugar and you should know how to do this. Also, if you do have medical conditions such as diabetes, high blood pressure (hypertension), a seizure disorder, or others or allergies to medications, beestings, peanuts, or other substances, then it is your responsibility to make sure this is recorded and updated if new conditions arise on your health records at your school; and you should also wear a medical identification tag or bracelet or carry a card indicating exactly what medical condition(s) or allergies you have so that in the event of an emergency, first responders will be aware of your medical condition(s). If you have a dangerous allergy to beestings or certain foods, you should go to school knowledgeable and readily prepared as to how to self-administer an EpiPen® and you should carry on your person at all times two EpiPen® if this applies to you. Also, make sure you inform your roommate(s), fraternity or sorority brothers and sisters, dorm floor and residence hall leaders and friends, and even your professors and instructors to make them aware of any serious medical conditions that you have in the event you experience an episode in your dorm room or class for which they may need to intervene on your behalf when you may not be able to effectively communicate to them in real time what is happening. If you are taking antiseizure medications that require frequent or occasional monitoring of medication levels, make sure that your levels are checked and normal prior to matriculating to your college campus and consult with your managing physician regarding how often you need to have your medication levels checked. Also prior to arriving on campus, contact your college campus health facility and the local hospital near your college campus to ensure that you will be able to go there for whatever medication monitoring your doctor recommends for you at the times such monitoring is recommended.

Another Word Regarding Exercise: Exercise in the Company of Others

I advise that you always exercise in the company of others being around in the vicinity, and I strongly advise you against going off on your own isolated or in a desolate location late at night (on or off campus) or during the day for that matter for a walk or run. Please read and study very carefully the chapter in this book on safety tips.

Make Sure Your Immunizations Are Current, Get a Flu Shot, Know How to Take Your Medications, and Know the Side Effects of Your Medications

Other general health tips include making sure that your immunizations are up to date. Get a flu shot annually in the fall, unless you have an allergy to the flu shot or ingredients of the shot (you may wish to ask your parents if you are unsure about this). Assure that you keep any special medication with you if taking special or extended trips. If you are taking, for example, also insulin that requires refrigeration, then of course make sure you have a reliable refrigerator that maintains the required temperature either in your dorm room or within your dormitory building that is close by and readily accessible by you and the leadership of your dormitory. Consult with your physician well in advance to you going away to college regarding perhaps your getting switched to medication alternatives that do not require refrigeration. Above all, while away at college, do not—and I repeat do not—simply stop taking prescribed medications without the expressed approval of your or another qualified physician. There are medications, such as antihypertensive (high blood pressure medications), that if you are taking and abruptly discontinue can result in dangerous and even deadly consequences. Regarding prescription medications, make sure your doctor provides you with enough refills on your prescriptions that will last you several months.

Before, or upon arriving at campus, identify a pharmacy on or in a safe location close to campus where you will be able to pick up prescription refills as well as commonly used nonprescription medications. As I did for my own kids when they went off to college, I recommend that you keep a supply of commonly used nonprescription medications and remedies in your room (e.g., Tylenol, nonsteroidal anti-inflammatory medications, cold and allergy medications, skin lotions, Benadryl and hydrocortisone cream, antidiarrheal medications, Vicks VapoRub®, muscle ache creams, and ace wraps) that are readily and conveniently available to you in the event you have headaches, muscle strain, common cold symptoms, etc. Learn how and when to use these medications and adhere to the directions. Be aware of your allergies before taking any medications. Please note that even nonprescription medications if inappropriately used can be quite dangerous. If in question, go to your college student health service for treatment and advice, and don't forget you can also call your parents for advice. Take note of the expiration dates of medications and cold medications, etc. When you seek to take over-the-counter medications for seasonal allergies, colds, or for congestion, use of nondrowsy antihistamine medications during waking hours is preferred over medications that will make your drowsy or fall asleep. As a busy student especially around exam time, the last thing you want is to be falling asleep during your exams. Also don't use such medications long term, and do make sure you do get as much rest as you can. Careful sparing use of antihistamine medications to help you sleep better at night when you have a severe cold or flu generally will help you rest better; but remember to read the directions on all medications, even over-the-counter medications, prior to taking any medications.

The Covid-19 Virus and Pandemic: A Must Read

In late 2019 and 2020 as we all are aware, the Covid-19 pandemic devastated nations across the globe including the United States. Millions upon millions of people were affected and infected with the virus and in the United States at the time of publication of this book, several hundred thousands of people died. Individuals with preexisting conditions and chronic health infirmities, such as diabetes, hypertension, heart disease, kidney disease, cancer and other conditions, as well as elderly and minorities, especially African Americans, were found to be more predisposed of acquiring and dying from the disease due to having lower innate immune systems from such chronic preexisting health conditions. Young people, including those of college age and those below age 50 were initially thought to be immune or less susceptible to acquiring and dying from the Covid-19 virus and because of this, many young people including high school and college aged students did not adhere to recommendations for social distancing, mask wearing, hand washing and other methods/recommendations that doctors and public health officials put forth to mitigate against the disease. Many young people did not take the Covid-19 virus serious and continued to congregate in large groups and have parties. However, with time, the epidemiology of Covid-19 bore out that young individuals in fact are carriers of the disease who can spread the virus to others and that young individuals themselves do acquire and die from Covid-19. Most colleges and universities at the time of this writing closed down for periods of times and went to online virtual classroom education and social distancing/mask wearing, mandatory Covid-19 testing requirements for on-campus in person classroom settings.

As a young person reading this chapter about ways in which to remain healthy, please visit the Centers for Disease Control Website (CDC) as a reliable source of health information and frequently for updates regarding infectious disease, pandemic information and vaccination/immunization recommendations and requirements. Also, please pay particular attention and adhere to you school's health information requirements and recommendations.

As a physician, I also recommend that everyone take the Covid-19 Vaccine, unless you have a specific contraindication to taking the vaccine. Please consult with your personal physician and pubic health officials regarding the specific Covid-19 vaccine that is available and recommended. At the time of this writing, two vaccines are available that require two separate inoculations. Consult updated information as future vaccines and schedules will become available after the writing of this chapter.

Get Yearly Eye Exams and Have Spare Eyeglasses and/or Contacts

For those of you who wear glasses or contact lenses, I also recommend that you purchase and take to school with you a spare pair of eyeglasses or contact lenses so that your ability to read and complete your assignments won't be hampered should you lose or break your eyeglasses or contacts. Prior to or upon your arrival to your college campus, locate and identify a reputable optometrist and eyeglasses store in the event you need to have urgent repairs to your eyeglasses. Your student center on campus may or may not offer such services as may your student health center. Be proactive and find out in advance where these services are and don't wait until exam week when you are in a time crunch and are in urgent need of such services. Make sure you get an annual eye exam to detect for any visual changes. Routine eye examinations by an ophthalmologist can detect a variety of series medical conditions that you may not be aware of, such as hypertension, diabetes, glaucoma, and other conditions. Whether you wear glasses or contacts or don't wear any prescription glasses, it is my recommendation that every student, before you head off to college, get a visual examination by an ophthalmologist and to do so yearly. Also ask them to give you a hard copy of your prescription that you can take with you to school and have on hand in the event you may need to order a replacement pair of glasses or contacts.

Maintain Your Dental Health

Maintaining your dental health is also a must. Maintain your oral and dental health with routine dental cleanings and dental checks. In fact, make sure you get your dental checkup and dental cleaning before you head off to college. Poor dental and oral hygiene is a leading cause of cardiovascular disease, not to mention very painful and annoying toothaches and painful tooth drilling by your dentist and also results in your needing painful root canals, which I am certain you will want to avoid.

Protect Your Ears and Avoid Hearing Loss

Other health tips include your minimizing the use of headphones with loud music to avoid possible and probable ear damage, which will occur gradually and often insidiously over a time period. As you know, the trend nowadays is for people of all ages to routinely listen to music wearing earphones. In my college days as I said before, we didn't use the portable technology that allowed us to listen to music on the move. We could only listen to music by playing records on our turntables or at parties or at concerts or on car stereos or radios. But I was guilty of listening to loud music playing records in my room wearing headphones while in high school and in college and afterward. I didn't always consider the fact that I should lower the volume of the music I was blasting through my headphones into my ears. I was damaging my hearing and I didn't appreciate it. Don't let this happen to you.

As an aside, it was not until I was almost done with medical school in 1987 that it came in vogue for people to walk around playing cassette tapes and later compact disks on large boom boxes, and I remember buying my boom box on Forty-Second Street in New York City when I was an intern at NYU. I took it up to Central Park with me on the weekends when I went there to walk and study. But I didn't blast my music aloud in public. By the way, I still have my boom box. LOL.

A Comment on Alcohol, Marijuana, and Recreational Drugs

You really should know by now that the use of alcohol, marijuana, and recreational drugs is not something in which you should participate or engage. I am not going to devote a great deal of attention to this subject in this book because I am sure you have heard from your teachers and parents and a multitude of news media and other sources about the health threats and dangers associated with the use of these addicting substances; and yes, alcohol, marijuana, and recreational drugs are in fact addicting and often lead to the user escalating to even stronger, more addictive, and more destructive drugs, heroin to mention one. The improper use of your or someone else's prescription medications falls into this category, for example, opioids such as Percocet. It is not uncommon for high school and college students these days to experiment with all sorts of drugs and even household medications. A word to the wise—you are intelligent. You already know that this is not wise to use alcohol and recreational drugs. As I said previously, as a physician and surgeon, I have encountered many incidents of young people who have overdosed on alcohol, LSD, narcotics, barbiturates, and any number of other illicit and prescription medications. While in college, I saw some of the students feel as if they had to get so filthy and stumbling drunk to be the life of the party that they had to be taken to the hospital. Stories are in the news often about high school and college students who were killed driving while drunk or who overdosed.

Does anyone think that to be cool, one has to get so drunk or high that they can't even walk and are throwing up all over the place? Guess what, other students are standing around watching and laughing and deriving entertainment and amusement at those students who are the ones stumbling drunk. Don't let this happen to you. Avoiding the peer pressure of using alcohol and drugs, "It isn't difficult to do if you know how to do it." And how to do it is just say no. If your roommate(s) and friends are exerting pressure upon you to participate in this type of activity, then they really aren't your friends and you should seek to associate yourself with different people. One final note of which you may not even be aware is that alcoholism, in many situations, does run in families. In other words, in some families, there may be genetic or hereditary predisposition for one to develop alcoholism. Does alcoholism run in your family? Find out if it does. If it does, then you yourself may be at greater risk for developing alcoholism. So play it safe and don't get started drinking. Lastly, if you have developed a drinking or drug or substance abuse problem, get help immediately. Go to your student health service or find other organizations that can and will help you. Don't think it can't happen to you and don't be embarrassed or too scared to seek help. See the next section also on maintaining your mental health.

Sexually Transmitted Infections, Urinary Tract Infections, and Safe Sex

Parents, I cannot tell you what to do in this case with your student because I understand that in some religions, contraception is discouraged or prohibited and because I realize that the subject matter of sexual activity can often be a difficult subject to have with your child. I can however give you my advice that ideally you will have open communications with your student regarding birth control and avoidance of pregnancy and sexually transmitted diseases. Students, you too should ideally have candid conversations with your parents, but again, I understand the sensitivities and awkwardness that this may bring. Therefore, at a minimum, I stress the importance of you consulting your physician to discuss this sensitive often private topic. This is nothing for which you should be embarrassed, but if you are, please help facilitate that your son or daughter consult with a physician to have this discussion.

As a physician and urologist, I treat patients weekly, including young people, for sexually transmitted infections, of which there are many different types. Some are easily treated, some are not easily cured, and others cannot be cured. These include nongonococcal infections (e.g., chlamydia), ureaplasma and mycoplasma infections, trichomonas infections, gonorrhea, syphilis, hepatitis C, hepatitis B, HIV (human immunodeficiency virus), HPV (human papilloma viruses), and others. Some of these infections cause signs and symptoms rather suddenly after exposures; others don't cause immediate symptoms because a person can be a carrier of such conditions and suffer no signs or symptoms for years if ever with certain infections. Go immediately to your school health service or a medical facility for evaluation and treatment if you suspect you may have been exposed to any sexually transmitted infection or have signs or symptoms of such.

The best way, of course, needless to say, to avoid these conditions is abstinence. However, those engaging in sexual activities are encouraged to practice safe sex by use of condoms and vaginal barriers to which you have been educated about in high school and about which there is ample literature and information available from your student health service, health professionals, and online from other reputable sources that are easily accessed. One of my main points here also, as a medical physician, is that if you have acquired an STD, you *must* comply with all medical treatment recommendations—meaning that if given antibiotics, you must complete the full course of your antibiotics treatments. Do not simply stop taking the medications just because your symptoms may have resolved. In addition, your sexual partner must also be evaluated by a physician and receive treatment. If only you are treated and your partner is not treated, then continued exposure to them will result in your getting reinfected.

Another important point I wish to make here also is that if you have taken your recommended treatments and you continue to suffer from signs or symptoms of infection, such as pain or urethra or vaginal discharge, return to your healthcare provider as soon as possible because you may have an infection, a resistant strain, or an infection that is not susceptible to the antibiotics prescribed to you. The organisms that cause many of the STDs are oftentimes fastidious—meaning that when your doctor takes a culture, they oftentimes do not grow in the culture medium and the laboratory results indicate that you do not have an infection, when in fact you do. The way in which I approach treating individuals who present to me with signs and symptoms of STDs or urinary tract infections is to collect cultures and then treat them with broad spectrum antibiotics because in my experience often simply treating patients based upon the results of culture results, which as I say may be falsely negative, means that many patients who need treatment won't be getting treatment and they will continue to suffer symptoms and they will continue to spread infections. There can be serious long-term health consequences of having untreated STDs, including chronic pain, orchitis, epididymitis, and prostatitis in men and pelvic inflammatory disease in women as well as infertility, urethral strictures, and widespread infections in both males and females. The consequences of untreated hepatitis C can be liver and kidney failure, and untreated syphilis can cause neurological deficits and more.

Urinary Tract Infections

Regarding the presentation and treatment of simple urinary tract infections (UTIs), note that it is more common for women to experience UTIs than men, because of the shorter urethra in women. Many consider that men with UTIs should undergo a urological evaluation because in most situations, men do not just get

UTIs, especially young college-age men. My recommendations, as a board-certified urologist, is that both males and females who develop symptoms consistent with UTIs, such as painful urination with or without visible blood (called hematuria), should go to their school health facility or local urgent care facility to get a urine culture. Some doctors will give women one antibiotic or a course of antibiotics with or without obtaining a urine culture. Some doctors will only obtain a urinalysis and treat based upon the urinalysis. However, in my practice, I prefer best to obtain a urine culture but to start treatment prior to the results of the urine culture because cultures take about three days to be finalized. Men with symptoms of a UTI should have a urine culture and receive five to seven days of antibiotics started immediately after obtaining the culture. Read more on your own regarding STDs and UTIs, and if you have not already, read the section earlier on maintaining your health; please do so.

Remember I am a urologist and I know the importance that you routinely inspect the color and consistency of your urine. If you should ever see blood in your urine, do not panic, but schedule an appointment with a physician for evaluation of this. In most instances, it may represent just a case of a UTI, but seeing blood in the urine (gross hematuria) may represent a serious medical or urological condition, for example, urinary tract stones or kidney or bladder cancers or medical kidney disease. Also, as part of your routine yearly physical examination, please make sure your physician performs a routine microscopic examination of your urine to check for the presence of blood (microscopic hematuria) or protein, which could be a sign of kidney disease. Speak with your family to see if kidney disease runs in your family.

Perform Your Recommended Monthly Self-Examinations

This book is in no way meant to be a full-compressive medical textbook. However, as a physician, there are additionally some important health tips I wish to give you to help you maintain your health while away at college and after college. These tips include that you must be aware of the routine self-medical examinations that are recommended for you to perform. In men, this means that you need to know how to perform and that you do perform monthly a self-testicular examination beginning at the age of fifteen and then lifelong to monitor for testicular cancer, which most often presents with a painless hard lump within the testicle itself. The most common ages for males to develop testicular cancer are between the ages of fifteen and thirty-five, but men even over the age of thirty-five can develop testicular cancer. Treatment for testicular cancer is more successful if detected in early stages before it spreads.

Both men and women should also become educated in knowing how to perform monthly breast self-examinations. Yes, men can get breast cancer too. Go online and watch a video or read a resource that visually shows how you should perform the breast self-examination or ask your doctor to show you. Generally, but not always, breast cancer is first suspected by one finding a nonpainful mass or lump in the breast.

Both men and women should also routinely, monthly, palpate (feel) they groin (inguinal), axillary (armpit), and neck areas for evidence of enlarged lymph nodes. Perform monthly also a self-examination of your skin, including your back, by using a mirror (or have a friend help you with this) to detect new areas on your skin that could, for example, represent skin lesions (tumors or cancers). Most people don't realize that your skin represents the largest organ of your body, and it serves many important functions. You want to maintain healthy skin. Again, the purpose of this information is not to scare you but to inform you that you are responsible for helping maintain your own health, and self-physical examination is one way in which to do this.

Gastrointestinal and Stool Health

Acute and/or chronic abdominal pain or discomfort may represent a variety of conditions for which you should seek medical attention. Don't simply drink antacids for an upset stomach that persists more than a few days. It could be something serious, such as an ulcer, significant gastritis or esophageal reflux, or pancreatitis. Pain in the right upper quadrant is sometimes associated with gallstones and right lower quadrant pain may represent appendicitis. The purpose of me including this information in this book is to not have you try to diagnose yourself with a medical condition or to make you fearful that you have a medical condition. My goal is to alert you that if you don't feel well, don't simply ignore it, but seek medical advice to ensure that you are okay. The challenges of college (and the abuses that some students place upon their bodies by also drinking excessive amounts of alcohol, which can lead to severe gastritis and even life-threatening pancreatitis) can present you with a great amount of stress that can become manifested by true physical illness, and you don't want to ignore the signs and symptoms of what could be a serious medical condition.

Again, I am a doctor, and even though you may find this to be gross, any doctor will recommend that you routinely examine the color and consistency of your stool. Again, this is not meant to make you panic or become paranoid about your health, but monitoring your stool can help you remain healthy. For example, changes in the caliber of your stools could indicate a serious medical condition or may represent the presence of internal or external hemorrhoids. External hemorrhoids are often but not always painful and represent protrusions of dilated veins through your anal canal, but internal hemorrhoids may occur also without pain, and both can narrow the caliber of your stool temporarily. If in question, consult with a physician for further evaluation. Prevention of hemorrhoids is by remaining hydrated and ensuring that you have enough fiber in your diet. Fruits and vegetables are an excellent source of fiber, and there are fiber supplements in the form of powders and fiber gummies that are also effective. Should you see blood in your stool, you should consult with a physician for further evaluation. Dark blood in the stool may represent blood in your gastrointestinal tract coming from up in your stomach or small or large intestines, whereas bright red blood may be blood coming from your large intestine, but either way, if you see blood in your stool, go see a physician. Also, please speak with your family to know whether gastrointestinal disease including colorectal cancer runs in your family history.

Maintain Healthy Feet

It is important also that even as a young person, you pay close attention to maintaining healthy feet and avoiding foot injuries. Get and maintain a good pair of walking shoes and sneakers that have good support that will keep your feet comfortable and healthy as you walk the many miles daily that you will likely be walking across campus. Get a good pair of recommended running shoes for use in jogging, running, and participating in aerobic activities. How often you get new running and walking shoes depends upon your level of activity. Consult with a local athletic shoe store and even your school's athletic trainer to advise you regarding the best shoes to get and how often you should change them to new ones. Running in shoes that are old and worn down trust me can lead to significant foot, ankle, calf, knee, and other injuries. For example, I developed severe plantar fasciitis as a result of running in old shoes that lacked the proper treads and support. Healing from plantar fasciitis and other orthopedic injuries takes a lot of time, is very frustrating and uncomfortable, and at times even requires surgery and months of physical rehabilitation. I cringe when I see people (students) wearing sandals and even high heels walking across campus. If you need to wear high heels to an event across campus, it is best to walk in comfortable shoes and carry the high heels in a bag and change into them when you arrive at your event. Also, regarding proper foot care, make sure you take to college a toenail clipper and fingernail clipper and file to keep your toenails and fingernails trimmed, neat looking, and clean. If you have the resources to do so, periodic visits to receive a manicure and pedicure is reasonable. Men, this applies to you also.

First impressions are often lasting impressions, so dress neatly, look neatly, and smell neatly. Maintain the appearance of and take care of your hair and clothing. Use deodorant daily and be prompt to class and meetings.

Men, you also need to care for your hair, and if you maintain facial hair, make sure you maintain it neatly, and periodically as necessary, trim the hair in your nose. Men and women, use antiperspirant and deodorant on a daily basis, and I don't need to remind you at this stage of your life about the absolute importance and necessity of showering daily, if not more than once daily, depending upon your activities and amount of perspiration. I know your parents told you about this. This means that if you need to get up earlier in the morning to make sure you have time to shower prior to going to class, then that's what you must do—get up earlier. Women, you can and should use perfume, and men, you can and should use cologne, but women and men, use these sparingly and don't douse yourself in perfume or cologne to where it is excessive and offensive smelling to others. Take an iron and ironing board to college and make sure your clothes are nicely pressed and clean at all times. Learn how to safely use an iron before you go to college because an iron can be a burn hazard and a fire hazard if you don't use it properly and turn it off. Hang up your clothes to help maintain them and keep them wrinkle free and don't just throw them on the floor all over your dorm room. Put dirty clothes in a hamper and plan to do your laundry once weekly. Take a bunch of coins to college to use in the washing and drier machines. If you have the financial resources to do so, investigate the options of using a laundry service at college to help save you from having to take the time to launder your own clothes. Doing so however does not replace the importance of your knowing how to launder and press your clothing. Don't just roll out of bed and put on dirty, wrinkled clothes unshowered. These are not only health tips but also tips to improve upon the first impressions that people have when they meet you. You want to not only look neat and well-groomed but also smell fresh. First impressions may often be lasting impressions, so you want to put your best foot (and armpit) forward. LOL.

Women's Health Examinations and Reproductive and Sexual Health

Further physical examinations that are recommended for sexually active women are annual Pap smears performed by your gynecologist or primary care physician. I am sure you were educated about these recommendations in high school health classes or by your primary care doctor or your parents. This book is not intended to cover a complete discussion on reproductive health and recommendations as to whether you women should use contraception or other methods to avoid pregnancy. I advise you to consult with your doctor and parents (if you are comfortable speaking with your parents about this) to get advice and guidance regarding sexual health. Men, I do advise the use of condoms should you have sexual activity to avoid impregnating a woman. Men, I advise that you too consult with your physician (and parents if you are comfortable in having this discussion with your parents) regarding the proper use and recommendations to use a condom during sexual encounters. Please see also the section on sexually transmitted diseases. Parents, I cannot tell you what to do in this case with your student, but ideally you will have open communications with your student regarding birth control and avoidance of pregnancy. This is nothing for which you should be embarrassed, but if you are, please help facilitate that your son or daughter consult with a physician to have this discussion.

Human Papilloma Virus Immunization

Lastly, there are recommendations for both males and females to receive three human papilloma virus immunizations starting at the age of fifteen. Speak to your physician about the details of receiving these immunizations including immunizations for hepatitis, which most colleges require. Your health provider will provide you with the risks and benefits of such immunizations, including immunizations for the influenza virus. I have included in the appendix the current immunizations and health screenings that most colleges and schools require that their students to have received prior to their matriculation, which includes screening for tuberculosis.

Pay Attention to Your Mental Health: Do Not Hesitate to Seek Assistance and Help as Needed

I have mentioned the importance of maintaining your physical health while you are in college and away from home. I would be remiss if I did not mention that you must also take deliberate steps to ensure that you maintain your mental health and wellness. College can be a very stressful experience for any student, and the stress can be further exacerbated if a student is experiencing difficulties in their classes or experiencing problems in their social situations. It is not uncommon for students to feel isolated and alone in college and feel as if there is no one whom they can speak with about their problems. Students having academic difficulties often not only feel pressures about their class performance but also feel stressed that if they don't succeed in college in their stated choice of study, they will have let down their parents and other supporters and they feel embarrassed and ashamed as if they are failures. Trust me, your parents and supporters will in no way love you less if you confide in them that you may be struggling and that you need to reduce your class load or even take a quarter or semester off from school. I am not attempting to scare you by saying this, but there have been many cases of students who became so depressed and stressed in school that they committed suicide. Services do exist for college students who are anxious or depressed for whatever reason, and trust me, there is nothing taboo about a student or any other person admitting that they need help and assistance in dealing with stress, anxiety, and depression. Before or upon arriving at your college campus, look up, write down, and record in your smartphone the contact information for your university's mental health services and mental health hotline. You may never have before in the past experienced stress or depression in your life, but that doesn't necessarily mean that you won't experience such problems in college or beyond. Proactively prepare yourself so that if you find yourself in this situation, you will know how to acquire the mental health services you need.

I have included in the appendix of this book a commonly used validated national stress, depression, and anxiety survey, along with the grading rubrics that will indicate your mental health risk status. You may wish to look at this survey for yourself to assess your situation as it stands now. Should you answer yes to question number 9, which is a question asking if you currently wish to hurt yourself, then it is recommended that you seek immediate mental health services.

Note that this survey is in no way meant to replace the services of expert mental health providers.

A Short Word about Living Off Campus

I could have inserted this section about living off campus in any of a number of other chapters in this book, but I intentionally am including a discussion about living off campus under the health section because in many respects, believe it or not, living off campus may impact your health. Some colleges and universities guarantee their students and opportunity to live on campus all four years, but others don't have enough dormitory rooms for all their students, and therefore, they consequently force upper classmen to move off campus. One option that colleges do generally offer to off-campus students is an option to continue to purchase an on-campus school dining (meal) plan, of which there are many different options. Many, but not all, off-campus students do chose to stay on-campus meal plans.

If you live off campus, I would seriously advise that you do maintain a student on-campus meal plan, unless you are a master chef and you have complete control of your off-campus house or apartment kitchen. Why do I say this? I say this because I have seen situations whereby three or four students team up to share an apart-ment that has a common living room space and a shared kitchen and refrigerator space. As such, I have witnessed that some roommates tend to be filthy and not clean up the kitchen for days or weeks after they make a huge mess and have dirty pots and pans and dishes with dried decaying food lying around in the kitchen as well as in the shared sitting areas. I have seen and heard stories of students eating other students' food, drinking out of the milk jugs of other students, and lacking basic sanitary habits; and this goes for bathroom messes that I have seen and heard that students living in shared spaces leave for their roommates to clean up. Living off campus and sharing spaces with other students require that each student do their part in helping clean the apartment and helping purchase needed supplies, like toilet paper, disposable clothes, cleaning supplies, and trash bags. It is not uncommon for students living off campus who don't have meal plans to routinely eat very poorly and to rely on ordering unhealthy fast food to sustain them. Also, many times, students living off campus must have a car or have access to friends who have cars and who can and are willing to give them rides to and from campus when needed. Many colleges and cities have bus lines that run routes close to campus, but others do not. It depends upon how far and where one lives off campus. Also consideration should be given to how severe the winter weather may be where your campus is located or how much snow and rain is typically occurring in your college town.

Also, in considering living off campus, of course one must first and foremost also consider how safe the after-hours is. In addition, in living off campus, the student must deal with a landlord, the quality, personalities, and characteristics of which can vary greatly with respect to how willing or quick they are at fixing clogged drains and overflowing toilets and air conditioning and heating. My oldest daughter lived off campus her junior year in a lousy apartment in which she shared a bathroom with another apartment. For the entire year, there was no showerhead in the bathroom. I called the housing company that managed the building, and they refused to even speak with me because my daughter was an adult, and they would not deal with me, the parent. The house in which she lives had huge holes around the base of the house; clearly there were some type of animals living under the house. It was dark and also secluded. The landlord also locked her bicycle up in the shed, and my daughter had to get an Uber® to go to the housing office, which was over five miles away, to get a key to unlock the shed to get her bike, and she had to pay a fee to do this. What student needs all of this headache when they should be focused on their studies. Not to mention with my daughter living off campus in this pit, her mother and I were more worried about her safety than if she were back living in an on-campus dorm. My daughter her senior year could not wait to get back on campus, and she did get back into a lovely on-campus dormitory for senior students.

In addition, living off campus requires that you and your roommates fairly and on time each pay your share of the rent and utilities. Of course, all these things you can consider to be learning experiences and they are. But faced with meeting the rigors of a challenging academic schedule, are you ready to take on these additional challenges? Think carefully before you decide to live off campus. If you do have a choice to remain in on-campus housing each of your four years, my vote is that you should stay on campus. Seriously, how many parties do you think you really need to throw in your off-campus apartment? Many students who move off campus live to regret it and wish that they had remained in on-campus housing, but the opposite is also true—many students love living off campus. It really depends upon your personality and your ability to find compatible off-campus roommates who will be responsible in helping keep the place clean and quite. Many off-campus apartments provide the student with a larger room with a private bedroom and some with a private bathroom. Weigh the potential pluses with the potential negatives and decide which is best for you and your abilities to maintain your academics and your mental and physical health, wellness, and safety. On other note of caution, sometimes students get off-campus housing by themselves and wind up feeling lonely and isolated. As I said, think carefully before deciding to move off campus. Your decision could affect your health. Lastly, whether you live on or off campus, before you go away to college, if you do not already know how to do so, please learn how to cook basic foods, such as pasta, hamburgers, and eggs, because you may be in a situation where it is late at night and you are hungry and the food service is closed or you live off campus and for whatever reason you can't get out to the cafeteria. I recommend for student's living on campus to have a small refrigerator in their room. Whether you are on or off campus, also pay special attention to discard food from your refrigerator before it spoils and take note of expiration dates on food packages prior to purchasing it.

Be Mindful of Your Posture

"Posture is the position in which we hold our bodies while standing, sitting, or lying down. Good posture is the correct alignment of body parts supported by the right amount of muscle tension against gravity."[7] Incorrect posture and unhealthy sitting and standing habits can also contribute to chronic back pain, which of course can complicate your ability to focus on your tasks at hand and divert your attention away from your success path.

[7] "Tips to Maintain Good Posture," https://acatoday.org/content/posture-power-how-to-correct-your-body-alignment, accessed September 16, 2018.

CHAPTER 9

Social Networking

Hobbies and Extracurricular Activities

You need an outlet to decompress from the stress and rigor of your academic studies or job. Your hobby may be active participation in club sports, jogging, hiking, window-shopping, playing pickup softball, soccer, basketball, yoga, sailing, painting, or playing a musical instrument individually. Or perhaps you are in the college wind ensemble, such as I was briefly at Northwestern and my daughter Sarah was each of her four years at the College of William & Mary (Sarah's wind ensemble toured nationally and worldwide), or playing competitive or noncompetitive chess, such as my son who played in high school and on his Texas Tech University competitive chess team. Extracurricular activities help you relieve your mind of the stress it endures on a daily basis. Allow time each week or even more frequently to distance yourself from thinking about your course major. A hobby does not necessarily require a significant amount of time or financial expenditure. Each person is different in the amount of time they need to decompress. Some people need more time than others.

But I emphasize the word and importance of your "active participation" to distinguish it from passive participation such as watching television or a sporting event. While in college, a limited amount of television viewing is okay, but you have to discipline yourself and

189

know when it is interfering with your studies. Active participation in a hobby will more effectively engage your mind and even your body in the activity. Your brain will effectively switch gears and focus on functions other than the stresses of your classes. Some people set aside a predetermined period to participate in their hobbies; others are more flexible depending on the circumstances. I recommend that given your varying obligations in college, it is more prudent to remain flexible. Group or club activities often require committing to set times in many instances more so than individual hobbies or activities. However, if you find yourself pressed for time due to looming deadlines or upcoming quizzes or tests, then you will have no choice but to place the priority in completing your academic responsibilities instead of your hobby activity.

When I was a sophomore at Northwestern, my roommate and I often liked to watch the television sitcom M*A*S*H from 7:00 to 8:00 p.m. Watching M*A*S*H was something we both anticipated and looked forward to, but afterward, we went back to studying. As an aside, as both my roommate and I were premedical students, we enjoyed watching the zany activities of the cast of M*A*S*H along with the dedication to his patients that the main character Hawkeye exhibited. The show served to energize me. Further, M*A*S*H did have a positive impact on my desire to become a surgeon. But to avoid the distraction of television when an exam was looming, I would often not return to my room until late. I would go to the Northwestern University Deering Library or University Library and find a nice quiet place to study.

Deering Library in
purple at night

Magnificent ornate Deering
Library Reading Room,
Northwestern University

Deering Library staircase statue

A success tip that I do have for you is that it is best for you to minimize the amount of time you spend watching television, and in fact, it is best to not watch television at all, except for the news and programs that offer educational content. Of course, I am aware that many students are sports fans and like to watch their favorite sports teams play on television. I just advise that you do this in moderation because you want to spend the majority of your time reading and studying, and it is more advantageous for you to play sports and exercise than it is for you to be sitting down and watching sports.

While in college, my hobbies included playing my trumpet, taking sailing courses on Lake Michigan on Saturday mornings, and going for walks down Sheridan Road and the Northwestern University Lakefill to gaze at Lake Michigan and the mighty Chicago skyline to the south. As I gazed out over Lake Michigan and down to the Chicago City skyline, I envisioned myself living in downtown Chicago and attending the Northwestern University Medical School, which was located on Lakeshore Drive next to the Chicago Magnificent Mile. Speaking of sailing classes, one of my fondest memories was when our instructors had us intentionally capsize our small sailboats so we could practice the technique of righting them following an unsuccessful tacking or jib. The Lake Michigan water was very cold in the springtime. Regarding taking long walks and runs, we did not have iPods or even the Walkman back then. We did not have the luxury of listening to music while we ran or walked. But we somehow survived. It was not until later in the 1980s that the boom boxes became fashionable to carry around, but even so, those were far too big to carry while running or jogging.

Sailboats on Northwestern's South Beach

Looking south over Lake Michigan to Chicago Skyline from
Northwestern University Lakefill, Evanston, Illinois

A Quick Word about Fraternities and Sororities

A decision many of you may want to entertain during your freshman or later years of college is whether you wish to become part of the college Greek systems, which refers to joining a social fraternity or sorority. The time periods for which fraternities or sororities can "rush" prospective members vary. To "rush" means the act of the fraternities or sororities actively attempting to exert influence and in many cases escalating pressures on students to join their fraternity or sorority. Many schools nowadays do not allow rushing to occur early on in the school year. It is a personal decision as to whether you wish to become part of the Greek system and if you do, which house should you join as often you will be rushed by more than one house. This is also a very important decision for which you need to do your homework because there are many added responsibilities in joining a Greek house. Often there are additional financial fees associated with this, such as membership fees, meetings, house chores, mandatory attendance and participation in parties and outings, and other events, often massive peer pressure exerted upon members to also partake in alcohol consumption, sometimes hazing another, and other things associated with being part of the Greek system.

Belonging to a fraternity or sorority does not mean that one must cave into the peer pressures of drinking; I belonged to a fraternity at Northwestern and I did not drink. There are many positives that can come from belonging to the Greek house, namely, you can become part of a lifelong brotherhood or sisterhood of friends if you match with students who fit your personality. Another potential advantage is that after your freshman year, depending upon the size of your fraternity house, you might have the opportunity to live in the fraternity house. Select very carefully and do not be forced into joining at all or joining a particular house. Even if you do join, remember that you have the right to leave the fraternity or sorority should you wish to. One main consideration in your decision as to whether you should join is determining if whether or not the amount of time you need to commit to study will be adversely affected. Remember also, you don't have to choose to join a fraternity or sorority house as a freshman. You can join in future years if you are rushed.

The Art of Networking

So what is networking, and why is it important for you to become proficient in the art of networking? When I was growing up, my father was always actively and intentionally introducing me to the elders of the church and of the community and taking me with him to visit them. My father was a lay and servant leader of our church, the Wiley United Methodist Church. He was often going around town helping the elders of the church, the shut-ins, and especially running errands for our pastor, the Rev. Calvin T. Word, who was blind. Reverend Word became blind as a child and had attended a school to learn braille. He was married to his wife Dorothy, and they had a son named Bryce, who was about five years younger than I. I recall my father putting me in the car and taking me on his *rounds* to visit Reverend Word, Mr. and Mrs. Eugene Bailey, and many others. Mr. Bailey was the Henry County Court Bailiff. On Sunday after-noons, we would drive out to the Henry County "old folks home" to visit Ms. Kaiser. We visited Louis and Beryl Poindexter, Cool Breeze, my grandfather Wayman at his home and workplace, Newby Paul Auto Shop, Uncle Buddy (Gerald Modlin), and Aunt Twilla Basset and my cousins. I would also travel with my father downtown to the bank, utility companies, and other places to pay his bills. My father believed in paying his bills in person whenever possible and not rely-ing on placing his bills in the mail. We would also visit the Cole's residence, a wealthy white family who employed my father to do yard work and odd jobs part time in addition to his job at Firestone or the foundry (and at times when he was laid off from his factory job). Whenever my father took me on his rounds, he would always expect me to stand tall and upright, be very respectful, and extend my right hand to give a firm handshake to whomever we were meeting. My father would always tell whomever we were meeting how proud he was of me. Hearing his words made me feel that much more proud of myself and made me even more desirous to please him. I didn't understand it or appreciate it at the time, but he was strategic in doing these things. Spending times like this with my father also gave me an opportunity to observe how my father communicated with those whom he met, observe how he greeted people and showed them respect, and how he had a genuine sense of compassion for others. I observed how my father was a servant leader, and ultimately watching my father in these social situations taught me how to be a man.

I was always very shy and soft-spoken and did not know what to say to these elders, but my father would later explain to me that it was important for me to meet these people and know who they were because each of these people possessed their own areas of knowledge and also because someday I might need their help or assistance. He wanted me to learn how to speak and converse with them. He let me know that no matter whom I was meeting, it was important for me to realize that I could learn from each person whom I was meeting. They all possessed wisdom, which my father wanted me to recognize. My father never used the word networking, but in retrospect, that is what he was patterning for me and trying to teach me, the art of networking. This included teaching me the importance that I lose my timidity to get out of my comfort zone when needed.

When I was a senior in high school, I met Mr. Eugene Bailey, who lived in the old parsonage behind Wiley Church, to ask for a letter of recommendation regarding a college scholarship application. My father told me to call Mr. Bailey on the telephone and ask him if I could personally schedule a meeting with him about writing a college recommendation for me. I bet my father had already told Mr. Bailey that I was going to be calling. LOL. I highly suspect he did. But my father insisted that I personally make the phone call myself and that I be confident enough to request the scholarship recommendation, which I did. I recall Mr. Bailey opening his door and inviting me into his home and to sit down in his dark living room in a small chair next to his front door. The fact that I still so very vividly remember this experience, which occurred over forty years ago, serves to reinforce within me just how important this event was in helping me further develop and enhance my self-confidence in speaking with elders.

Thank you, Mr. Bailey. Likewise, I am grateful to my dad teaching me the art of networking. The letter was no more than a paragraph in length, but the fact that Mr. Eugene Bailey, who as a court bailiff was a highly esteemed member of our local black community of New Castle, Indiana, took the time to write the recommendation letter for me was one of the greatest honors I had ever received up to that time. I attribute one of my greatest secrets of success to be the fact that my father taught me the importance of networking and taught me about the value and knowledge that I could gain by learning from my elders because they do possess a great deal of wisdom, which if asked they are usually more than eager to share. I utilize the art of networking in my professional life on a daily basis both in the care of my patients and in helping me build upon the minority health initiatives that I have established at Cleveland Clinic and in other situations.

The art of networking does not have to be limited only to associating and interacting with older individuals or those of the same skin color as you. Quite to the contrary, you can and should also seek to network with and learn a great deal from those even younger in age than you and others outside your race, ethnicity, culture, or county of origin (nationality). Please take a look at the editorial in the appendix of the book that I wrote in the school newspaper as a college student at Northwestern with respect to my pleading for students to associate with and network with students of all races. Sometimes it takes putting your ego aside to admit that you can learn a great deal from even children and youth. I learn from my kids and from the school students whom I mentor and coach all the time. Even though my family lived on South Twenty-Third Street in New Castle, which was in the black community, and attended a black church, both of my parents, as well as my grandmother Hampton and my older sisters, taught me the importance of interacting with people other than just "colored" people. Yes, growing up in the 1960s into the early part of the 1970s, we referred to ourselves as "colored" and did not take offense to this terminology. It was not until the mid-1970s that society started referring to us as blacks, which I didn't care to be called. I am thankful to my parents for proactively teaching us not to be hateful or resentful of white people, even though they had told me and I had obviously heard and learned about the plight of our people as slaves and of the racism my parents and other colored people experienced in a segregated America. Growing up in New Castle in the 1960s, it's true that I do still remember seeing segregated restaurants and drinking fountains in some locations, and I too did experience and was victim of multiple episodes of racism that often challenged my self-esteem.

One of the most impactful experiences of my youth was when we as a family every night for an entire week sat in our family room watching the Alex Haley television miniseries *Roots*, which detailed the trials and tribulations of generations of blacks from their capture in Africa and slavery in the American south. Watching this miniseries served to further instill even a greater sense of self-dignity and pride within me, and this was extremely important given the environment of the time, which was more pervasive in making especially black youth question their self-worth. Yes, my parents, church, and community taught me the facts of life that included the existence of racism. But neither my siblings nor I were raised to summarily dislike or hate whites or any other groups of people. We were taught to understand that we were important and "just as good as everyone else." My parents and family taught us to have self-esteem and to understand that life is not always fair. We knew that as colored people, we would have to work even harder than white people to be respected and to acquire opportunities that they could obtain while not working as hard. These were the hard but necessary lessons my parents had learned from their parents and from their own life experiences. I learned the importance of learning to network with everyone including with white people.

In a literal sense of the word, my parents taught us the importance of meeting with people and learning from their wisdom, whether they be black or white. In reality, growing up, my best friends Jeffrey Ayres, Ian Sheeler, David Hamilton, John Herndon, Brent Maze, Alan Broyles, and their families and Jeff Rust, Brian Hacker, Jamie Miller, and others, as well as important people such as my baseball coaches, trumpet, band and art teachers, and others, were all white people. New Castle, Indiana, had a town population of around 18,000 people, and the black populace I would guess when I was growing up was probably 250 people or less, so I could see how important it was for me to learn to interact with, work, and play with people outside my own race. I do however know that there are many of you reading this book who live in large cities and in areas that are composed predominantly of the same race and ethnicity of which are you, whether you be black, white, Hispanic/Latino, etc. And there is nothing wrong with this, and you have much to learn from those people all around you. Nevertheless, my sage advice to you, whenever possible, is to expand your horizons by making a special effort to get to know and interact with people outside of your own race or ethnic background so that you will develop a better appreciation and derive the benefits of the growing diversity of our nation and our world. I am so grateful, and a better person, because my parents and family taught me to truly not see people by the color of their skin, but rather by the content of their character, which the Rev. Dr. Martin Luther King Jr. of course eloquently stated best in his "I Have a Dream Speech." Also, I am grateful to Jeff, Ian, and my other friends back in New Castle and in college who upon meeting me and interacting with me did not judge me by the color of my skin, but rather by the content of my character.

There were times when I could tell that my father was frustrated with me when I was young, mostly between the ages of eight and fourteen, because I was overly quiet, often timid, and appeared incapable of (or initially perhaps unwilling or unaware of the importance of) engaging many of the elders in substantive conversations, despite his attempts to help me get dialogues started with others. However, as I matured, I developed a greater appreciation and realization of the importance of what my father had been attempting to do for me and why. I, in large part, came to this epiphany because, as I was becoming a man at the age of fourteen, I came to have a better appreciation of the magnitude of the sacrifices that my father and mother and family had made for me. I had a better appreciation of the hard work they had done and were doing on a daily basis on behalf of my siblings and me. I came to appreciate that it was my responsibility to uphold the high expectations that my parents and family had placed upon me.

When I was six years old, my mother took me one night to visit her college class at Ball State University Teacher's College, which was located in Muncie, Indiana, about sixteen miles north of New Castle.

I remember running up and down the aisles of the classroom auditorium steps before the actual class started, and I remember vividly her stopping me to proudly introduce me to her class. I clearly remember her saying, "This is my six-year-old son, Charlie. One day, he will be going to college too." And I remember the class and professor clapping for me. It was then, at the young age of six, that I realized that my parents had placed expectations upon me to be a high academic achiever and that I was expected to attend college. Up to that point, I do recall vividly that I had wanted to be a trashman because it seemed like fun to be riding on the back of the garbage truck that used to come by every Tuesday on Twenty-Third Street and because my favorite toy at the time was my metal white garbage truck, which I am proud to say that still have and cherish over fifty years later (see me with the picture of my trash truck).

Pictured with my metal trash truck from my
childhood that I still cherish to this day

And I am in no way being condescending against trashmen or garbage collectors. What would we do without them? My father used to voluntarily at four o'clock in the morning (as a form of exercise and community service) collect trash on the streets and in the parks of downtown New Castle that teenagers carelessly and deliberately spewed while cruising in their cars on Saturday nights. I didn't like the fact that he was expending his time and energy to clean up after disrespectful people, but he was trying to teach me, my siblings, and the community (students, this is another success tip I am giving you now) about the importance of community service and not being afraid to step up to do what is right. Another success tip—my parents always taught me as did MLK tell us that whatever it is we wish to be, we need to be the best at it that we can be.

Daughters Hannah and Meredith at MLK
Monument in Washington DC

It was not until I was around twelve or fourteen years old that I finally *fully* recognized what my father, in particular, was attempting to impart within my character and awareness (here are more success tips)—that there is a wealth of knowledge in the form of older people that I could harness for my benefit. It would mean losing my timidity and being brave and wise enough to access this information to enhance my education and knowledge to improve my life skills. As I have indicated in this book, my mother had returned to college around the age of forty to become an elementary schoolteacher, but my father in eleventh grade, at the age of seventeen, had to leave high school to enter into the US Navy during World War II. He never had an opportunity to complete his high school education, let alone to go to college. So he really continuously hammered into our consciousness the importance of education as a means to a better life.

The first time I recall hearing the formal terminology of "networking" used was when I encountered two books published by a local Cleveland African American author named George Fraser. It was in the summer of 2003 when I purchased two of his books, the groundbreaking classic *Success Runs in Our Race* and also *Race for Success*. I read the first of his books during the summer that year while my family was vacationing at Lakeside. Lakeside is a United Methodist Church gated community retreat on the Marblehead, Ohio, peninsula located about an hour and a half west of Cleveland on the shores of Lake Erie. These books were a revelation for me and represented what I call the bible of networking of establishing meaningful, substantive, positive, supportive, and business relationships between and among blacks. I highly recommend that you in particular read *Success Runs in Our Race*. For those of you who are not members of the black community, I still wholeheartedly advise that you read this resource as many of the lessons contained within will benefit you greatly regardless of your race or ethnicity.

For me, the contents of these books set in motion the roadmap that allowed me to create and establish the Cleveland Clinic Minority Men's Health Center and our annual celebrated Cleveland Clinic Minority Men's Health Fair. Coincidentally, I had just finished reading the second of Mr. Frasier's book when on June 30, 2004, Dr. Andrew Novick, the chairman of Urology of Cleveland Clinic at the time, held a ribbon-cutting ceremony at Cleveland Clinic to celebrate the official opening of our Minority Men's Health Center. We had held two previous Minority Men's Health Fairs in April of 2003 and 2004, and now we were formally opening our year-round Minority Men's Health Center clinics and celebrating receiving a substantive two-million-dollar governmental HRSA grant. The *Cleveland Plain Dealer Newspaper* had published an article announcing the opening of our Minority Men's Health Center. On the first official day of seeing patients in our Minority Men's Health Center, upon opening the door to see the first patient presenting to the center to see me, behold, whom other than Mr. George Fraser himself did I find sitting in the exam room. He had read in the newspaper about the Minority Men's Health Center opening, and out of curiosity, he wanted to see the center firsthand, meet me, and assure that the center as advertised was there to provide benefit to minority men. I had never personally met Mr. Fraser but recognized him the moment I opened the exam room door to see him sitting there in the flesh, and I was both honored to be in his presence and in awe that he was sitting in my Minority Men's Health Center.

After meeting George, I excused myself for a moment, retrieved my briefcase, and came back into the room. I pulled out of my brief-case both of Mr. Fraser's books and informed him that I had recently read them. We both had a hearty laugh and immediately bonded. I told Mr. Frasier that, along with my father, I credited him and his black community networking books for helping guide me as to how to establish our Minority Men's Health Center as well as how I could best disseminate information within the black community as to the existence and purpose of the center and how it would benefit them and their families. In short, Mr. Fraser's books summarized what my father had been showing me in his actions and attempts to teach me at an early age about the importance of networking within and outside of my community and comfort zones. Mr. Frasier's books expounded upon the more precise art of networking specifically within the black community and the importance of learning and building from the accumulated generations of knowledge and exper-tise contained within this community.

Author George Fraser in the Minority Men's
Health Center with Dr. Charles Modlin

Keep in mind that I am not from Cleveland or Northeastern Ohio. The community that I was attempting to engage in order to substantively improve upon their health outcomes did not know me. Because of my busy schedule as a kidney transplant surgeon, I initially did not have much time to become actively engaged or known within the local black community. However, through reading and absorbing the knowledge within the pages of Mr. Fraser's books and through many years of hard work, I was able to put into practice the lessons contained within Mr. Frasier's books. I had to dig deep within my character and remember the lessons taught to me by my parents and their admonition that it is my responsibility to give back to others less fortunate than I by utilizing my talents acquired in large part due to the countless sacrifices of the many generations who had laid down their lives for my generation (success tip). Therefore, I had to first become a visible, proactive community advocate whom the black community could trust. People needed to know that I had their best interests at heart. Securing the trust of the community required much sacrifice. I spent countless hours away from my family on nights, weekends, and holidays becoming active in the black community in an effort to gain the trust of the community so that my messages regarding the importance of preventive health screenings and self and community empowerment to foster improved healthy behaviors and establishing continuity of care with physicians could be heard. I had to very carefully juggle maintaining my full-time kidney transplant and urology practices in the early stages of my professional staff career at Cleveland Clinic with my community outreach activities and family obligations.

For the first seven to eight years as a staff kidney transplant surgeon at Cleveland Clinic, I was assigned to staff and operate on patients not only at our main campus in Cleveland but also at hospitals in Youngstown and Akron. Doing so required that I sometimes drive three thousand miles or more every other month and in the final year before closing these satellite programs three thousand miles monthly to commute to this satellite programs. I am not proud to say this, but I do recall the misfortune of falling asleep at the wheel driving as the rigors of the job required that I work at all hours of the day and night. One day, I was so tired that I had to pull off the road to a truck stop to take a quick nap while still in the car driver's seat. While napping, I recall having a nightmare that I had fallen asleep while still driving the car, and this made me suddenly wake up from my nap and slam my foot on the car brakes while screaming. I sometimes tell this story now and get some laughs, but in reality, it was no laughing matter because I quite literally thought I had fallen asleep while driving and that I was going to die. My heart was palpating, and it took me many seconds to realize that I had only dreamed I was still driving.

Were it not for the lessons taught to me by my father about networking with my elders, I would have lacked the courage to go out into the black community of Cleveland to establish the Minority Men's Health Fair and the Minority Men's Health Center. Also, were it not for the concrete lessons contained in Mr. Fraser's books, I am not certain the center or the Minority Men's Health Fair would be the successes that they have become today. I encourage anyone reading this book to purchase Mr. Fraser's books and digest the wisdom contained within his pages.

The definitive message to you is the same advice that my father told me, "The greatest teacher is at the foot of an old person." But don't forget that you can also learn from those of the same age or younger than you. Finally, don't disregard the importance of networking and interacting with people from different generations, genders, races, ethnicities, religions, and cultures. They possess a wealth of knowledge, and you'll be surprised at how willing people are to disseminate much of the knowledge and information they have learned as a way of giving back and assisting you in achieving your goals. It is the theme of this entire book. Success tip, networking. "It isn't difficult to do it if you know how to do it."

CHAPTER 10

Aspire to be a Leader in Your Field, Not Just a Follower: Master Business Basics and Develop an Appreciation and Working Knowledge of Office Politics

Regardless what your major area of study is in college or what your particular career aspirations are, it is imperative that you acquire a broad-based education. In other words, if you are a science major studying to become an engineer or surgeon, it is imperative that you also take college-level courses in literature, the arts, and the languages, to name a few other areas. Likewise, if you are a humanities or theater major, it is in your best interests to take, for example, a science class such as biology or geology. Doing so expands your knowledge base. I was a chemistry major in college, and of course, I took the science premedicine courses in biology, physics, and mathematics. But I also took Latin, Spanish, French, Chinese Art, and, as an extracurricular course and activity, sailing classes on Lake Michigan. I always looked forward to going to these classes outside of my major area of study because doing so allowed my mind to get away for a while from studying the hard sciences. I looked forward also to taking these additional humanities classes because doing so allowed me to meet other students and make additional friends, most of whom I probably would have never met, even though the Northwestern campus was not large. Most of my science classes were on the north campus, whereas almost exclusively the arts and humanities classes were on the south campus. Remember, while in high school, college, and beyond, by intentionally making an effort to experience and learn new things as well as meet new people, you actively broaden your intellectual capacities, which serve to further expand your opportunities in life. By meeting new professors and fellow students, not only do you grow academically, but also you mature in your interpersonal communication skills, which will exponentially serve you on your journey to success.

Take Some Business Classes

But even more than simply taking courses that are out of your major area of study, I believe strongly and assert that it is important that you also strategically take some business classes while in college and to become financially literate. During my senior year in college, I took an introductory course in economics, which I thoroughly enjoyed. I had taken an economics course when I was a senior in high school, and I enjoyed that class very much also.

A Word about the Importance of Developing Financial Literacy for Personal and Business Purposes: Securing and Maintaining Your Financial Information

Financial literacy refers to one's education, understanding, and appreciation of the aspects as to how one makes money, budgets their income, and saves and grows their money, as well as the ability to have the skills and capabilities to utilize financial resources to make decisions regarding investments. I advise you to commit time into further reading and study of financial literacy and to improve upon your understanding and practice of financial literacy techniques in your daily life. The basics involve, as early as you can in your life, to start a checking and savings account and in high school or college to open a credit card account with a low spending limit. If you are going a distance from home to college, I advise you to open a checking account with a bank that has a prominent presence in your college town and preferably one that even has a presence in the student union building on your college campus. Not all banks have a national presence, and the bank you have in your home city may not be located in your college town. Of course, online banking will be more convenient for you as a busy student. Remember for security purposes to choose a secure password and to frequently change your online banking and other passwords. Remember also to of course refrain from going to cash stations at night and in isolated areas. Opening a credit card account and making regularly scheduled payments at an early age are excellent ways for you as a young adult to establish a great credit rating for yourself, which will be beneficial to you following your formal education, for example, help you purchase a car or a house. Keep a locked security box in your dorm room in which to keep your sensitive financial and other important documents. I purchased lock boxes for each of my kids when they went to college. Also copy and keep a copy of your credit card information (as well as other important documents) in your lock box and a keep copies at home in the event your credit card is stolen or lost so that you will be able to notify the credit card company to immediately cancel your card. With online banking, you will readily have this information online as well. And please don't forget the combination to your lock box. LOL.

The MBA Degree

In 2011, long after my college days, I graduated with my master's degree in business education. I recall Henry Pak, one of my best friends at Northwestern and who is still to this date, advising me, even though he knew I had aspirations of becoming a physician, to acquire my MBA degree. I did not appreciate at that time his advice regarding the value in my doing so, but many years after having been practicing as a surgeon at Cleveland Clinic, I realized that taking business classes would potentially expose me to additional leadership opportunities as a physician at Cleveland Clinic and give me a broader perspective regarding the business aspects of medicine and even entrepreneurialism and other aspects of business outside of medicine.

In business school, I was able to interact and work with a number of students, many of whom were working in a variety of areas other than medicine. I further realized what Henry Pak was trying to teach me almost thirty years earlier that becoming proficient and developing basic levels of business acumen would not only make me more educationally well-rounded but also provide me with certain advantages in my pursuits in the field of medicine. For example, Cleveland Clinic is a physician-led healthcare organization consisting of more than ten hospitals in Northeastern Ohio, in Florida, and across the world. The CEO of Cleveland Clinic and other key leaders are physicians, all of whom must possess knowledge and appreciation of business principles necessary to run the network of hospitals in collaboration with nonmedical business professionals. Not only is it important for physician and nursing executives to possess such business acumen, but also it is increasingly becoming more important for all physicians, all of whom are leaders in their own right, whether working in academic institutions or running their own private practice offices, to have more than rudimentary knowledge regarding hospital cost containment, healthcare economics, budgeting, organizational development, medical and surgical operations management, corporate communications and knowledge of media, and marketing principles necessary to sustain and grow their hospitals and medical practices. Likewise, no matter what your professional objectives, it is highly likely that you will be more marketable and value-added to your organization if you possess business acumen.

During my MBA, my favorite courses were in organizational development, media, marketing, corporate communications, team building, and leadership development and business principles. I have actively utilized the knowledge I have learned from my business courses in the growth and development of the health disparities programs I have created, established, and facilitated throughout Cleveland Clinic, namely, our Cleveland Clinic Minority Men's Health Center and Minority Men's Health Fair. My business and leadership development education has also benefited me in becoming a productive and value-added member of Cleveland Clinic's board of governors and has made me more value-added to, and I believe more appreciated by, my organization that in turn has served to further reinvigorate and reenergize me in my daily activities as a practicing physician and surgeon because I have been given opportunities to have more of a voice and seat at the table in participating in making many critical decisions and to help set substantive policies for our hospital.

The following is a list of some of the business courses I recommend you study at college or even self-study:

- Operations management
- Organizational behavior
- Management communications
- Business law
- Business quantitative principles
- Accounting
- Finance
- Economics
- Entrepreneurship
- Strategic thinking for entrepreneurs
- Venture capitalism
- Others

Learn Fundraising Techniques, Become a Loyal Alumnus, and Maintain Communications with Your College Alumni Office

As a leader in your given profession, it is almost certain that at some point you *will be called upon* by community not-for-profit organizations to serve as a member on their boards, each of which has various missions to provide a benefit to the community. Each organization, in order to sustain themselves operationally and achieve their mission and objectives, must successfully develop focused efforts on fundraising or else perish as an organization. To be an effective board member and provide a legitimate community benefit, you need to understand techniques of fundraising. As a board member of a not-for-profit, or even a for-profit entity, you also need to understand the particular legal and financial obligations that come with serving on such boards. Such information is beyond the scope of this book, and you should read the fine print prior to joining such organizations and, if necessary, consult with a business attorney prior to joining a board.

Your college alma mater, to which I hope you will remain forever loyal even after your graduation, will call upon you yearly following your graduation to be philanthropic and make a financial pledge to the university, commensurate with your means. As a student, as well as an alumnus, you can distinguish yourself to your school by serving in a leadership role or participating in your college's fundraising campaigns. I participated as part of my thirtieth collegiate undergraduate reunion class at Northwestern whereby we raised over two million dollars, and I have been personally asked again by the university president to serve on my thirty-fifth college reunion committee, and I am honored to do so given how Northwestern has vastly contributed to my successes. As a class representative of my medical school class and member of the school of medicine alumni board, I started and led an initiative to establish an endowed chair scholarship campaign for my Class of 1987 Northwestern University Feinberg School of Medicine. We successfully raised over $100,000.00 to endow an annual scholarship to students in need. Perhaps you too can establish such an initiative to help out future students at your college.

As an undergraduate student and as a medical student at Northwestern, I also participated in fundraising phone-a-thons to raise money for the university. I did this as a way of showing the university I was appreciative of being a student there and as a way of giving back to my university and helping create opportunities for current and future students.

Having a fundamental knowledge of fundraising techniques only serves to enrich your life by enabling you to more effectively give back to the community in which you live as well as where you originated and to give back to your school. By doing so, you validate the people who showed you support along your journey to achieving your dreams. The basic ingredients that go into developing basic fundraising skills center around one developing and constantly maturing one's communication and relationship skills that enable one to communicate effectively, credibly, and influentially and with a passion to others what is the mission of the organization you are representing to which you wish them to contribute. Being an effective fundraiser does take practice, and with practice, you become more effective and successful in fundraising and ultimately in achieving your objectives to give back to your communities. This makes you into a more valuable member of your organization. Depending upon where you work, it is quite likely that not only during your career will you be called upon to fundraise for not-for-profit organizations, but also you likely will be asked to serve on a committee or play a leading role or contribute your voice to fundraising objectives, for example, capital campaigns for your place of work. Having an ability to do so will additionally make you more value-added to your organization.

Dr. Charles Modlin pictured with Class of 1983 thirtieth reunion cochair classmates presenting 1983 Class Gift Check in 2013 Northwestern University Football Homecoming Game

How to Schedule and Manage a Meeting

Whether you want to become a physician, attorney, business-person, teacher, professional car racer, or rocket scientist, you will find yourself in a position of needing to schedule and manage meetings, and there are a multitude of ways to be successful at this task. I am in no way an expert on *Robert's Rules of Order*, which is the most widely used manual of parliamentary procedure in the United States originally published in 1876. Nonetheless, I advise you now, no matter where you are on your journey, to purchase a copy of this book and become proficient in developing a working knowledge of the parliamentary procedures of organizing meetings. In the business environment, leadership and board-level meetings usually adhere to such principles, and to function in such environments, you will need to be proficient at least in the basics of parliamentary procedure. No one shared this information with me in college, and I wish I had known about the importance of such procedures earlier. Purchase a copy of this book and read it cover to cover, starting now. You'll be glad you did. But just reading the contents of *Robert's Rules of Order*, which is true of reading any book concerning developing proficiencies, it is not enough to only *read* about proficiency in that area. You must *put into action* what you learned from reading books through practice, practice, and more practice until the knowledge becomes second nature for you. This is true in every area of education and life. Put the book learning into action until it becomes part of your fabric. By learning parliamentary procedure, you will be more prepared in officiating meaningful, efficient, and effective meetings.

The success of the many meetings that you will conduct and lead largely depends on your (1) communication skills (verbal, nonverbal, and written), (2) active listening skills, (3) organizational skills, (4) capacity to relate to and respect your colleagues (publicly and privately), (5) and your emotional intelligence and (6) ability to demonstrate to others that you value their input and that you hear their input and other attributes. Likewise, the success of your meetings also depends upon the amount of quality time that you place into your meeting preparation. The success of operating a meeting starts long before the actual meeting itself. Prior to meetings, it is of paramount importance that you also effectively engage in some pre-meeting conversations with others who will be attending your meeting. Does this make sense to you? In reality, many decisions that are to be decided at a given meeting have already been decided before the actual meeting. In reality, opportunities for you to advance and be promoted within your organization often depend upon your awareness of the importance of conducting effective meetings and your ability to successfully communicate to other stakeholders and leaders within your organization your thoughts, ideas, and vision before the actual formalized meeting occurs. These measures are what fall under the term office politics.

Office politics is a real phenomenon, to which you may easily fall victim especially if you are naïve to its existence. I refer you to the section below on office politics as well as to the reference list in the back of this book on resources that discuss office politics.

There are a multitude of ways to schedule meetings. In high school or while in college, you perhaps have already become familiar and proficient in scheduling and conducting meetings for your clubs, fraternities, or sororities or other organizations. The manner and ease with which you accomplish this vary according to how many individuals you will be inviting to attend a given meeting. Some meetings may be placed as regularly occurring meetings on your calendar of which you might notify people in your organization or group via e-mail or letter or announce at a prior meeting. In my days during school and early in my professional career, we did not possess cell phones, e-mails, or social media networking capabilities; and consequently, notice of meetings were more commonly via office memos, newsletters, the school newspaper, word of mouth, or announcements at other meetings or over the high school public announcement system. Now, there are a number of online programs available to assist you in scheduling meetings whereby you can solicit optimal meeting dates and times from individuals whom you wish to participate in your meeting.

GoToMeeting, Doodle, and Survey Monkey are just some examples of such modern Internet-based programs available for you to schedule meetings. You should also become familiar with techniques of scheduling Skype meetings, video and teleconferences, and three-way calls. When I was in school, I commonly heard people saying that you don't have to worry about things like learning to type or perform office functions because as a doctor you will have a secretary to perform these duties for you. Well, in this modern era of corporate cost cutting, it is increasingly more common that professionals often have to schedule their own meetings, manage their own schedules, type and distribute their own office memos and e-mails, and place their own phone calls. With desktop computers, laptops, tablets, and smartphones, I don't need to tell any of you about the importance of learning to type. Probably, looking back, the most important course I took in high school, aside from my English and Latin classes, was the one-semester typing class during my senior year. Back then, we had to use manual typewriters (or electric if we were lucky, which I was because my mother purchased one) to prepare all of our college applications, school essays, and many other formal reports. We didn't have Word processors. Our spellchecker was a dictionary and thesaurus. To correct typographical errors, we used whiteout and often had to retype the entire page over. I encourage each of you students to find an old manual or electric typewriter, some typing paper (and carbon paper), and see for yourself how difficult it was to use typewriters. LOL.

In summary, the bottom line is that it is to your advantage to familiarize yourself with the multitude of ways to schedule and conduct meetings, including in-person meetings and remote meetings, incorporating both a small number of attendees and large groups of attendees. It is also to your advantage now at your early age to acquire a working knowledge and expertise in conducting meetings based upon *Robert's Rules of Order* and to develop the understanding that the ultimate success of your meetings rests in your abilities to properly prepare in advance your meeting agenda and to effectively communicate to those whom you wish to be in attendance the purpose, goals, and intent of the meeting. It is also important to adhere to start and stop times as advertised and to allow for those in attendance to actively participate in the meeting.

A Word on Office Politics

Your success at conducting meetings (and even surviving at your job) also rests upon your awareness and understanding of the fact that office politics do exist. Familiarize yourself with the nuances of office politics. This takes much effort and time. The heights at which you will be able to soar during your career may ultimately—unfortunately but true—in large part, depend upon your ability to partake in office politics ethically, and I emphasize the word ethically. Under no circumstance do you want to lower or compromise your standards and ethics by taking the low road by playing dirty office politics. You may have already experienced students in school or colleagues at work who have unscrupulously compromised their character as a means to advance their own careers. Under no circumstance should you ever resort to playing dirty office politics. Read some of the recommended resources that I provide on office politics. Keep your eyes and ears open and become alertly aware of what is going on around you in school and at your workplace throughout your career. My purpose in discussing this is not to scare you, but to teach you.

In reality, in school, and in the workplace, the vast majority of people whom you will encounter are good people who are not attempting to impede your progress. However, there are people whom you will encounter, perhaps at school, but more so in your workplace, who may have malice toward you and who may intentionally and strategically actively attempt to divert your attention and impede your progress. Sometimes they do this out of displaced over competitiveness, sometime out of jealousy and/or insecurity they may have within themselves, and sometimes for other reasons. Speak with your parents, coaches, and mentors about some of the office and workplace politics they have encountered so that you can develop a better understanding of this dynamic early in your career. It is unfortunate, but true, that I, and many of my colleagues and coworkers, must often spend an inordinate amount of time and energy trying to avoid office politics and avoid falling prey to office politics. Many of us also dedicate a good deal of time assisting others in solving difficulties they have encountered at the hands of office politics. Unfortunately, avoiding office politics and not falling prey to office politics can be difficult to do in many instances because, often unbeknownst to you, others around you may be actively engaged in dirty office politics (e.g., spreading false and hurtful rumors or attempting to character assassinate or discredit you) and your boss or supervisors may actually believe them. This is why I implore you to proactively learn as much as you can about the existence of office politics and not be naïve to the existence of office politics. Resist the temptation of lowering yourself to playing dirty office politics even against those attempting to hurt and derail you. Instead, maintain constant open communication with your supervisors, managers, bosses, and colleagues in your workplace so that your true character and work ethic will be known to them. For more important information on this tough but necessary subject matter, please read my section on "Haters" and don't hesitate to discuss this subject matter with your parents, friends, coaches, and mentors.

CHAPTER 11

The Importance of Community Engagement, Coaching, and Mentorship

Give Back to Your Community

The Northwestern University motto incorporates into it the phrase "whatsoever things are true," which is derived from the latter part of Philippians 4:8, which reads, "Whatsoever things are true, whatsoever things are honest, whatsoever things are just, whatsoever things are pure, whatsoever things are lovely, whatsoever things are of good report; if there be any virtue, and if there be any praise, think on these things." My father so loved this Bible passage as did the founders of Northwestern University, which is why they incorporated "whatsoever things are true" into the motto of the university. It is indeed true that you understand early in your life that you must "use the education, knowledge, and expertise you have been fortunate to have acquired to give back to your community and serve those in need." These were the words and instructions given to me by my father. He understood that the trailblazers who came before me and their many sacrifices contributed to whatever successes I achieved. These leaders do not only include the Rev. Dr. Martin Luther King Jr., Ms. Rosa Parks, and other civil rights leaders whom we read about in history books. Those who have created pathways are all around us and include our parents, guardians, spiritual leaders, teachers, professors, coaches, mentors, friends, relatives, role models, and many others. They guide us on a daily basis by being part of our support system and mechanism as we advance our educational objectives. In acknowledging how others have benefited our progress toward our goals and our development, we, in turn, should clearly understand that we indeed do have a responsibility to give back by devoting our time, knowledge, wisdom, advice, advocacy, and resources for the benefit of others.

Find a Mentor, a Coach, an Advocate, and a Sponsor and Be a Role Model

Dr. Charles Modlin pictured on Saturday Hospital
Rounds with several student mentees from Cleveland
Clinic Office of Diversity Saturday Academy

This book focuses on helping you realize at early an age that your path to success depends on many factors; some of which are in your control and some of which are not. You have a choice of finding a mentor. Some people have already achieved success in the field to which you aspire, and many are available to assist you. Other seasoned professionals outside your chosen profession can also provide you with guidance to help you get from where you are now to where you want to be. Both parties can serve as mentors. Mentors can come from varying backgrounds, but all possess unique educational and life experiences that equip them with wisdom to share with you.

Each mentor can provide a different benefit. Some mentors may use more of the Socratic methodology of helping by posing questions to stimulate your critical thinking skills thereby helping to enable you to derrive your own answers and solutions. Others may be more direct in delivering you advice about how they might approach a particular situation, while others utilize a combination of both techniques. A coach and mentor are not synonymous. There may be value in your establishing a relationship with a coach as well as with a mentor. A coach can often be more hands on by more actively intervening to facilitate your progress and is often willing to provide direct instruction or exact steps when addressing an issue. A mentor is present to listen to you and then utilize their knowledge, expertise, and life experiences to help you derive answers to your questions or problems. However, the personality of the individuals helping you will vary of course, but the bottom line is that both coaches and mentors are valuable resources for you to seek and have in your stable.

Special Importance of Finding Advocates and Sponsors

In addition to seeking a mentor, coach, or both, I strongly advise that you seek out and find an advocate and also that you find a sponsor for you. An advocate is someone who publicly supports your virtues and attributes and recommends you to others. A sponsor is similar to an advocate, but even more than advocating for you, they take you under their wing and vouch for your work ethic and authenticity (and they often use their own political connections, authority, and influence), as a very influential person in their own right, to actively intervene on your behalf to help you obtain a particular position, job, or opportunity. They often in some instances also use their influence and political connections to help, assist, and guide you in your professional development once you attain the position for which they sponsored you. A sponsor may be a member of the particular organization for which you seek to enter or they may not be. Many times, in order to acquire and attain a certain position, job, or opportunity, your resume, as impressive as it may be, may not be enough to secure that position, job, or opportunity for you. In addition to having impressive credentials and preparation, you may oftentimes need a sponsor to introduce you to employers and to "the powers-to-be" in order for you to attain that position, job, or opportunity.

To be frank, identifying a sponsor is not always an easy thing to do. At times, your sponsor may be the same person as your mentor or coach, but in many situations, it is a different person and someone who has taken note of your work ethic, credibility, and leadership potential. In most cases, but not in all cases, a sponsor is someone whom you have encountered and in many cases worked with or interacted with and they have taken note of and been impressed by your performance. Sometimes a sponsor is a very influential person whom you have not met and don't personally know but whom your mentor, coach, advisor, or advocate has identified as being influential and approached on your behalf to request that they assist you and shine a light on you to help you advance into a particular position or opportunity. Do you understand here what I mean?

When I was a student and even into my professional life, I never really understood the concept or importance of sponsors. I did of course seek out advocates to write letters of recommendation for me for various opportunities. As a young student, I also never really sought out formal mentorship or coaching relationships; however as I indicate throughout this book, I have indeed learned and benefited from others who have offered me advice and guidance, a few of whom I would consider mentors, coaches, and advocates. An example of a sponsor on the college social scene level would be a member of a fraternity or sorority who has met you and likes you and believes that you would be value-added as a member of their fraternity or sorority and then who actively takes steps to help you gain entry into the fraternity or sorority. A sponsor at the academic college level might be a very influential professor who very actively advocates on your behalf for you to obtain a particular job or internship. Another example of a sponsor would be a powerful and influential congress-person who advocates and actively takes steps (sponsors you) to get you hired to clerk for a Supreme Court justice. This is the secret methodology as to how many students actually acquire many of these high-profile prestigious opportunities. Many of these students (and those coworkers you interact with during your professional career) are not any more qualified than you are, but because they have sponsors, they are able to acquire such opportunities. An example in the professional world would be an employee who is able to get the corporate CEO or other influential individual to sponsor them to get a promotion. A sponsor helps give certain people advantages over those equally or even more qualified than they are to acquire certain positions and promotions. Without such sponsorship, for example, you may not, just rely upon your own outstanding merits and qualifications, be able to attain such positions.

Much of what I am relating to you now regarding sponsors is not common knowledge and is kept secret by many. Obtaining and utilizing sponsors is an advanced success tip and technique. Most people won't outright tell you or confess that they have sponsors. This is an advanced technique and success tip of which you must familiarize yourself with how to do it. Do you understand what a mentor, coach, advocate, and sponsor are and their differences? Their boundaries in some instances are blurred, but as you mature on your success path, I am sure you will develop a better appreciation and understanding of the importance of mentors, coaches, advocates, and sponsors. The sooner you understand the importance of these individuals and understand their roles, the better advantaged you will be. Always be on the lookout for mentors, coaches, advocates, and sponsors.

The question that you may be asking yourself is, "How can I identify someone whom I can call upon to serve as a mentor, coach, advocate, or sponsor for me?" There is no one answer to this question. I have addressed above ways in which many find sponsors, and often, by not in all cases, sponsors are secured for you indirectly by your advocates who actively intervene on your behalf to help you connect with and secure sponsor to help you advance to the next level. When approaching mentors and coaches, research to make sure they are a good fit for you. Be respectfully assertive and respectfully contact them in person, via e-mail or a well-constructed letter. If they say that they cannot be your mentor or coach, do not be offended. There may be personal or professional reasons such as time constraints or others as to why they cannot serve you. We will discuss later in the chapter in greater detail how to approach and secure a mentor or coach.

Placing a priority on finding a mentor and/or coach will help you accomplish the task. You will likely have more than one mentor depending on where you are on your life's journey. A mentor may be one person while in high school, but in college, you may benefit from identifying one or more person to advise and mentor you.

I have benefited from mentors, coaches, and role models, but in doing so, I never consciously approached a person with the terminology in my mind that I was seeking out a coach or mentor. I thought of them more as advisors. In my day, the concepts of mentoring and coaching, which we commonly speak of today, were not popularized as they are for today's students. My father was my mentor until the day he passed away on August 13, 2010. He still mentors me, for not a day passes by that I don't recall and even now call upon him for his guidance and advice. He continues to motivate, move, and guide me every day. In addition to my parents, while I attended high school, I looked up to a number of people in New Castle, Indiana. Many of their names are in the "Acknowledgment" section of this book and include family, teachers, professors, coaches, friends, and my friends' parents. Their encouragement and expectations of me helped drive my determination to succeed in my goals.

While in medical school, there were professionals whom I respected and admired. Dr. James Holland, a urologist at Northwestern University Medical School and Evanston Hospital, and Dr. Paul Cauldron, an internist who served as my junior medicine rotation mentor at Evanston Hospital, are two examples. Both of these men showed genuine interests in me and offered me advice and guidance. Dr. Jack Snarr, the dean of Students at Northwestern University Medical School, served as my medical school advisor and also advised each of my medical student classmates. He was an excellent resource. These professionals gave me valuable advice. I encourage students whether in college or on the job to develop a formal student-mentor relationship. At Cleveland Clinic where I have now been on staff for over twenty-two years, there is a recently developed professional staff mentorship program. The professional staff ourselves are encouraged to seek a mentor(s). Additionally, Cleveland Clinic trains members of the professional staff to formally serve as mentors to their staff colleagues as well as other health caregivers, employees, medical students, and other students.

However, the majority of mentors and coaches available to you will probably not be part of a formalized mentorship or coaching program. You will identify most of your mentors and coaches through the relationships you have developed with people whom you recognize as having your best interests at heart. Most of the time (but not always) you will be able to tell, you will sense, who the people are who have your best interests at heart. As such, many of them may be or have been your current or former teachers and professors, spiritual advisors, college advisors, family, friends, sporting coaches, or a professional whom you have shadowed. I mentor and coach high school, college, and medical students whom I initially met because they actively sought me out as a physician to shadow. Over a period of time, many of these students distinguished themselves to me (e.g., some through research projects with me) as being highly motivated and ready to enter the medical profession or other areas. By showing and demonstrating their sincere interests in pursuing a career in medicine, or at least their desire to learn, it was natural for me to desire to help them achieve their goals, even if they wanted to pursue areas outside of medicine. These mentees executed an intentional and well-thought-out plan to initiate a student-mentor relationship with me. Many students had researched me, the work I perform, and my long track record of mentoring and coaching and offering letters of recommendation/reference for students applying to college, scholarships, and jobs.

The importance of acquiring a mentor and coach never stops. During my kidney transplant fellowship training, I was fortunate to meet and train under the leadership of Dr. Stuart Flechner who arrived at Cleveland Clinic as a staff urologist and kidney transplant surgeon just a few months before the start of my fellowship. He already had held staff positions at other kidney transplant programs in Texas and California. Dr. Flechner was an excellent teacher for me in the operating room, on the wards, and in the transplant clinics. To this day, I consider him both a friend and the most important professional mentor, coach, and advocate I've ever had, other than my parents whom I consider as having been both personal and professional mentors to me. Other important mentors to me at Cleveland Clinic include Dr. Robert Fairchild, Dr. William Braun, Mr. Martin Moon, Mr. Thomas Bennett, Dr. Craig Zippe and Carlumandarlo Zaramo, PhD, and Lateef Saffore, PhD. Keep in mind that mentor(s), coaches, and advocates can also be your friends and remember that you may be seen as a mentor, coach, or advocate or even a sponsor to one or more of your friends. Mentoring, coaching, advocacy, or sponsorship is not mutually exclusive.

Make a bullet list of the names of people in your life whom you feel you can approach to serve as a mentor, coach, advocate, and sponsor to you. Think about how each one would be advantageous in helping you achieve your short-term and long-term goals. Do your homework. Research and plan how you will approach them, and in the case of sponsors, think of how you might also enlist the help of others to advocate on your behalf to help you acquire an influential sponsor. Remember, mentors, coaches, and advocates can also serve as sponsors under particular situations. In fact, anyone who advocates you to help you identify and secure an influential sponsor is in fact acting as a sponsor you for you to obtain another particular sponsor. So you see how the boundaries between coaches, advocates, and sponsors are blurred. Any of the individuals may ask why you selected them. Be prepared to answer their questions.

There are times when you will not need to ask a person to become your mentor, coach, advocate, or sponsor. The relationship will grow naturally over time as you interact and work with a given individual under various dynamics. Don't overlook the fact that one of your peers who may be your age or even younger than you may also serve as a valuable mentor coach or advocate to you. It will depend upon the sum of their life experiences. The following are a few pointers to remember:

- It is not your mentor's job to provide you with "the answers." Coaches more commonly try to provide you with answers. Mentors help you derive the answers on your own.
- Be mindful of your mentors' and coaches' schedule. He or she is likely very busy with a job and life.
- Different mentors and coaches will have varying amounts of time for you. At the beginning of a relationship, have an open conversation about what will be the approximate frequency of your communication with them and get an idea as to the preferred time slots for appointments and best forms of communication (e.g., e-mail, cell phone, visit, or text). Both mentee and mentor should agree to remain flexible to respect each other's schedule. Remember, there may be situations where your time schedules don't mesh, but in most situations, you should be able to find mutually beneficial times to communicate with each other.
- As you progress in life, mentors and coaches may relocate. Be flexible. With today's technology, it is still possible to keep in touch through texting, e-mailing, Facebook, Instagram, Skype, and of course via telephone.
- Remain open to identifying new people who might be ideal candidates to serve as mentors and coaches.

Your mentor and coach are with you out of a genuine desire to be of assistance. In return, I strongly believe that you, as a mentee or coachee, as a simple gesture of your gratitude, should extend an offer to be of help to them. This is not a requirement but something that

I personally suggest and advise and in which I believe. For example, if your mentor, coach, or advocate is researching in a particular area, while you may not be available to complete in-depth analyses, offer to assist investigating a critical article or utilizing the Internet to help them in their research project. Providing or just the act of offering such assistance is helpful in nurturing the relationship and giving back to your mentor. Others may disagree with me, but this is how I feel. I consider it a simple act of kindness and gratitude.

You may also express your gratitude by writing a thank-you note or card of appreciation to your mentor or coach. It is very likely that your mentor regardless of their age or status would appreciate such a reminder that their devotion of time is appreciated. I have served as a mentor, in various capacities, to dozens of students over my professional career as a physician and surgeon and even while in college, medical school, and residency. Receiving cards, notes, letters, and words of appreciation from the students whom I mentored has greatly served to reinforce to me personally that I am providing a worthwhile service to another person. Receiving small tokens (nothing extravagant or expensive is necessary) of appreciation and positive feedback from my mentees serves to motivate further, encourage, and reinvigorate me even to do more. Let your mentor, coach, advocate, and sponsor know that you appreciate what they have done and are doing to assist you. Expressing your appreciation to them will assure that you stand out. It is good common sense, don't you agree? Lastly, I believe it is very important as a mentee to periodically update your mentor as to your progress on your success journey even, for example, after you have moved on to the next phase of your journey, that is, following high school or college graduation or upon getting your first professional job. They will be thrilled to hear about your progress in life. Keeping in contact with your mentor, coach, advocate, and sponsor shows them that you appreciate what they have done for you and that you remember them.

Become a Mentor, Coach, Advocate, and Sponsor: The Importance of Giving Back to the Community

A manner in which I have actively given back over the years is through mentoring, coaching, advocacy, and sponsorship. Just as there have been people helping you throughout your life, you have the opportunity to utilize your knowledge and wisdom to benefit others. You might not realize just how much knowledge you already possess that you can use to benefit another person. For example, perhaps in high school, you took chemistry or calculus from a particular teacher. You may be able to benefit students yet to take some of the classes you have already taken by tutoring them or giving them a heads-up about what information was taught in the class. You may also benefit other students regarding some of the nuances and idiosyncrasies you learned regarding a particular teacher, for example, their teaching style. Of course, there are ethical ways in which to do this as it is not ethical for you to "give away" test answers, for example, to other students. You get what I mean? Nevertheless, even small amounts of advice you can share with others can immensely benefit their lives. You'll also find out that when you tutor someone, you yourself benefit by revisiting course materials and you also are learning techniques of teaching.

Your role as a mentor is to help empower your mentee with the ability to think critically. Your job is to help them with the tools and skill sets needed along their journey toward success. Communicating the challenges that you faced is one valuable tool of mentorship. For example, providing your list of recommended books on such topics as leadership, self-development, public speaking, time management, and networking is helpful. Included at the end of this book is a list of such resources that I have found to be helpful in some of my development. I wish I had kept a list of books and resources I had utilized throughout my journey, but unfortunately, I did not have the foresight at the time to do this. I remember some but not all. Perhaps it would be a great idea for you now to start keeping your list of valuable reference resources that you in the future will be able to reference for your own purposes as well as use as a resource to help facilitate others in their development.

As a mentor, your job is not to provide all the answers to your mentee. No one's background or journey is exactly alike; therefore, everyone must be able to make important decisions in life that are unique to their circumstances.

Mentorship takes many shapes and formats. Various organizations offer formalized and substantive mentorship training programs in mentoring specific ways. The main component in serving as a mentor is that you do have a genuine desire to assist someone else. Serving as a mentor is not the same as serving as a tutor. A mentor's purpose is also not for a quid pro quo. In other words, mentors don't enter into a relationship with a mentee with the goal of obtaining anything in return other than satisfaction in knowing that they are genuinely striving to help someone else. If you have not yet done so, please go back and read my section on how to find a mentor.

You will learn in life that the more you give back to someone else, the more benefit you also will gain. This reminds me of the books, included in the appendix section, I had the pleasure of reading and presentations I attended by author Dr. Dwayne Dyer who talked about how one is repaid severalfold when they are generous to others. The bottom line is that by serving as a mentor, coach, advocate, or sponsor to others, you will learn more about yourself. By guiding others, you will be forced to reflect upon the specific reasons for your successes, which in turn will allow you to appreciate how others have contributed to your life. You will develop your mentorship, coaching, advocacy, and sponsorship capabilities over time through the more mentoring, coaching advocacy, and sponsorship you do. As I said, you don't have to wait to become a mentor, coach, an advocate, or sponsor until you finish your training. Go ahead, jump in, and get started. Really, "It isn't difficult to do it if you know how to do it." The main prerequisite that you must possess is a genuine and unselfish willingness to assist others. "It isn't difficult to do it if you know how to do it."

Dr. Charles Modlin with Cleveland Clinic
Saturday Academy student mentees

Mentoring students at Cleveland Clinic in the operating room

Dr. Charles Modlin visiting professor with
Northwestern University Premedical Students at
Undergraduate Campus in Evanston (2009)

Dr. Charles Modlin mentoring Shaker Heights
High School MAC Scholar students

Dr. Charles Modlin mentoring students in the operating
room, promoting diversity in the health professions

Become a Role Model to Your Community and to Society

I am certain that you know what a role model is and that there
are people whom you have looked up as role models to you. Some
of these people you personally know, but some you have never met.
Role models are not limited to celebrities or sporting figures. They
are prevalent and abound around you. Please see in the appendix
an article featuring my father who was a role model to many in his
hometown and around the nation. A role model is someone whom
you admire for their positive characteristics. Of course, no one is perfect and no one will ever achieve perfection. Nevertheless, I believe
that one of your goals is to live your life as best you can so that you
will be a person whom others can look up to as a role model. As a
role model, you possess the ability to inspire and motive many people
who have taken note of your accomplishments, many of these people
in many cases being people whom you have never even personally
met and may never meet.

Renowned surgeon recounts struggles, encourages today's scholars

By Donna Cronk

NEIGHBORS EDITOR

As one of just a few African-American transplant surgeons in the country, as well as a community activist and busy father of four, Dr. Charles Modlin's credits, honors, awards and distinctions are numerous.

Yet of all the awards he has received, he says the one of which he treasures most was taking the stage Thursday as featured speaker at New Castle Chrysler High School's 44th annual Achievement Day.

He said the invitation came as an affirmation by the New Castle community and school system that he was a success, and was a tribute to his parents, Charles and the late Grace Modlin.

Modlin spoke in Bundy Auditorium. He said the last time he was on that stage was during a Christmas band concert his senior year when he played the trumpet. He reminisced about other memorable moments in that room: Taking driver's education and going with his father to hear Pete Rose speak.

A 1979 graduate of NCCHS, Modlin went on to graduate from Northwestern University Medical School in 1987. After a six-year residency in urology and surgery at New York University, Modlin went on to serve a three-year fellowship in basic science transplant immunology and clinical renovascular and renal transplantation surgery at the Cleveland Clinic Foundation. In 1996 he joined the Cleveland Clinic Foundation's Urological Institute staff where he remains today. He is both a transplant surgeon and urologist.

Modlin spoke about the stresses of becoming a doctor. He credits his parents for inspiration, motivation, a strong work ethic, and God for His blessings.

As a high school student, Modlin thought about becoming either a doctor or pursuing a career in music. He credits various high school teachers, townspeople, local doctors and churches, along with his parents, for encouraging and seeing the potential in him.

He was influenced and touched by watching his mother care for her elderly mother.

At Northwestern, Modlin was with some of the brightest students in the country but away from the

O-T Photo / John Guglielmi

The green jacket recipients were Marci C. White, Philip W. Shaffer, Baily D. Benson, Michael G. Metroka, Luke A. Meyer, Matthew P. Younts, Jennifer L. Smith, Stephanie M. Stearns and Keshia A. Polston.

no ethics and made things difficult for him.

Loans and scholarships helped pay his way but Modlin still was short on cash and took a wide range of odd jobs to make ends meet. "I considered it a privilege to attend college. I did not see it as a God-given right," Modlin says.

He felt his parents had sacrificed enough for him and he didn't want them to know some of his difficulties such as going hungry because he didn't have money for food. After all, he reasoned, they had

school as a junior to serve with the U.S. Navy and they had worked hard and reared five children. And his mother at the age of 40 with five kids and three grandchildren, decided to attend college to become an elementary school teacher. He says some nights she would go sit in the car with a flashlight shining on her studies. She went on to become the first African-American teacher in New Castle, Modlin says.

The doctor says he made the conscious decision to

◼ Continued from page A1

Scholars

endure and make his own sacrifices to accomplish his goals and dreams.

There were times he was depressed, stressed and exhausted. But his father gave him persistent encouragement to continue.

"Did I do the right thing to become a physician?" Modlin asks. He goes on to answer his own question. He has helped cure patients of cancer and save lives. He is credited by saving his brother-in-law's life by performing a kidney transplant.

And, Modlin continues, on two separate occasions, he provided a diagnosis for colon and prostate cancers to one man. That one man "is the same man who taught me how to ride a bike, throw a ball and the same man who taught me to become a man." That man, of course, is his own father.

Says his father after the speech, "I wouldn't be alive if it weren't for my son."

The younger Modlin said there is an unwritten secret in succeeding in life. "It's the

C-T Photo / John Guglielmi

National Honor Society President Michael Metroka talks with guest speaker Dr. Charles S. Modlin Jr. before the start of the Achievement Day program at NCCHS.

decisions we make in life which determines the outcome."

He encouraged all present to take that road to success by making good decisions and decisions that lead them toward whatever successes of which they dream.

Also during his speech, Modlin announced that he and his family are establishing two scholarships in Grace

Modlin's memory. One will benefit a Greenstreet Elementary School student and the other a high school student wanting to pursue a career in education.

Also during the program, the band and chorale performed. Academic winners were announced and the Spirit Bowl's flame ignited and the bowl presented to the Class of 2004.

Dr. Charles Modlin was invited guest keynote speaker for his high school alma mater's New Castle Chrysler High School 2004 Achievement Day Ceremony, recognizing and honoring academically talented high school students.

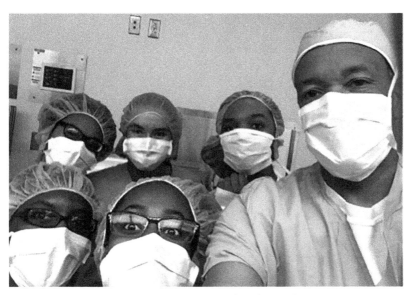

Dr. Modlin mentoring Cleveland Clinic
Saturday Academy Students

CHAPTER 12

Now for the Tough Love

Haters

This is not a pleasant topic about which I now write, but this subject matter of roadblocks, which I now discuss, is of paramount importance and I am compelled to include this information in this book to optimally benefit you. This chapter is not meant to scare you in any way; quite to the contrary, my goal is to help benefit you from my life experiences. There are many names for the roadblocks that may come into your life. Some are situational. Others originate from people you will encounter. These people may be obstructionists, intentional blockers, or as some call them haters. Let me just state again that the majority of people whom you will encounter in school, in your workplace, and in life are good people who are living their own lives and pursuing their own dreams and are in no way trying to interfere with yours. However, in life, not everyone will be on your side. Be prepared. Do not let detractors depress you or deflect you from your plans. The earlier in life you come to appreciate these facts of life, the better prepared you will be in recognizing these situations and the better prepared you will be to confront such challenging situations and *difficult* people. Even following completion of your college experience, your path to success may not always go smoothly. Expect delays in your progress and also disappointments. It is a part of the learning process and part of life. Sometimes the best way past an obstruction or obstacle is right through it. In other words, many, if not most, times, it is best to confront obstacles and obstructionists head-on. However, in confronting obstructionists head-on, often you will find that many of them are bullies who sometimes will back off if confronted head-on. Or they will resort to using other deceptive, subversive, or passive-aggressive tactics of which you may not even be aware. As I indicated previously, in college, you will experience much greater levels of academic and social situational competition; however, the subject matter of obstructionists and detractors is beyond that which one would consider as normal academic competitiveness.

Other times, it may actually be best to not confront obstructions head-on, but to instead go around obstacles and obstructionists, hence the necessity for you to also learn how to try to navigate around obstructions and obstructionists. Knowing which approach to take depends upon the situation and requires thought and strategy.

If you find yourself in a difficult situation, speak to your support system earlier rather than later. Try to avoid too much damage being done. Spend time documenting specific occurrences. You may need to present evidence as you seek resolution. Trust me. I speak from experience. Despite a great upbringing and preparation for the real work provided to me by my parents, I readily admit that I did not anticipate the level or magnitude of hate (yes, indeed, some of it based on racism) I have encountered during various parts of my journey. I wasn't totally naïve to the fact that it existed, but I wasn't as extensively prepared in techniques of taking "haters" on head-to-head, and I wasn't as prepared as I would have liked to have been in knowing how to engage detractors in the crucial conversations and ways necessary to combat some of the roadblocks I have experienced. I learned a great deal from my experiences in real time, and in retrospect, I often tried to ignore certain challenges rather than confront them head-on. A quick tip here that my father taught me about overcoming some challenges is to try to make an internal game of competition within you out of certain challenges. In other words, in many instances, you can make overcoming challenges a goal that you try to achieve, a competition in which you are really competing with yourself. Does this make sense to you?

In many situations, in retrospect and analysis, I have been too "polite" in dealing with haters and obstructionists. In many situations, haters and obstructionists have misinterpreted my politeness and quiet nature as a sign of weakness on my part and perhaps have felt that they could therefore take advantage of my friendliness, politeness, and good nature. Don't let this happen to you. As a general rule, as I am sure you were taught also, it is always best to be polite and good-natured to those whom you meet. However, you must learn to identify early on when people are trying to take advantage of you because of your politeness. If you see or feel this is happening to you, you must take action sooner rather than later to have critical and crucial conversations with those who may be misinterpreting your good nature as a sign of weakness and let them know that you demand to be respected. I have learned this lesson the hard way during my life, especially during my surgery residency at NYU when I had to in certain situations adopt almost an entirely different personality (a very aggressive personality) in confronting bullies in the workplace in order for me to get my job done. Do not immediately resort to having to become aggressive in confronting obstructionists. It is best to first attempt to have a civil conversation with them in hopes that they will understand that you demand respect and that you will not be bullied by them.

But again, sometimes, however, depending on the situation, I stress that it might be best to ignore certain situations or ignore certain people altogether. My father often stressed to me to "just ignore those people." As the saying goes, one must know which battles to pick and choose. But sometimes you can't just ignore situations or the people causing such situations. Realize also that there are some bullies out there who will repeatedly try to obstruct you if they feel you are afraid of them and afraid to confront them. Remember, consult with your mentor, advisors, parents, trusted friends, and even a counselor if necessary to help you decide how to deal with specific situations. We have all heard about real-life tragic stories of how victims of bullies resorted to taking their own lives, and we say to ourselves that if only they had gotten some help, the tragedy would have never happened. Again, I am compelled to discuss this unpleasant topic as a way of reminding each of you reading this book that if you find yourself in what you consider to be a desperate situation as a result of being a victim of an obstructionist or hater, help is available in many forms for you. Don't suffer in silence. If you need professional help, go get it.

I experienced some negative people while I was in college (please read two of the articles I wrote as an undergraduate student in the school newspaper, *the Daily Northwestern*, included in the appendix of this book), but most distractors did not surface until I was in medical school (in particular one chief resident whom I had as a medical student and whom I will never forget how mean and hateful she was toward me), during my residency, my kidney transplant fellowship, and over the last twenty-plus years as a practicing staff physician and surgeon. By the way, you may or may not agree with the subject matter and conclusions in the articles I wrote in *the Daily Northwestern* newspaper. If you disagree with me, that's okay. At the time, there were students who wrote editorial responses in agreement with me, and there were students who disagreed with me. The bottom line is that I saw what I believed to be on campus some problems that I was brave enough to address publicly. Regarding the article I wrote about self-imposed segregation, the point I was trying to make way back in 1982 was that of the importance that the student body embrace and benefit from the diversity of the student body. I was not trying to speak against students forming bonds with individuals who resembled them as some students completely misinterpreted. Rather, I was encouraging students to associate with, embrace, and experience students also who did *not* look like them. Do you get what I was saying in the article on self-imposed segregation? This is the same point I have made to you in this book. You see, back then no one ever spoke about diversity in the same way in which it has become popularized today. Regarding the article I wrote about premeds being too intense for their own good (also in the appendix of this book), the point of this article is that future doctors should learn how to work together and not against one another. It is interesting that both of these articles became part of the subject matter of a few of my Northwestern Medical School interviews, because I included both articles as part of my medical school applications. Regardless, I find it both interesting and I feel proud that I wrote this article on premeds because some forty years later, the medical profession has now fully embraced this concept (as if it is now a new concept) as evidence has shown that collaboration among medical professions leads to better patient outcomes. Looking back, do you think I was well-ahead of my time? LOL. My point here to you, students, is that if you feel strongly about an issue at your school, don't be afraid to take a stand against it—a nonviolent stand of course. I would be interested in what you think after reading my articles. Please e-mail me with your comments at Charles.Modlin@gmail.com.

Everyone at some point will encounter detractors or haters. In looking back on things, I, however, now realize that I have received quite an extensive education in real life as to how best overcome obstacles, obstructions, and haters. Even for me, as it will be for you, it is a work in progress and this is one area in which a person is never finished learning. But what has been the source of my strength and ability to deal with these unpleasant experiences and people? Remember that some of my initial success tips that I want you to remember and internalize is for you to remember from whence you came, remember the people who have supported you, remember the self-belief and substance you have within your character, and remember the success path that you are on. As Philippians 4:8 (KJV) says, "Whatsoever things are true, whatsoever things are honest, whatsoever things are just, whatsoever things are pure, whatsoever things are lovely, whatsoever things are of good report; if there be any virtue, and if there be any praise, think on these things." Likewise, if you are true to yourself and if you remain steadfast and true to your mission, then I assert to you that you too will be effective and successful in dealing with the obstructions and haters whom you *will* encounter. This being said, the primary advantages that has allowed me to persevere in the face of repeated obstacles and needless opposition are the lessons taught me by my parents, family, and community, which I have outlined in this book and which represent the very purpose and essence of this book. Always remember your roots and your goals. Be persistent, resolute, and confident in your abilities. Ingesting these tools and becoming proficient in the art of conducting crucial conversations and crucial confrontations will help you navigate the burdens that may be placed upon you by rivals or those who are jealous or even racist. I have included in the appendix section of this book some great resources on the subject matter of crucial conversations and crucial confrontations.

Me at New Castle Baker Park Swimming Pool,
remembering from whence I came

The main thing for you to remember is that if you experience these trials, remain strong, remember your mission, and do not be defeated. As stated, there will be many situations and people whom you can ignore. You have to acquire the ability to identify those situations that you can ignore and those that you cannot, and this is not always easy to discern. However, if you are receiving threats or dangerous advances, it will be dangerous to ignore the situation, and you will want to first and foremost make sure you are safe. And yes, this does mean that if you feel in danger or that your life or safety is threatened, you must immediately notify the police and security services at your college.

So why am I making such a deal about detractors and haters anyway? Why can't you just ignore all of them? Well, quite frankly, detractors can do a great deal of damage to your reputation by negatively influencing and biasing those in essential positions who may begin to doubt your abilities and forgo providing you with opportunities. Such people can threaten and do grave damage to your career and make it very difficult for you to achieve your goals. Be observant of your work and school environment, and keep yourself in a position to recognize threats to the best of your abilities earlier rather than later. There is no need to be paranoid, but assess to the best of your abilities your school and work environments so that you can determine those who can be friends and support systems. This is not a one-time thing you will need to do. Different people will come into your school and work environments, and different situations and dynamics within your environments change, so your assessments will need to remain ongoing. In addition, don't be afraid or hesitant to seek professional psychological and emotional support counseling that is readily available to you on your college campus or in your vicinity. Seeking such support is in no way a sign of weakness and something for which you in no way should be ashamed. It is a sign of maturity and self-recognition that there are times when we all may need some additional assistance in finding solutions to overcoming certain hurdles and obstacles for which we might not ourselves otherwise feel we can handle or cope. There are many people available to help you with such dilemmas, and it is important for you also to be aware that prolonged mental anguish and stress can escalate and lead to serious depression, apathy and lack of desire to achieve one's goals, helplessness, and hopelessness and even suicidal thoughts, as well as manifestations of physical illnesses. If you find yourself in a situation that you feel is beyond your psychological and emotional control, seek the immediate advice of your support system and seek professional counseling services immediately.

My additional advice in general for you as you embark upon your college career and even beyond is to make as many "good" and "emotionally intelligent" friends as you can, and I emphasize the words good friends and also emotionally intelligent friends because you need to surround yourself with quality people who are likewise striving for excellence and success in their own lives in such a way that does not harm or impede others. You will be much better off if you have a few good, true, emotionally intelligent friends than many acquaintances. This theme that having a few good friends is better than many acquaintances was the topic of my son's eighth-grade Shaker Heights Middle School graduation by the principal Mr. Randy Yates. I still remember his profound remarks, and I hope you now will take note of the magnitude of what he was saying. Thank you, Mr. Yates.

When I look back on my journey and my life, I have had many friends, but I have definitely benefited by having especially a handful of great friends. Your instincts will help guide you in terms of who are your really good and great friends. Don't try and redefine yourself just to fit in with the in crowd. Ideally, of course, you do want to be able to associate with all sectors of your class and workmates, but when it comes to developing true close friendships, your instincts will help guide you. You should be able to confide your inner thoughts and concerns to a good friend and vice versa. Remember that a good friend is not someone who automatically agrees with you on every-thing, but someone who actively and intently listens to you and gives you their best, honest, heartfelt, commonsense, and emotionally intelligent sage feedback and advice based upon their understanding of who you are and your personality, as well as their understanding and knowledge of your dreams and ambitions.

Now getting back the subject matter as to how to deal with obstructionists. To help prepare yourself for some of the obstructionists you will likely encounter at some point during your journey, you should rehearse in your mind and even discuss with people you trust how you might best respond to various scenarios you feel you are likely to encounter with obstructionists, and this is where good friends can come into play. In other words, prepare yourself by anticipating various difficult situations and encounters that you might perhaps encounter and think through in your head (and even rehearse aloud) options as to how you might approach and deal with such situations should they occur. You won't be able to anticipate precisely every situation you may experience, but advanced preparation by anticipation and forethought will help you greatly as to how to respond to potential future unpleasant situations. Inquire of your friends, family and parents, professors, mentors, and others how they responded to various situations of obstructionists, haters, and hurdles they have faced. Learn from others' experiences. Students, when friends approach you with their problems and concerns, realize that by listening to them, you can also, in turn, learn from their experiences, trials, and tribulations. Realize, however, that you will not always be able to help your friends solve their situations and issues and vice versa; when you go to a friend with a problem, please be aware that they won't always be able to solve your problems either. In knowing your friends, however, if you note or have a fear that they may be in a situation over their head, do please encourage them to notify their parents and to seek professional help. As a friend, you do owe it to them if you see or feel that they are getting into a dangerous situation, including abusing alcohol or drugs or are even in an abusive relationship. Don't turn an eye to it. As the saying goes, if you see something, say something. Do not put yourself into a dangerous situation while trying to solve a friend's problems. Be an advisor and an open ear to them, but if you sense danger, then encourage them to get help. In certain situations, you yourself may need to call for help on their behalf. These are advanced lessons of which you need to become aware, sooner rather than later.

Importantly, in summary—and I am being repetitive for a reason, concerning facing hurdles and challenges—it is imperative for you to remember that others around you are also experiencing hurdles, so it is important that you be a friend and be a resource for others. So remember, when you arrive at college, the relationships you establish with advisors, college professors, and other students may be handy in helping you face, confront, and overcome the challenges you may be facing both during and after college life. Also, be sure to remember that your parents, guardians, family, and friends who supported you in the past are resources whom you can still call upon for support. Don't be afraid to seek professional counseling services to assist you as well.

One final word about haters and obstructionists—do not allow them to get you to lose your cool. Often, this is their goal, for you to, especially in public, have a nervous breakdown, have a temper tantrum, cry uncontrollably, hit your fists into the wall, get drunk, scream, shout, and lose your cool. Haters derive a great deal of pleasure and satisfaction when they visually can see that they are getting under your skin. This makes them want to continue to try to do harm to you. Don't wear your emotions on your sleeves. Do you understand what I am saying? They want you to decompensate publicly so that others observing you will develop negative impressions of you and question your abilities to maintain your control under pressure. If you feel and sense that haters are seriously getting to your emotions, do not make a public display of it. Take a deep breath. How you handle the immediate situation varies according to the circumstances and location in which you find yourself. Collect yourself. If in a public place, options include walking out of the room, changing the topic of conversation and/or the people with whom you are speaking, and laughing and using humor to politely make the other person look foolish or suspect. You have to anticipate in advance derogatory comments that a particular person may say, based upon prior interactions you have had with them, and work out and rehearse in your mind in advance an example of a retort you will give to check the offending person if need be. These are advanced techniques and part of your maturation process, but such techniques can be perfected with practice, time, and experience. Note that there are some stand-up comedians who are great at using witty humor and comedy (whom you can observe) in making hecklers look foolish, for example. There are also many comedic actors on television and in movies who also do this very well. It is unfortunate that one has to waste precious time dealing with haters. Once again, many times, the best approach is to avoid them altogether, but that's not always feasible or the preferred way to approach haters.

The Difficult Roommate

Please read chapter 13 where I relate a true story of a college roommate who literally terrorized one of my daughter's friends. I won't repeat the story here in this section; nevertheless the incident highlights the fact that you, as a college student and as a human being, have certain rights and dignities to be able to "live" at peace in your college dormitory room. If you have a college roommate, 50 percent (half) of that dorm room is yours to use to put your things in. Your roommate, for example, has no right to occupy your closet or desk space for their things. Your roommate has no right to allow visitors in your room when you are trying to sleep or study. If you are having serious issues and problems with your college roommate that the two of you cannot solve, then I advise that you go to your college residence assistant (RA) to help in finding a resolution to your problems. If your RA refuses to assist you or is incapable of doing so, then you need to take steps to meet with the college's housing office administrators and put in a request to transfer to another dormitory room if possible. An unruly, unkempt, and obnoxious roommate can go a long way to seriously negatively impacting your ability to focus, concentrate, and study, which can definitely throw you off your success path.

While you are away at school, your dorm room is your home, and you have a right to feel safe and comfortable in your dorm room. Do not simply sit and suffer in silence if you are experiencing serious issues with your roommate. If the problems are more easily solved, such as your roommate being too noisy or talkative when you are trying to study, sometimes the best approach is to simply go to the library or to a study room in your dormitory hall to avoid the roommate. Sometimes, also, you can drown out your roommate by listening to music using your headphones, but remember what I said about not listening to loud music especially via your headphones. Again the best approach if you are having problems with an otherwise amicable and reasonable roommate is to voice your concerns to them and try to find mutual solutions to the problems. Likewise, you need to be receptive of any problems your roommate might be having with you. You, for instance, don't want to be the roommate who is taking a greater share of the room than is yours and who is hosting friends over in the room when your roommate is attempting to sleep. My tip to you is also when you make your final selection on which college to attend, contact your college and find out the process for selecting roommates. Most colleges nowadays allow students opportunities to submit a list of their personality traits that the colleges then use to help match compatible roommates with each other. For instance, you can indicate if you are early to bed and early to rise or if you are a night owl who loves to sleep in. Be honest and as accurate as possible in submitting what are your character traits. The process is not perfect, and incompatible roommates will continue to be matched.

Accepting Delayed Gratification

Your journey to success will not be completed overnight. I labored seventeen years in training after graduating from high school to finally become a kidney transplant surgeon. It takes persistence and being steadfast in your determination because your journey may be bumpy at times. While I was in college and medical school, many of my friends from high school and other acquaintances I met along the way, by their admission, were not particularly ambitious. They seemed to be more carefree and have more fun than I, who was motivated and operating from a reference that I needed to sacrifice now and accept delayed gratification so that I might realize my goal in becoming a medical doctor. Many of my friends partied and lived day-to-day for the sake of having a good time *now*, immediately, not in some distant future, but now. They did not worry about studying, taking tests, or achieving goals to have a good future. It often resonated with me that I was sacrificing and forgoing many present-day pleasures that others around me were experiencing to focus on achieving my goals. As a note, it *will* help and benefit for you to take time out to engage in activities that you enjoy. I reassert of course that I do not believe that this requires for you to use alcohol or drugs for you to enjoy yourself. Nevertheless, my point here is for you to fully understand, however, that for you to succeed, you will need to understand, accept, and embrace the concept and practice of delayed gratification, regardless of what seemingly carefree lifestyles are occurring around you.

It is important not to assume too much about other students' lifestyles or study habits. Not all careers require the same level of time commitment or even mental focus. Even people who are on the same career trajectory as you possess different abilities and talents that might allow them to spend less time, for example, studying a particular subject compared to the amount of time you have to commit. I've seen students who fail in their journeys because they try to keep up with the party schedules of their friends because they can't accept the fact that they need to spend more time studying than their friends do. The sooner you understand these nuances, the less they will distract you. Utilize these observations to your advantage and learn from those individuals around you, both those who have lofty aspirations and those who do not.

You may have heard the phrase "living vicariously through others," which means experiencing something indirectly compared to others who are directly living it. Recognize that your time constraints and the different demands you face compared to others may lead you to live vicariously through others at times. Often, by discussing with your roommates some of their experiences, you may almost feel as if you were there. For example, your roommate attended a concert and you could not because you were studying for a test or had to work. Getting all the details of the event can allow you to visualize that experience. You are deriving some benefit from your roommate's experience. Another person's entertainment or lifestyle does not need to serve as a mechanism for which you need to be distressed or jealous. You are now accepting of the reality of delayed gratification. You are making sacrifices now (e.g., acing that chemistry examination) to achieve your long-term goals. On a serious note, also you must come to realize earlier rather than later that some of the students around you may actually embellish and vividly exaggerate some of their own experiences as a way to show off or brag to you about how much fun they are having. Don't always accept at face value or believe what others are telling you. Sometimes they are only trying to make you jealous, and sometimes they may even be trying to throw you off your focus of concentration. When I was in college, I did in many cases live vicariously through others around me. Some examples included situations where many of the students whom I knew on school breaks and vacations went on beach vacations or skiing trips, whereas I had to return home to work to make some additional money to help pay for school expenses. Not once, however, did I feel jealous or resentful that I was not able to live that lifestyle, because in the forefront of my mind, I always remembered the many sacrifices that my parents and family had made for me to provide me the educational opportunities that they had not been afforded. Besides, I personally always looked forward to going back home during vacations to see my family. I will be repetitive in saying that remembering from whence you came will help you maintain your focus and objectives and help you accept delayed gratification.

If you can embrace the concept of delayed gratification, you will have cleared one of the most significant hurdles and stumbling blocks that cause countless numbers of students to give up on their dreams. Too many students cannot understand that they must routinely forgo many of the joys of today for the benefits of tomorrow. It is your challenge to learn new ways to enjoy life even if it means sometimes living vicariously through others. The rigors of competition in college will exist at a much higher level than high school. Consequently, that which worked for you in high school may not work for you in college.

Continue to make objective reassessments of your work/study and recreation balance. If you are serious about achieving your long-term goals, sacrifice and delayed immediate gratification for the benefit of fulfilling future goals will be the rule of the day. Remember to learn ways, even little ways, of still enjoying your journey while maintaining your discipline and direction. Challenge yourself and even make a personal private inside joke or game out of accomplishing your goals while delaying gratification. One inside joke I had for myself was visualizing how some particular students in college had expensive sports cars and I did not. Sometimes I would picture in my mind those same students in racing helmets and racing gear driving

CHARLES S. MODLIN, MD, MBA

their fancy cars finishing last place across the checkered flag. It's stupid, I know, but is just an inside joke that maybe only I understand. The point I am making is that I found sometimes ways to derive amusement in accepting the fact that there were things I did not have that others had and that I was not going to be jealous, but instead understand that, in time, I too would have many of those same "nice things." Does this make at least some sense to you? Do you have any private jokes inside your own head that amuse you and have allowed you to accept delayed gratification? "It isn't difficult to do it if you know how to do it."

Safety First: Be Street-Smart

As you know, some college campuses are urban, some are suburban, and some are rural. Some college campuses are safer than others. How safe a particular college campus is should be of paramount importance to you in selecting your college and should be a question you and your parents ask of the college officials when you tour a college campus or are considering applying to a particular college. Considerations of safety should be first and foremost also when you are selecting a location in which to live, either on or off campus. Look around campus to see if there is sufficient campus lighting, emergency telephone stations, and the presence of campus police, and inquire about whether the school offers security-operated and/or student-operated late-night campus escort services for students who are studying late at night in the library, etc. Most colleges these days do offer such services and have even developed dedicated apps that you can download on your smartphone to request for security escort services. As I stated above, it is wise for you to also establish accounts with the transportation services Uber® and/or Lyft® as you can rapidly access these services to transport you back to your campus and dorm room if needed. Paying attention to safety and not intentionally placing yourself in harm's way, I stress, equally apply to both males and females. This is another success tip by the way. Don't be mistaken to think that male students are also not vulnerable to being victims of crime and assault. Be and remain vigilant and aware of your surroundings at all times. Be street-smart. Do not put yourself in dangerous situations. Travel in groups and don't be out alone late at night on or off campus. I do advise that you download and establish an account with one or both common transportation apps (Ubcr® and/or Lyft®) onto your smartphone so that you can quickly summon a ride out of a dangerous environment to take you back to your campus dorm room if necessary. Please note that I do not work for any of the corporations or products I mentioned. I am sure there are other transportation apps that you can access. I only mention these two companies because I have used them and have found them personally for me to be reliable. Your college may have a reliable and dedicated safe transportation escort service also that you can access for purposes of your safety.

While in your dorm room, also make it a habit to lock your door. Make plans and provisions to not put yourself in such situations of vulnerability. Also don't think it is childish to make sure someone knows your whereabouts. In these modern times, it is quite easy to use texting and cell phones to alert your friends as to where you are and when to expect you. Be smart. Do not be out walking around alone intoxicated, and of course for that matter, don't be intoxicated at all, whether alone or in a group. Use your head and use the common sense that got you to where you are today. It's not cool to be intoxicated or stoned and it definitely is not safe. In the news often are stories about college students who wind up hurt, missing, or deceased due to alcohol or drug overdosing. No campus is safe of all threats, and the victims of crime are not to be blamed for the fact that they are victimized. All I am trying to relate here is to practice common sense vigilance on your part while on or off your college campus. Use your head and take advantage of the safety mechanisms available to you. You owe it both to yourself and to those who love and care about you.

One lesson my mother taught me at an early age—and I am not insulting anyone's intelligence here, but sometimes people tend to forget important ways in which we can help maintain our safety—is to not leave any of my food or drink unattended so as to avoid an opportunity for anyone to spike my food or drink with drugs or substances. The importance of this speaks for itself and includes not accepting food or drinks at a college fraternity or sorority function or another event (especially from someone you do not know well or trust, just as an example) that you did not personally see poured or served up with your own eyes. As I am sure by now, you have heard the news that there have been many cases of students and others being drugged and sexually violated by others spiking their food and drinks. A case in point is the Bill Cosby case that has been prevalent in the news. Be attentive and don't accept food or drinks, alcohol or nonalcoholic beverages, from someone you don't closely know or trust, and it is always best to personally get your food and drinks yourself and personally see them poured or served up. Again, I am telling you this not to scare you or make you paranoid but to help you remember to practice safety at all times. Does this make sense? Also, do not go to an isolated or secluded location with anyone whom you do not know well or trust, and when going to a party, remember to let someone you know where you will be.

A helpful technique to enhance personal safety that many people now employ when walking by themselves, or even with a friend or a group, is to carry their cell phone in their hand with 911 punched and ready to be called with the press of the "send" button if the need arises. Also, many self-defense experts advise people when they are walking alone at night to call a friend on their phone or at least appear to be engaged in a real-time conversation. This technique gives a potential assailant the indication that a "person" on the other end of the phone is aware of your location and can be alerted if danger approaches. Many saftey experts also advise that you keep you GPS locator activated on your cell phone in the unlikely event authorities might need to track your location.

Another important safety tip is for you to at all times be visibly aware of your surroundings, that is, glance around you in all directions periodically and avoid walking near areas that could conceal someone hiding. Be sure that your sense of hearing is not obstructed. Far too often with modern technology, we walk around wearing headphones listing to loud music and are totally oblivious to hearing what is happening around us. People have been injured and even killed because they walked in front of moving traffic unable to hear the cars, trucks, trains, and even bicycles approaching them. Also, avoid wearing headphones with loud music playing. Over a period of time, the decibals can lead to irreversible hearing loss. As a high school and college student, I was guilty of wearing headphones and playing loud music. Protect your precious hearing.

Self-Defense

Another piece of advice that is important for both males and females alike is to take some self-defense training with the hope that you will never need to use any of these skills, but in the event you are forced into having to defend yourself from an attacker, you will be in a better position to protect yourself. Most college campuses or locations near college campuses offer classes in self-defense. The goal is not to become a martial arts expert like Chuck Norris or Bruce Lee but to acquire certain fundamental self-defense skills that may serve to help you or even save your life should you need to use such techniques. I am not endorsing any particular products; however, there is a handheld self-dense device called TigerLady (it's for men too) that is legal across the country that I have bought for my children to carry. I have no stake in this company, and I am not implying that you purchase this product. I reference this particular project only to suggest that you might wish to conduct some of your research into additional options for your safety. Other approaches are to carry bright flashlights, whistles, alarms, and Mace if legal in your area. Again, I am not endorsing or advocating that you use or carry any harmful or illegal devices not allowed on your college campus, city, state, or country. Of course, under no circumstance should you carry or possess a firearm or a weapon on your college campus.

Again, the best approach to your personal safety is to avoid putting yourself in dangerous and precarious environments and to remove yourself from such environments and situations expeditiously should you find yourself in dangerous areas and situations. As part of the discussion of not placing yourself in precarious situations, I must say a word about several situations that have occurred at parties or gatherings on and off several college campuses over the years and have highlighted in the media. Specifically, I am referring to cases where groups of male college students have been arrested, implicated, accused of, and prosecuted by the law for participating or being present during rape assaults on or off college campuses. The Duke Lacrosse case that dominated the news several years ago is just one example. Whether you are a male or female, if you see such a situation happening, don't get caught up in such illegal and immoral activities, remove yourself from the situation immediately, and call the police in real-time. You do not want to be implicated in such a crime because even if you are innocent but present, you will be also arrested. Don't let this happen to you because your life will be ruined. If you see something, say something. Also, please take note of the #MeToo climate and always behave yourself so that you don't place yourself into a situation where you can be accused of improper sexual harassment behavior.

On a similar note and word of caution regarding dating in high school or college. Be aware of the laws in your state regarding having sexual relationships with what your state may consider to be a minor. If you yourself are not a minor and even though the other party may be only a few years younger than you, having sexual relations with this person will place you in legal jeopardy if you yourself are considered an adult by the law and if this person presses charges against you. Know the laws of the state you are in. Men and women, when going out on a date with someone you don't know well, for safety reasons, make sure you are in a public place when going out with this person. There have been too many cases of foul play (abductions or disappearances) where students have met up in isolated locations with someone they met from the Internet, for example. If you don't know well your date, for safety purposes, it would be wise for you to see and take a photo of your date's driver's license and share this photo with a friend and let your date know that you have done so. Keep yourself safe and don't place yourself in dangerous situations. Does this make sense to you? I hope it does.

A Word about Social Media and Safety

In my college days, there was no such thing as social media. We didn't even have cell phones, let alone smartphones or laptops or personal computers. All college students are now savvy regarding how to use social media, whether it be Facebook, Twitter, Instagram, Snapchat, or other forms of social media with which I am not familiar. The bottom line is that social media platforms are a potential source through which people sometimes unknowingly and unwittingly compromise their safety, and this is unfortunate but potentially dangerously true. Be aware of the fact that there are people monitoring your social media sites and postings for unsavory reasons of which include to try to determine your whereabouts (where you are going to be and when) as well as to gain personal information about you that they may wish to use for nefarious purposes. Make special attempts to not announce, whenever possible, in advance, online where you are going to be and when. Also, be aware of the fact that there are people who are monitoring your social media also to gain access to your personal information, such as your address and your financial accounts when you conduct online banking or online purchases. Make sure your computer security system is up to date as far as virus protection monitoring and be cautious in opening e-mailed files from people you don't know or from people you did not solicit. Most colleges nowadays offer information technology services to provide you with up-to-date computer virus protection. Take advantage of these services from your IT department. Bottom line, take care in "friending" people you don't know on Facebook or other social media sites, and be careful as to what you post on social media sites so as not to compromise your safety or professionalism. On a side note, because computer users are always at risk of acquiring viruses, please make sure that you do back up your important files routinely on an external hard drive, on flash drives, and on the cloud. You don't want to lose your important files, documents, and school projects because of a computer crash.

In addition, during my professional life, I have witnessed situations where search committees and prospective employers examined the social media posts of candidates for high-level professional positions and have even harshly judged them and disavowed their candidacies based upon how they were dressed and otherwise portrayed years before online on their or other people's social media. Try not to let this happen to you. Rule of thumb, before posting something online, stop and reconsider as to whether you would want your future employer viewing it. You may feel that this seems unfair and maybe it is, but this happens more often than you might imagine in real life.

Also, cyberbullying and online stalking are real phenomena that do occur and have destroyed lives of young people. Don't become a victim of cyberbullying or online stalking, and don't yourself be a cyberbully or stalker. If you find yourself becoming a victim of cyberbullying or online stalking or feel as if you are being threatened online, don't simply ignore it, but take this seriously and seek help by going to the authorities.

In conclusion, of all the chapters in this book, the lessons contained in this section may be the most important of all for you to comprehend and put into practice immediately and consistently not only as a student but also for the remainder of your life. Help your friends and loved ones adopt such practices as well. Along with the joyful topics, I felt an obligation to include in this book these unpleasant topics that are not meant to scare you, but to inform you and better prepare you for the next stages of your life and for the rest of your life. You may have already been exposed to much of this information. Also to be certain, there are additional safety tips that I have not included within the pages of this book. I hope that you will take the subject of maintaining your safety very seriously. It's not a laughing matter.

Anyone can become the victim of violence regardless of their size, strength, gender, or how street-smart they are currently. No one, not one single person, is immune to being the target of malice. Therefore, regardless of your background, you have an obligation and responsibility not only to yourself but also to those who love you to be vigilant at all times and to keep your safety as the number one priority. The intent of this chapter is not to scare you, but to keep your radar in full force and your antennas up regarding potential dangers that may be lurking around you. Being naïve to the fact that there are people who may want to harm you (physically and/or psychologically) will make you less vigilant and a larger target for dangers that may exist. There is no guarantee that any of us will not become a victim of violence or misfortune; however, if we remain aware of our surroundings and aware of threats, we can reduce our risks of putting ourselves in potentially dangerous situations. Even though the blame is never on the victims of violence, but always the perpetrator, the victim is still the one who suffers.

This chapter is not meant to be comprehensive of each way in which you might be able to protect yourself, physically, emotionally, mentally, or psychologically, but it is a reminder to keep and make safety your first priority. Included in the back of this book is a list of helpful resources.

CHAPTER 13

A Final Word

So what's it going to be? Do you have what it takes to be successful in college and beyond to achieve your goals and dreams? Did you already know each of the success tips that I have detailed in this book before reading it? When I was entering college, I can unequivocally state that I did not know everything contained in this book. It was not until I was repeatedly approached by literally hundreds of students over my many years of mentoring and after I had been asked to deliver commencement addresses, etc., regarding my journey in becoming a surgeon did the light bulb go on that I could, should, and must package my life experiences in this book form in an effort to further give back to others. In other words, I suddenlty realized that much of what I had learned, and in many cases learned the hard way, could help students (including my own four children) who are themselves desirous for successes in school and in life. Writing this book I consider to have been my responsibility and in keeping with the admonition my parents taught me—to give back because my successes are in large part the result of the sacrifices made by others who came before me. This is something I strongly believe, and I hope by reading this book, you too will have taken the time to reflect upon the many reasons for your own successes, which I am certain are many. The material contained within this book is meant to be thought-provoking and will hopefully help guide your journey and cause you to think more consciously, deliberately, intentionally, willfully, determinedly, and strategically with each decision and step you take moving forward. These words are a labor of love that have taken me many years to put into this book form. I admit that my day-to-day work, personal, and home schedules got in the way of me sitting down and completing this book in a more timely fashion. I advise that you please read and reread this book as many times as necessary to fully digest the messages, lessons, and success tips included within its pages. Everything in this book is intended to be for your benefit. I advise that you save this book in your personal library as a reference for years to come. Share this resource with your family, friends, mentees, junior high and high schools, and city libraries and encourage them to get a copy.

There is an anonymous quote that says that the greatest waste in the world is the difference between who we are and what we could've become. Madame C. J. Walker, America's first black female millionaire, was quoted as saying, "There is no royal flower-strewn path to success, and if there is, I have yet to find it. For if I have accomplished anything, it is because I have been willing to work hard… Don't sit down and wait for opportunities to come—get up and make them!" Author Dennis Kimbro was quoted as saying, "Our Todays are what our Yesterdays made them; our tomorrow must inevitably be the product of our todays."

If you remember but two things from my many success tips contained within this book (and I hope you will learn, retain, and put into practice many more than just three of my success tips), it is 1) to appreciate and build upon the strengths that have already brought you great successes, 2) also remember from whence you came, and 3) always put your safety first. If you follow these three pieces of advice, then everything else I have detailed within this book will fall into place.

The contents of this book only represent portions of the knowledge and wisdom I have gained during my lifetime. I continue to learn new things on a daily basis, and of course over the course of my life, I have learned predominantly from people older than me, but increasingly I am learning many things now from people younger than myself. My goal in writing this book was to create a comprehensive listing of the many success tips that worked for either me in high school or in college as well as lessons I have learned since during my life. Many of the lessons I learned the hard way. I wish I had when I was younger a type of reference such as this book of success tips while I was in high school so that parts of my journey might have been made a little easier (and in some cases a lot easier).

Additionally, I have included in this book some examples of how you might apply the success tips contained in this book and my reasoning why such tips will facilitate your success. Each item included represents an important element in the armamentarium of any person's success. However, these tips are not all-encompassing, and many of them require you to practice them so as to acquire efficienices in doing so. There are certainly other people who may have additional tips that can augment your success, and for this reason, I have included a list of books and references at the end of this book that you might wish to access for additional information and perspectives. Likewise, because your life experiences are different than mine, you will have additional perspectives on what it takes for *you* to personally be successful, which in turn you will be able to communicate to others as one of your contributions to giving back to others. As such, I invite you to e-mail me and post to my Facebook, Twitter, LinkedIn, and website any positive words of wisdom, advice, guidance, and success tips for which you believe others could benefit.

I wish you the best of success and I wish that you reach your full potential in this life.

CHAPTER 14

A Special Message to the Parents and Providers (Students, This Chapter Is a Must read for You Too)

Parents, providers and caregivers, you are to be greatly commended for the dedication, sacrifices, love, and nurturing you have provided to your children so that they are in the position they now find themselves, poised to step out into the world to pursue their dreams and goals to become the future leaders of this nation and the world. You have stressed to your child that his or her opportunities for successes in life will exponentially become amplified by them achieving a strong and well-rounded education. Most importantly, you have infused within your child a love of learning. You have provided your child with the tools necessary for them to learn, including teaching them effective time management skills. Moreover, you have helped them develop into responsible, respectful, and self-confident young adults; and through good times and difficult times, you have been out there in front cheering them on and also behind the scenes helping facilitate their forward progress, even when they not have even been aware of your presence. You have helped instill within your student the strong work ethic, stamina, determination, grit, and ethical principles that will guide them in their decision-making abilities for the rest of their lives. You have done all these things and more, and

I realize that many of the lessons for success that I have highlighted in this book you more than likely have already voiced to your child. However, if your kids are anything like my kids, they are not always receptive to messaging from their parents and providers, and they, often, are more readily willing to "hear" messages of advice from someone other than their parents and providers. I'm sure this is as frustrating for you as it is for me, but that's how it goes. When my kids were younger, parents and providers of kids older than mine would commonly warn me that when my kids got older, they would not want to listen to what I had to say, and I often didn't believe these other parents and providers because I thought for my kids it would be different. Perhaps your kids still heed your advice.

Regardless, if you were responsible for getting this book into the hands of your young adult, I thank you. Also, I thank you for taking time to read this book and for reinforcing within your student the lessons contained in this book. My goal in writing this book was and remains to assist you in getting through to your children, as early as possible in their lives, regarding some important lessons that will serve to benefit them and help them navigate the long and often arduous journey, which I know you know awaits them.

This book *will* help empower your student to reach their full potential by helping keep them on track, by helping them anticipate and plan for pitfalls and challenges awaiting them, and by helping them understand proactively how to formulate and conduct crucial conversations, confrontations, and strategies necessary to confront obstacles and difficult people. This book while not spoon-feeding or detracting from the life experiences your student needs to experience for himself or herself, I have no doubt will to the contrary exponentially help accelerate and expedite the knowledge and self-awareness they will need to soar to new heights. This book will ultimately benefit your students for the rest of their lives. This book will provide your student with, many years ahead of when they might have otherwise learned the hard way, the critical information and skill sets necessary for them to succeed.

Oh, the Places You'll Go by Dr. Seuss

When your children are little, you as their parent understand the importance of allowing your child to dream. Likewise, even as they enter and complete high school and begin and complete their college education, please don't kill their dreams. Instead, encourage them to continue to pursue their dreams. Encourage them to dream big and to reach for the stars. Serve as jet fuel for their excitement to learn. Reinforce within your student that with proper preparation, work ethic, and planning, they have the potential to accomplish their goals to be whatever it is they dream to be. I recall reading the Dr. Seuss book *Oh, the Places You'll Go* to my four kids when they were young. If you have never read this book or don't remember it, I encourage you to read it, because it serves as a reminder of the power you as a parent or caregiver have in stimulating and empowering your child to aspire to greatness. I am gifting this book to each of my kids upon their high school and/or college graduations to serve as a reminder of just how far they have come in life and to encourage them to continuously strive for even greater successes, because successful people know that the journey to achieve great accomplishments never ends. *The Cat in the Hat* book can also serve to remind your student of his or her responsibility to, in turn, play the role of *the Cat in the Hat* character and serve as a mentor and inspiration in helping encourage and guide others to succeed as well.

Daughter Meredith with the Dr. Seuss book I
gifted her for high school graduation

Don't Dictate, but Support Their Career Choice

Always support your students. Don't dictate to them what area of study they must pursue; rather, help them make informed decisions about selecting their desired career path; and once they make their career path decision, help, advise, encourage, and support them on their journey. Also, please don't attempt to force upon them which college they must attend. Understandably, financial constraints my severely limit your student's choices of colleges. If this is the case, please have a critical conversation with your student and make informed collaborative decisions with your child as to which colleges they can financially afford to attend. Remember, where your child attends college, what they study, and what career path they seek are matters that are critical to your child's happiness. It is critical that your student finds a work career in which they are going to be happy doing, because it is their life, not yours, and in many cases they may be working in this area for the next forty years of their life.

So in helping students select their college of choice and their career paths, you as a parent sometimes may find it necessary to remind your child where their current strengths lie and also remind them of their attributes that have contributed to their current-day successes. You can and do have a right to constructively recommend ways in which your student might be able to work to overcome particular areas of weaknesses or deficits (which they, their teachers, you, or others may have noticed), but simultaneously, in doing so, offer solutions to assist your student and reinforce to him or her that you are not being critical of them.

Sometimes, you may find it better to choose a teacher or counselor to offer such advice to your student, depending upon the personality of your child and your relationship with them. It is true that at different ages, your student may react to you differently than they did when they were younger, and they may not always receive your input as constructive despite your best attempts and despite the fact that you have your student's best interests at heart. This is frustrating, but unfortunately true, and something you will need to learn how to navigate for the benefit of your child. Students, the sooner you learn that your parents and providers do have your bests interests at heart, the better off you will be and the more advantages in life you will truly possess.

So what are some ways in which you as a parent can provide an atmosphere of, upon observing your student, being able to voice your observations and concerns to your student for the purpose of offering solutions to help make them more well-rounded and improve whatever deficits they may have and, additionally, to enhance further their strengths? Such solutions rest on your ability as a parent to make your student understand that you love them and want what is best for them and that you are supportive of their dreams. As your student grows and matures, the ways in which you must approach this may vary but is an ongoing process. With this being recognized and established, one of the first steps you must take in order to be able to assist in helping mold your student into a more well-rounded individual includes you, as a parent, identifying your students learning styles, study habits, and strengths. You do this by being both an active and a passive participant in your student's education throughout their school years, pre-K throughout high school, and into college. Taking both an active and a passive role in your child's education is not incompatible but essential. This is a balancing act that you as a parent must learn how to do. You, in many cases, must actively step in to assist your student; and as they advance in years, even though active in attending parent-teacher conferences and school events, etc., as a parent, it is essential that you transform your role into that of more of a supporter, mentor, and advisor who allows your student to figure things out on their own.

However, in the case of your child having difficulty in a particular class or with a particular subject matter, you as a parent should actively conduct research to identify potential tutors and ancillary educational programs and learning materials to augment their education. A starting point is for you and your child to meet with your child's teacher(s) and guidance counselor (if necessary) to pinpoint areas and gain clarification regarding areas where your child might be struggling. One very important note here is that you as a parent should seek ancillary educational resources and educational materials and meet with your student's teachers and counselors even in situations where your student is excelling. This is a technique that many parents and providers don't consider. We did this with our children on many occasions, even in situations to enhance their strengths in areas that they already excelled. I recall enrolling our children in extracurricular math classes and bringing home brainteasers and extra math workbooks when they were in elementary school. Their eyes would light up when they received such educational and fun resources. Things like this greatly enhanced their self-esteem, which then served to even further enhance their desires to excel.

Similarly, you can provide your students with extra educational opportunities and advantages even when they are older in high school. Enroll them in SAT and ACT preparation courses to help prepare them for these important college entry examinations. But please don't overdo these things. You don't want to burn your child out, and you need to recognize that your child does need to focus also on their classroom assignments and that they also do need some downtime to rest their minds and to socialize with their friends. When I was coming up, we didn't have access to opportunities to enroll in SAT and ACT preparation courses; however, my parents and providers always stressed the importance of education as did my aunt Mildred Faye, who was a schoolteacher in Indianapolis, Indiana. I recall her, knowing that I excelled in Latin class in high school, bringing me some Latin flash cards to further enhance my abilities and interests. I was very moved, and her doing this even gave me more fire and intensity to live up to her expectations for me to excel in Latin. Likewise, she and many of my other relatives, parents, providers, family, and friends, in a positive way, often reinforced their belief in me that I had the stuff to become a doctor. I say that they did it in a positive manner because their doing so did not make me feel obligated to pursue a career in medicine should I decide to change career choices.

Parents and providers: Talk with Your Students and Be Actively Engaged in Their Schools

While your kids are in school, including high school, talk to them and ask them questions about what they are studying. You may not necessarily understand the physics or chemistry that they are studying; nevertheless, inquire of them what they are studying because this demonstrates to them that you care and are interested in their education. Students are different, of course, and many may not want to be bothered in speaking with you about classes. To this day, I remember my father often when I got home from school asking me, "What did you do at school today?" And I remember often saying to him, "Nothing," and I recall him saying, "You must have done something. You couldn't have done nothing all day in school." LOL. I guess I should have not been surprised by the fact that as my kids entered high school and even the middle school, they normally said nothing to me also when I asked them what they did in school that day, which brings up another important point. *Always* attend your kid's school's parent-teacher conferences and school open houses. Doing so gives you an opportunity to firsthand meet and speak with your student's teachers to learn what is being taught in class and what their teachers are expecting them to be learning and doing. When you attend your student's open house curriculum evening and parent-teacher conferences, be proactive and ask the teacher to give you a list, in advance, of the reading materials your student will be expected to read that quarter or semester, and then you as a parent be proactive in obtaining these books in advance. What's more, attending these school conferences shows your children that you do care about their education and that you place their education as priority number one.

What I found that my kids really appreciated was when their mother and I would leave a parents and providers note in their desk at school indicating that we had visited their classroom and that we were proud of their work. Even when your kids are in college, I highly recommend that you make every effort possible to attend their college family weekend. I have found out doing so makes your student feel very proud to have their parents and providers come visit them, and it gives you an additional opportunity to check on them to see if they need anything for their dorm room, etc. It gives you a chance to also take them out to a nice dinner and to meet many of their college friends. One thing I have noticed is that many of the students whose parents and providers or families did not attend their college family weekend did feel and look disappointed that their parents and providers were not there. Of course, not all college students care if their parents and providers visit or don't express that they care, but believe me, it is important to most college students to have their parents, providers and family visit them at college and great memories are made during such events. Colleges actually go to great lengths to plan out fun and active events for parents, providers and families to enjoy during family weekends. I advise you to look online months in advance to find out which weekend is the college family weekend event so that you will have time to take off from work if necessary and make travel and lodging plans, because hotel rooms during college family weekends usually fill up quite early. "It isn't difficult to do it if you know how to do it."

Similarly, please attend your student's college orientation and attend the orientation sessions for parents and providers. Purchase and proudly wear your student's college shirts and hats with their college's name and logo and even college mascot. Place one of their college sticker placards on your car window or bumper. Fly their college flag outside of your home. Send them letters and e-mails and texts periodically to let them know you are proud of them. These small things show your students that you are proud of them and remind them that you support them. Send them care packages of healthy snacks for their college finals week. Join and become an active parent member of their college or university parent-teacher organization and even join and be as active as you have time to be in their college parent support groups. Whenever possible even in college if your student is in sports or in band or choir, please attend as many of their sporting, band, or choir concerts as you can. These points I cannot stress enough because doing these things only serves to keep your student inspired and further motivated to continue to perform to the best of their abilities. Remember, no matter how old is your student, it is still important that your student know you are proud of them.

Parents and providers, an important tip that I highly recommend for both students and parents and providers to implement is to keep a running, ongoing record of your student's accomplishments and activities. You will use this list to help facilitate your student in creating their resume, and this resume will go a long way in assisting teachers and high school counselors in preparing college recommendation letters on behalf of your student. Trust me, your child's high school advisor and teachers have loads of students for whom they have to write letters of recommendation for college entry as well as for awards and scholarships, and there is no way they are going to remember everything about your child when they go to prepare their college entry and scholarship recommendation letters. You can greatly assist them prepare their letters that will allow them to highlight important information about your student that will make their letters standout rather than the counselors simply reciting your student's high school academic record. At my kids' high school, the counselors actually request that parents and providers provide them what they call a parent brag sheet. Your ability to provide your student's counselor and teachers with an impactful parent brag sheet will be greatly enhanced if you keep an ongoing record of your child's accomplishments rather than try to rush to remember what to include at the last minute. Trust me, "It isn't difficult to do it if you know how to do it." And I just told you how to do it. So do it. LOL.

Parents and Providers: Learn with Your Students

So what are some additional points of information and several questions you should consider and ask yourself and be honest with yourself as your child is preparing to take their journey to success? Students, do you know how your parents and providers will be affected by your going off to college? Parents and providers or students, do you suffer from separation anxiety? It happens. I have friends who have suffered from separation anxiety when their kids went off to college. If this is you, I advise that you seek counseling well in advance of your child leaving for college because you don't want your separation anxiety to negatively stress out your child or even become an influence as to where your child decides to go to college. It's not fair to your student. Don't be ashamed of having separation anxiety. My point here is that if this is you, please don't be in denial. Admit it and seek professional help so that when the time comes for your student to go off to college, you will be capable of accepting it and dealing with it. Your child will have enough to worry about with moving to college, making new friends, dealing with their roommate, professors, and classes. I'm sorry for being so blunt here, but you as a parent don't want your student worrying about your separation anxiety. They have serious work to do in college. It is not taboo to see a psychologist to help you manage your separation anxiety. Make sense?

What are some of the ways in which you as a parent or caregiver can stay involved and remain connected with your student when they are away at college? Well, parents and providers, I encourage you to learn along with your student whatever it is that they are into and studying at college, for example, chess, music, history, foreign language, art, or acting. As an aside, no matter at what level of school your students are in—grade school, middle school, high school, or college—parents and providers, the secret to your being of maximal assistance to helping facilitate your student's journey is for you, yourself, to a certain extent (in moderation) step into the shoes of your child. This will allow you to have a better feel for what it is your student is experiencing. Also, students, it is imperative that you recognize that in some situations, just as it will take you time to get acclimated and comfortable being at college living away from the people you love, in turn it may take a while for your parents and providers to get used to you, their child, being off to college, especially if you are the first child from the family to go away to college. Be sensitive to this. Don't just go off to college and act as if your parents and providers don't matter anymore. Students, don't be selfish. Maintain lines of open communication with your parents and providers and family while you are off to college. One way in which to facilitate ongoing connection with your parents and providers and siblings who are still at home is to expose and communicate back to your parents and providers, siblings, and family some of your interesting experiences in college and to inform them about some of the subject matter you are learning and discussing in your college classes. Examples include encouraging your parents, providers and other family members to learn chess if you yourself are a chess player in college or develop an appreciation of Chinese art if you are taking a Chinese art class. You could even visit your local art museum with your parents, providers and siblings when you are back home on break and point out to them some interesting facts you learned about Chinese art. Students, invite your parent(s) to participate on a mission trip that you are going on with your college.

My daughter Sarah invited her mother, who is a physician, to join her and her college classmates on a mission trip to Central America where she served as the mission trip physician. Other things we also did for our daughter Sarah was to sponsor one of the outings of her College of William & Mary Wind Ensemble when they performed in Philadelphia, and we helped support our daughter's wind ensemble fundraising efforts for their UK tour. There are a multitude of ways in which you too can remain connected with your student while they are away at college, and ways in which to do so that in no way result in your becoming overbearing or intrusive. The extent to which your student will wish you as parents and providers to be involved will vary according to your student's personality and the dynamics of the family. However, students, I do seriously encourage that you do allow your parents and providers opportunities to remain engaged and involved in some of your college activities, even if it is only to invite them to visit you at school to watch you perform in your college band or observe you play a few games for your college sports team, even if an intramural team, take a jog across campus with you, take you out to a nice restaurant in your college town, etc. Be creative in ways in which to remain connected to your family. Students and parents and providers, "It is not difficult to do it if you know how to do it."

Parents and Providers' Role in the College Search, Seeking Financial Aid, and Financial Concerns and Stressors

Parents and providers, be involved in a supportive role in your student's college search. I say be involved in a supportive role in differentiation from filling out their college applications (that's not at all ethical) or mandating where your student should attend college. Assist your children in obtaining information about prospective colleges and have discussions with them early with respect to limitations where they might be able to go based upon the family's financial situation. Be honest with your student as they need to know early what the family financial situation is. But actively and *proactively* help your student search for potential financial aid and scholarship opportunities. Importantly, please sit down with your student to complete the FAFSA application as early in their high school career as possible. The FAFSA is the Free Application for Federal Student Aid and is a document whereby families provide the federal government with their family financial and tax return information to allow the federal government to determine how much federal aid your student is eligible to receive for their upcoming year in college. The application has to be completed each year your student is enrolled in college, and the first time filling it out is time-consuming; however, you'll be glad to know that subsequent FAFSA applications for your student allow options for automatically populating the FAFSA application with the family's prior year's financial and tax return and demographic information. Of note, the automatic importing options for some reason never worked when we completed each of our four kids FAFSA applications, but hopefully it will be functional and work for you. Register your child early with a FAFSA account. Your student and you as parents and providers will receive separate accounts and passwords. Write down the passwords and save them for easy future access.

Speak with your high school and college counselors about other federally funded and state aid and other sources of potential funding. It is your student's counselor's and high school financial aid assistant's job to assist you and your student and inform you of these opportunities, but you must take the onus also upon yourself to be proactive and don't exclusively rely upon others to do your homework and research about seeking funding for college. Parents and providers, you have the right to do so, and I strongly recommend that you and your child jointly meet with your child's high school counselor and high school scholarship/college financial aid advisors to obtain as much information as you can about college aid. If your student knows what area of study they will be pursing in college, search the Web and other resources through your school to find out about scholarship opportunities that are specifically available for students wanting to study that particular subject in college.

However, when it comes to actually writing the scholarship applications or writing the college entry essays, parents and providers, do not do the writing for your student. You can proofread their essays and applications for spelling errors and grammar, and you can even offer them advice, but do not write the essay for them. This is unethical and not in the best interests of your student to do so. English teachers in most high schools these days, in class, assist students in construction of their college application essays and scholarship essays. The various types of financial aid your student may be offered include merit-based scholarships, financial (need-based) scholarships, grants and/or loans, and college campus work study options. I, as an undergraduate student as well as a medical student, held down work-study jobs, from being a residence hall desk monitor to being a chemistry lab technician as an undergraduate student to working at the Northwestern University Student Health Center when I was a senior medical student. These work-study jobs not only require the student to carefully budget their time but also in many respects offer your student a chance to learn certain skills. Speak with funding sources to determine which forms of aid, specifically, your student will need to repay to the government or other funding source following their formal completion of college. Also, make sure both you and your student fully understand in detail information regarding expectations, schedules, and requirements regarding repayment of student loans, both principal and interest.

Of particular note, there are some scholarships or grants that stipulate that the student recipient provide some specific type of service upon graduation, such as working in an underserved area or returning to work in the city that provided the funding. Read, know, and understand the fine print and details prior to accepting a particular award so that you know what the expectations are of you should you accept the award. In addition, if your student is considering enrolling in the armed forces as a way to pay for their college education, you as a parent need to and should be actively involved and actively present in all conversations with the armed services representatives as there may be specific stipulations regarding what type of study in college your student will be allowed to pursue while in the armed forces. I have heard stories—I cannot attest to their authenticity—of students who claimed they were promised by their armed forces college recruiter one thing only to realize, after the fact, that their understanding of the agreement was not exactly what they thought it was or believe they were accurately informed of the details by the recruiter. Parents and providers and students, do not be intimidated by a recruiter who tells you that the parent cannot be present and involved in the decision-making process, because this is not true. The same applies to you, students, who are being recruited to play college sports. The armed forces are an excellent choice for receiving college funding for some students, but may not be the best route to take for everyone. Parents and providers, you and your student must educate yourselves thoroughly before deciding to take a particular route. Always, always, always explore alternative routes that may be more efficacious to your student.

As a parent of four children who have graduated high school and with my two oldest children having already now graduated college, I, myself, have seen and witnessed firsthand many of the challenges and stressors that our children experience and must endure. Such challenges are great sources of stress for high school students who strive to achieve high academic performance and consist of pressures to perform well in school and stressors that dramatically escalate and peak during their junior year in high school. The junior year of high school represents the time period when high school students are under a tremendous amount of stress not only due to day-to-day academic classroom challenges but also as a result of pressures to perform well on standardized college entrance examinations (the SAT test with or without writing and SAT Subject Tests and/or the ACT test with or without writing) given during their junior year. Other stressors include pressures mounting (expectations, pride, ego, and self-esteem), which they have placed upon themselves and others have also placed upon them in applying to (meeting many deadlines) and getting accepted into college, that is, the college of their choice.

Let's face it. Not only are your students stressed from their schoolwork, but also, to complicate matters, they are stressed of course many times with their social situations at school, let alone with reality setting in that they will soon be leaving home to go off to college and with the pressures that accompany all these thoughts, concerns, and matters. They are starting to get emotional about leaving close friends from high school and unsure of whether they will meet good friends in college. In addition, many students start to wonder how they will be paying for the college they want to attend. Stress is abounding from all sides. Through all of what is going on in their heads, your students need your love, support, and understanding. Parents and providers, if you have not done so, read the section I wrote earlier in this chapter on separation anxiety and what also follows next. You need to remain a strong rock for your student.

Parents and providers: It Is Normal for You to Miss Your Student while They Are Away at School. But Don't Be Selfish. Let Them Soar

I do remember when I applied to Northwestern University and received my acceptance letter. I was lying on my bed when I heard my mother showing my father my acceptance letter. I heard my father say, "But he'll never come back with all that culture up there in Chicago." My mother responded to my father, "let him go." My parents and providers had not intended on me to hear this conversation, but I do confess that hearing my father's concerns that if I left home to go far away to college that I would never return to live in New Castle, Indiana, made me feel as if I was abandoning my family by wanting to go the four hours away to college. At that point in time going to college nearly 300 miles away from home was considered very far, especially for our family dynamic. My parents and providers had no experience with driving this far from home, especially in the big city traffic of Chicago. This is of course not what my father wanted me to feel and he was very proud of my acceptance into Northwestern. More recently, a student I mentored was accepted, with a full ride, into a highly prestigious national university many hours away from home. However, the student's parents and providers insisted that the student attend a university closer to home because they said they would miss their child; and so this student elected to turn down the full-ride scholarship from the prestigious national university to attend a closer college which was a highly respected university that also offered the student a full-ride scholarship but that the student was not as excited to attend. Again, I understand that the decision as to where a student will go to college is a student-parent decision and dynamic. But parents and providers, please try to suspend your rationale for trying to encourage where they go just on the fact that you will miss them. Parents and providers, I am speaking about these accounts to please encourage you to not restrict or hold back your students from spreading their wings and branching out into the big world that is out there for them to discover. Of course, if there are significant financial barriers which prohibit your student from selecting one college over the other, of course, that is another scenario to where you will need to speak with your student and be candid with them and explain to them the financial limitations that might prevent them from attending a more expensive and/or distant college. All I am saying is when finances are not the limiting factor as to where your child attends college and there are no other legitimate reasons as to why your student cannot attend a particular university which they have been accepted into and desire to go, please do not let your personal selfishness that you will miss them to prevent them from attending the best college they can attend and wish to attend. Modern communication, such as cell phones and smartphone technology and social media such as Facebook, Facebook Live, and FaceTime, allow parents, providers and their students to stay connected much more easily that when I was away from home in college. Back then, students didn't have a telephone in their dorm room. I had to use the phone downstairs in the dormitory lobby to call my parents and providers once weekly usually on Sunday evenings. They were excited to hear from me and I was excited to hear their voices. Whenever they tried to call me, again, we did not have cell phones, someone in the lobby had to hear the phone ring, answer it and then be willing to go find whoever the phone call was for to tell them they had a telephone call. So, I am sure we all agree that staying in touch with your student even when they are off to college is really not that difficult to do these days. "It isn't difficult to do it if you know how to do it."

Parents, providers and students, stay connected despite external pressures to separate you and your student. Maintain open communication

Now, parents and providers, with having had each of my four kids already attend college orientations, I have made some significant startling observations as to how, in my opinion, at some but not all colleges, many college orientation administrative staff, very actively, proactively, deliberately, and intentionally, in direct language at some college orientations and through other communications they have with your matriculating college students, physically and emotionally go to extreme efforts and spend much energy and dedicated planning to separate and place distances between students and their parents and providers. I've seen it firsthand when my son and I attended his college orientation. I must say that I was appalled and, yes, actually offended by the fact that many of the college administrators running his orientation actively spoke with the matriculating students about how their parents and providers should just get into their cars and leave the orientation and how because they were now eighteen years old, they don't have to show their parents and providers their grades and that their parents and providers had no rights to access any of their college grade reports, etc. And yes, I get that college students at the age of eighteen are young adults, and I understand that students must sign consent forms in order for their parents and providers to see any of their academic records, and in the case of even a medical emergency, parents and providers have no legal rights to even know anything that is going on medically with their students. I get all of these legal details. Trust me, I really do.

However, my point that I have clearly emphasized throughout this book to students reading this book is that they are where they are today in large part because of you, parents and providers, and the willing sacrifices, love, advice, role modeling, and mentoring you have provided them their whole life. For these reasons, I believe the colleges should leave it up to the parents, providers and their college students to determine whether the student will show the parents and providers their reports cards. To me, this is a family decision, and dynamic and college administrators should stop actively trying to undermine parents, providers and stop attempting to negatively influence the students to not share information with their parents and providers. It is one thing to inform students that they legally have the option to conceal information; however, the fervor with which I witnessed some of these college administrators go to actively place peer pressure upon the students to conceal information from their parents and providers to me was degrading, disgusting, and insulting and overly intrusive.

Parents and providers, given the fact that colleges do actively engage in mind control over your students (in some cases, not all cases, don't get me wrong), I want you to be aware of this phenomenon earlier rather than later so that you will be able to respond accordingly and take actions to establish open communication between you and your student prior to them attending their college orientation sessions and prior to them receiving such pressures from corresponding college administrators. Sometimes, sadly, even high school teachers and counselors, often in a joking but nevertheless destructive manner, start exerting pressure on students to hide information from their parents and providers. Again, students do need and require an opportunity to mature; my point here is that in my opinion, parents and providers and students, you should resist external influences from interfering between student and parent communication. Students and parents and providers, please do not allow college administrators and others to attempt to shame you if you wish to continue to communicate freely with one another. That decision is between you and your student. Of course, as your student matures, as I am sure you understand completely, your student will become more autonomous of which you will be proud to see happen. This is not to say that you and your student cannot continue to maintain open communication, which I believe will be greatly beneficial to both student and parent. Students, maintain open communication with your parents, providers and family. Remember, as have stated, your parents and providers have amassed a wealth of knowledge in many areas that they wish to share with you. Parents, I am not implying that you should be helicopter parents and providers, which is a term often used by college administrators to try to shame and lampoon parents and providers who maintain active communication with their students. Your students do need to learn how to manage their schedules, interact one on one with their college counselors and professors, and meet and interact and work with other students. You already know this. I am just saying from my experiences, some college administrators indeed do go out of their way to place thick and high barriers between the parents, providers and their student.

Parents, inform your student about their personal medical history and the family medical history, and discuss advanced directives and organ donation wishes

Another word to both parents, providers and students-parents, before your kids go off to college, and preferably as early as possible, make sure your student is fully aware of any medical problems or medical history he or she may have as well as what the family medical history is, both sides. For example, let them know if diabetes runs in the family. Let them know at early ages, for example, if there are other particular medical issues that run in the family, such as sickle cell trait or disease, hypertension, degenerative neurological disease, hypertension, or kidney disease. This is not meant to scare your kids but to alert them that there are conditions that run in your family that they should be aware of as they grow older. Speak to your student about their opinions and wishes regarding organ donation and what would be their own end-of-life decisions should an unfortunate tragic medical situation arise that you as their parents and providers need to act upon on their behalf if they do not have the capacity to make decisions on their own. Additionally, inform all of your children of your personal wishes regarding organ donation and your end-of-life decisions. Your students, as they finish high school and are college students, are young adults and you need to and should know of their end-of-live wishes (advanced directives and power of healthcare decision choices); and they, in turn, need to and should know of your wishes. Speak with them. Have a family discussion so that should an unfortunate occurrence happen, you (and they) will be informed to make the decisions that you (or they) would have wanted.

Stress, Anxiety, Depression, and Substance Abuse Can Happen even to Your Students

Parents, if you see something, say something. Don't ignore it.

On a serious note, visiting your student at college will give you an opportunity as a parent to also see where your child is living and how they are living. In some situations, visiting your student at college will also provide you with an opportunity to allow your student to tell you about or for you to identify, unhealthy situations in which they may be engaged. I recently heard a very sad story about one of my daughter's friends from elementary school through high school who excitedly went to the East Coast to attend the college of her choice, but she became psychologically traumatized by her assigned college roommate, so much so that my daughter's friend for weeks had been essentially living in the dormitory lounge and sleeping on couches, hardly eating, and hardly sleeping and was distressed. Her mother did not learn of the magnitude of what was happening until she visited her daughter and was shocked to see the bags under her student's eyes and the weight she had lost. The student's mother went to the school's administration and forced them to switch her daughter to a new dormitory room, whereas prior to the mother visiting and seeing for herself the dire situation, the administration completely blew off (paid no attention) to the student's multiple requests to change rooms. (Please read the section in this book regarding attempting to select a compatible roommate prior to matriculating to college.) This underscores how important it is for you, parents and providers, to pay periodic visits to your child at college so you can see for yourself where they are living and how they appear physically and emotionally to be holding up away at college.

Students, be open and honest with your parents and providers. They can't be of help to you if you are encountering serious situations if you are not honest and forthright with them. As I note in the situation with my daughter's friend, it is unfortunately common, but true, that some college administrators will not pay any attention or heed to complaints and concerns of college students. Students, even though you are young adults, you still sometimes do need your parents and providers to intervene on your behalf. You are not a failure nor should you feel embarrassed to have to bring your parents and providers into a particular situation about which you might be suffering at school. Parents, this important success tip is also for you to understand that at times you may need to step up and help your student solve and confront certain situations at their college. Again, unfortunate but true, sometimes parents and providers need to remind college administrators that they, through payment of their tuition, are ultimately paying for the college administrator's salaries. Of course, the best approach is for your student to attempt to solve the situation themselves, and if you as parents and providers need to get involved, the best approach is an amicable, nonconfrontational approach in interacting with college officials. If that approach is not effective, then at times you may have to escalate to going to higher levels of administration at your student's college, including going to the college president.

Another beneficial reason as to why it is important for you as a parent to visit your student at college is, for example, if you see in their room loads of empty beer cans and hard liquor or cigarette butts or joints or bongs, you should as a parent speak up and inquire about what you are seeing. I understand fully that college students do drink, but I also understand as a parent and as a physician that you as a parent have a responsibility to say something if you see or feel that your student may be excessively drinking alcohol or if you suspect they might be using illicit drugs or even abusing prescription medications. Similarly, keep an eye out for changes in behavior of your student and look for signs of stress, distress, anxiety, or depression. You should in no way consider that you're opening your eyes and observing your child's surroundings is an act of spying on them or not trusting them. I, as a physician, can tell you that some behaviors exhibited by both students and adults of any age represent an avenue and way in which a person may be crying out for you or someone to take notice of their situation and their way in which to nonverbally cry out for your or someone's help and assistance. Should you see such signs, parents and providers, do not be afraid to speak up and tell your student of your concerns and clearly stress to them in no uncertain terms that you are there for them and that you will facilitate them getting counseling if you or they feel it is necessary. You, as a parent, may hopefully have a great deal of insight as to whether professional counseling is warranted, even if your student does not consider it necessary.

If you feel that your child is overly stressed or depressed (to the point that they may consider doing harm to themselves), you as a parent have an obligation to proactively assist (or even insist) them in seeking professional assistance in the form of either professional private behavioral healthcare services, the school health service, or spiritual advisors or other avenues. Don't think your student is immune to the pressures of college that stem from the rigorous academics and competition they are facing in college, from the social pressures they face, and even maybe from even just being homesick. I was at times homesick when I was away at college. Students, there is nothing for you to be ashamed of because you may be homesick. Additionally, should your student need to take time off from school to go back home for a while, that is, a few days, a week, a quarter, or semester, then you as a parent should support their decision and encourage them to do so and stress to them that this is not a sign of weakness or failure on their part. If it is the case where your student needs to take time away from school to where they will be missing several classes or withdraw from school for a leave of absence, both you and your student should jointly approach the school administration to make them aware of the situation. Trust me, your student will not be the only student doing this, and there should be no shame associated with your student needing to take extended time off from college. In addition, importantly, you and your student should speak with the financial aid department at your student's college to determine how your student taking time away from college may impact financial packages in the form of financial aid and scholarships.

I recall when I was a surgical intern at New York University Medical Center, this is after I had completed medical school, I called my father almost in tears and told him that I wanted to quit. I was sleep deprived and alone in a big city and distressed from the abusive practices that I had to endure back in those days in the NYU surgery residency, and all I wanted to do at that point was to go home and see my family. I vividly recall my father saying to me, "Son, if you want to come home, that's okay. We love you, and if you feel you need to come home, that's okay." As I've expressed in this book, my parents and providers in no way encouraged any of their children to be quitters. My parents and providers themselves our entire lives were living examples to my siblings and to me as to how to persevere in life. But sometimes there does come a point in life when your student may need to take a break and return home to reset. This is not a knee-jerk reaction that your student should make, and I am not telling you to encourage your student to quit what it is they are doing just because the going gets tough. Nevertheless, you as a parent should be able to identify best, as you know your child better than anyone else, how they are coping and whether they need to take some time off from their studies. In the case of my father telling me that I had an option to return home, he did not immediately present this to me as an option. He told me this only after I had repeatedly called him over several weeks to months during the initial stages of my internship to relate to him my level of distress. I had lost, for example, thirty pounds during my first month of internship. The very fact that my father told me that I had an option to quit in fact served to give me that much more needed strength to preserver and endure the physical and mental abuse that surgical interns commonly had to endure at that time, especially in that particular surgical program, which was known for abusing its interns and residents. Relax, current national laws do not allow residency directors and hospitals to allow their interns and residents to work more than eighty hours per week. I was working sometimes 140 hours or more per week and taking in-house (in hospital) call every other night to every third night for six years straight, often being sleep deprived causing me many times to even hallucinate on the job while taking care of patients and even while standing in the operating room holding retractors. Again, those of you, students, seeking to go into the medical professions, relax, because current law no longer allow for this type of abuse to medical students, interns, and residents.

Lastly, a plea to you, students—maintain open communications with your parents and providers because they possess great wisdom, the sooner of which you recognize, the sooner from which you will greatly benefit.

Some Final Words of Advice, Inspiration, and Encouragement

Look for inspiration in nature, for example, the onset of spring, flowers, birds, baby chicks, the smell of springtime, and budding leaves on trees. Notice the smiles on the faces of others. Find and create things to look forward to. Create special occasions. Invite and encourage your parents, providers and family to visit you at school on parents and providers/family weekend.

Read inspirational poems and quotes and ponder their meaning. Read books and muses. Listen to music that inspires, motivates, stimulates, and energizes you and helps your creative spirit and helps you dream and think big.

Reach for the stars. Do dream. Innovate and invent. Don't be afraid to fail. Don't let the fear of failure prevent you from trying new things.

Listen to your body; know what time of day that your body and mind best respond to study and what time of day your body best responds to exercise and what time of day your body best responds to rest. Prof. Harold Zimmack reinforced this.

Parents and students,

I invite you to contact me via e-mail or social media to provide to me feedback on your opinions of this book and how you and your student have received the success tips and messages contained within this book. Please inform me as to how you believe this book may have, even in some small way, benefited you. Also, students (and parents and providers) please do give me status updates as to your (or your student's) progress toward success. Also, please recommend this book to other students, parents and providers.

Sincerely,

Charles S. Modlin Jr., MD, MBA
E-mail: Contact@DrModlinMD.com
Twitter: @CharlesModlinMD
Website: DrModlinMD.com
Facebook: https://www.facebook.
com/DrCharlesModlinBooks

CHAPTER 15

A Special Tribute to My Parents, Charles S. Modlin Sr. and Grace Hampton Modlin

This chapter about my parents is my honor and tribute to them for the love and guidance they provided me so that I would have opportunities they never had. Even though they have now both passed away, they both continue to serve as my strong source of guidance and inspiration. I would be greatly honored, proud, and happy if you, the reader of this book, would take the time to read this chapter about my parents to learn more about them. By your reading this chapter, I am confident that you will further develop a better understanding and appreciation of the importance of my success tip that you should and must always remember from whence you came as being a truly powerful and potent success tip and one the most important success tips for you to assimilate into your character.

Charles S. Modlin Sr. pictured with his four National Senior Games Association Record Setting Gold Medals (set in 2005 in Pittsburgh, Pennsylvania, for men eighty years of age and older for the 100-, 200-, and 400-meter runs and the long jump). Please Google Charles Modlin National Senior Games to read more about his track and field accomplishments.
Go to the following Internet link to hear inspirational interview of eighty-year-old Charles Modlin Sr., National Senior Games Association Track and Field Champion on Growing Bolder Radio Show: https://www.growingbolder.com/charles-modlin-3365/

Charles Modlin Sr., long jumping at the
National Senior Games Competition

Charles Stanley Modlin Sr., age eighty-five, surrounded by his family, passed away in Ohio at 5:45 a.m., August 13, 2010, after a long illness. He was born in New Castle, Indiana, on October 27, 1924, the son of Wayman and Mary Modlin and the oldest of two siblings, the late Twilla (Bassett) and Gerald (Buddy) Modlin. He grew up during difficult times and lived through the Great Depression and endured the laws and hardships of segregation. Charles, nevertheless, endured these hardships. He was a good student in school and always remained very physically active. He stated that the challenges he encountered during his childhood enabled him to develop an immense sense of civic responsibility and pride in his work. He readily recounts how the strict discipline administered by his father and teachers no doubt was essential to his personal development and ability to perform tasks during his life. He fondly remembered "how society used to band together to assist one another through hard times." Such a sense of civic duty and pride is what motivated Charles for years to voluntarily pick up trash off Broad Street and volunteer at the New Castle Senior Center and serve as a minor league baseball coach, among other things. Charles stated that the countless hours he spent with and learning from the "older" generation were critical to his development. He credits the older generation with imparting within him his sense of civic responsibility to feel obligated to helping the now "younger generation." "The best teacher is at the foot of an old person," he always said. He credits one of his most memorable and valuable learning experiences to have been his inclusion as the youngest member in the African American singing group called the Rose City All-Male Chorus, which included his father.

During his junior year in high school, at the age of seventeen, Charles' sense of obligation to his country and family led him to leave high school to join the US Navy to serve his country (1943–1950) where he said he "learned to become a servant." And he became well-known for serving and helping people throughout New Castle for the sixty years. In recognition of his service to his community and country, in 2003, Charles was the first World War II veteran in Indiana to be honored and awarded by the Veterans Administration with his high school diploma and New Castle Chrysler High School recognized him by allowing him to march with the 2003 graduating class. Mr. Leach, former New Castle High School principal, saluted him during the ceremony.

Charles married Grace Hampton in 1952 and was married to her for fifty-one years until her death in 2003. He was employed by World Bestos (Firestone) and Dana Corporation (from where he retired in 1989) and in the 1970s also worked for former mayor Gary Marcum and the city as superintendent of the water department and later superintendent of the parks department. He became very active in his church, Wiley United Methodist Church, eventually serving as lay leader and special assistant to the senior pastor, remaining active in the church for over for forty years. He and his wife became parents to four children, who survive him, Deborah Edmunds (Houston, Texas), Rebecca Modlin (Panama City, Florida), Dr. Charles Jr. (Shaker Heights, Ohio), and Pamela Modlin (New Castle) and was also stepfather to Beverly Williams (New Castle). He was always very active in the lives of his children and grandchildren. He is survived by his nine grandchildren and five great-grandchildren, including Charles III, his namesake.

Charles has been a role model to his family and community and was noted throughout his community, statewide, and nationally for being a very successful champion and proponent of the National Senior Games Association. He was featured in *AARP the Magazine*, *Indianapolis Monthly*, Cleveland Clinic Minority Men's *Mentor*, National Senior Games newspaper, Louisville *Courier-Journal*, New Castle *Courier-Times*, Muncie *Star Press*, the national radio show *Growing Bolder*, and *Who's Who in Black Indianapolis* by *Minority Access* as well as a number of other local and national media venues. The city of New Castle proclaimed August 9, 1999, as a special day in his honor, "Charles Modlin Day." Posted at the city limits marking New Castle for years were prominently displayed signs reading, "Home and Birthplace of United States Gold Medalist Senior Olympian Charles Modlin Sr." (As an aside, I, Dr. Charles Modlin, remain still very disappointed that a subsequent mayor of New Castle had the two signs removed because the mayor said they were an eyesore.) Charles had been recognized also by Indiana senator Richard Lugar, former president George Bush, President Obama, and National Senior Games president Phil Godfrey, among others, for his accomplishments as a National Senior Games record holder and champion.

Among the great honors received by Charles, aside from his family, the two of which he was most proud, was when Riley School principal Richard Bouslog dedicated and then rededicated and set the plaque for the Modlin Mile Fitness Track at Riley Elementary School in New Castle, Indiana, in his honor. Also, he cherished having been invited to march in cap and gown to deliver the invocation and benediction during his son's Northwestern University Medical School graduation in 1987. (That was one of my greatest moments in my life also, to witness my father do this at my medical school graduation. Thank you, Dr. Jack Snarr and Northwestern University Feinberg School of Medicine for giving him the opportunity to do this. I am forever grateful to you because of this.)

Charles participated in the Senior Games Association since 1990, at the age of sixty-five, when he first competed in the Area 6 Council on Aging in Muncie, Indiana, and won four gold medals. He since won countless gold medals in the areas of cycling but especially track and field. His first national event was in 1993 when the games were in Baton Rouge, Louisiana, where he won a gold medal in the 100-yard dash at the age of sixty-eight.

Since then he competed in every national event except one due to an injury. During the National Games in 2005 in Pittsburgh, Pennsylvania, he won gold medals in four track and field events, each representing National Senior Games Association (NSGA) records for his division of males over the age of eighty, and each of these records still stand at the writing of this book. In the 100-meter run, he set a record time of 15.65 seconds, a record of 32.97 seconds for the 200-meter run, a record of 1 minute and 17.59 seconds in the 400-meter run, and a record jump of 12.5.75 feet in the long jump. He was an inspiration to everyone he encountered, said former mayor of New Castle Tom Nipp, and countless others in New Castle, as well as in Shaker Heights and in the Cleveland, Ohio, where his son, Charles Modlin Jr., MD, resides.

Charles Modlin's last national competition was in San Francisco in August 2009, and he last competed in the Indiana Senior Games this June 2010. Neither colon nor prostate cancer diverted his attention away from his major mission in life, which was to promote for all people the importance of health through exercise and physical activity. The way he hoped to achieve his goals were through his activities as a senior athlete in the NSGA. His mission was not only to win gold for himself but also to more importantly continue to be an inspiration for both the younger and older generations. He said, "My whole purpose in life now is to promote to seniors the National Senior Games Association because the National Senior Games Association exists to make the lives of senior citizens better." Charles Modlin Sr. dedicated himself to encouraging everyone to remain or become active so that they can live healthier, more productive lives. He said that if everyone would go out and watch someone eighty years old running, then they themselves might realize that "if they can do it, what's wrong with me?"

The Modlin Mile Fitness Track Plaque, Riley Elementary
School, New Castle, Indiana (dedicated 2007)

Charles' favorite Bible verse, which he readily quoted and had embroidered on his running suits, was Isaiah 40:31, which reads, "But they that wait upon the Lord shall renew their strength; they shall mount up with wings as eagles, they shall run, and not be weary; and they shall walk, and not faint." Trust in the Lord, he always said along with "God is Love" and "Jesus, I want to be with you." "There is nothing in this world that is work, it is all exercise."

Daddy, we will always love you and you will be missed. You have finished your exercise here on earth; you ran the good race. We know you are now up there with Jesus, doing what you love to do, running for Jesus.

In 2003, Charles set up a scholarship fund for the Henry County Community Foundation in the names of his deceased wife, a retired New Castle Elementary School teacher, and himself, the Charles and Grace Modlin Fund, to assist high school students entering the educational profession as well as to fund teacher projects at Greenstreet Elementary School and now exists to also assist teachers at Riley Elementary School since Greenstreet School's closing.

Thank you, Dr. Barbara Messinger-Rapport,
Cleveland Clinic geriatrician of my father

The "3" Charles Modlins, Dr. Charles Modlin Jr., Charles Modlin Sr., Charles Modlin III

Grace Hampton Modlin, pictured with husband Charles Modlin Sr.

Grace Modlin, high school graduation picture

Grace Modlin, elementary schoolteacher photo

Grace Modlin, seventy-eight, entered eternal life after a long illness on February 27, 2003. She graduated from Anderson High School in 1943 and attended Butler University from 1943 to 1944 on a scholarship. She worked at the Finance Center in Indianapolis. She was a role model to her family and many others. Grace was active in the NAACP and civil rights movement in the 1950s–1960s and had been active in Wiley United Methodist Church and the Socialites Club. She was very dynamic in the lives of her children. Grace was a Brownie troop leader and organized troop outings to Chicago. She also served as president of the Weir Elementary School PTO. She was a member of the New Castle Chrysler High School Band Boosters organization from 1974 to 1979. She was tireless in trying to make a better life for her family, and she set high academic standards for her children to uphold. As a mother of five, she returned to college in 1968 (at the age of forty-four) and received her bachelor's degree in education from Ball State University in 1972 and her master's degree in 1973. She was a student teacher at Weir Elementary School and, following graduation, became the first black teacher of a main classroom in the history of the New Castle Community Schools.

Grace Modlin Ball State University master's degree graduation picture with children and grandson Richard Williams. Charles Modlin pictured in center

Grace Modlin with Grandson Trey

Grace was given much support from Alton Taylor, her first principal, and Ray Pavey, school administrator. She taught at Weir Elementary from 1971 to 1975, Hernly Elementary from 1975 to 1976, Westwood Elementary from 1976 to 1979, and Greenstreet Elementary from 1979 to 1988, retiring in 1989. She was born on August 15, 1924, in Carthage, a daughter of the late Walter and Clara Hampton.

At the time of her death, she was survived by her husband of fifty-one years, Charles, whom she married on January 1, 1952; a sister, Mildred Faye Varnado of Indianapolis; five children, Beverly of Muncie, Deborah of Houston, Rebecca and Pamela, both of New Castle; and Dr. Charles Jr. of Shaker Heights, Ohio; nine grandchildren, Richard, Ryan and Randall Williams, Jeniece Edwards, Sean Edmunds and Charles III, Sarah and Meredith Modlin, and her namesake Hannah Grace Modlin; four great-grandchildren, Emma and Anna Williams, Ashton, and Trinity; a nephew Kevin and great-nieces, Mia, Kristen, and Gina; and several cousins.

She was preceded in death by her parents and a sister, Virginia Hampton.

Appendix A

The Road Not Taken
(Robert Frost)

The Road Not Taken
Two roads diverged in a yellow wood,
And sorry I could not travel both
And be one traveler, long I stood
And looked down one as far as I could
To where it bent in the undergrowth;

Then took the other, as just as fair,
And having perhaps the better claim,
Because it was grassy and wanted wear;
Though as for that the passing there
Had worn them really about the same,

And both that morning equally lay
In leaves no step had trodden black.
Oh, I kept the first for another day!
Yet knowing how way leads on to way,
I doubted if I should ever come back.

I shall be telling this with a sigh
Somewhere ages and ages hence:
Two roads diverged in a wood, and I—
I took the one less traveled by,
And that has made all the difference.

Finally, brethren, whatsoever things are true, whatsoever things are honest, whatsoever things are just, whatsoever things are pure, whatsoever things are lovely, whatsoever things are of good report; if there be any virtue, and if there be any praise, think on these things. (Philippians 4:8 KJV))

But they that wait upon the Lord shall renew their strength; they shall mount up with wings as eagles; they shall run, and not be weary; and they shall walk, and not faint. (Isaiah 40:31 KJV)

Footprints in the Sand
(Mary Stevenson)

One night I dreamed I was walking along the beach with the Lord.
Many scenes from my life flashed across the sky.
In each scene I noticed footprints in the sand.
Sometimes there were two sets of footprints,
other times there were one set of footprints.

This bothered me because I noticed
that during the low periods of my life,
when I was suffering from
anguish, sorrow or defeat,
I could see only one set of footprints.

So I said to the Lord,
"You promised me Lord,
that if I followed you,
you would walk with me always.
But I have noticed that during
the most trying periods of my life
there have only been one
set of footprints in the sand.

Why, when I needed you most,
you have not been there for me?"

The Lord replied,
"The times when you have
seen only one set of footprints,
is when I carried you."

Self-imposed segregation at Northwestern leads to misunderstanding between races

Perspective

Charles Modlin

Premeds: too intense for their own good?

The Daily Northwestern

Two *Daily Northwestern* newspaper articles written by Charles Modlin as an undergraduate student at Northwestern University

NORTHWESTERN UNIVERSITY
CHICAGO ILLINOIS 60611

THE MEDICAL SCHOOL
Ward Memorial Building
303 E. Chicago Ave.

29 March 1983

Charles S. Modlin, Jr.
3217 Beechwood Dr.
New Castle, IN   47362

Dear Mr. Modlin:

A committee of faculty and students has carefully studied your credentials and has concluded that you should be recommended for acceptance
into our student body. On this basis, I am pleased to offer you a place
in the class entering Northwestern University Medical School in September, 1983.

We believe that you will find here an opportunity to build a firm
foundation for a career in medicine and that the associations you will
form with your fellow students and with faculty will be of lasting
pleasure and benefit.

You of course understand that acceptance here must necessarily be
contingent upon successful completion of all requirements for admission.
A statement of the further action you should take in response to this
notification is enclosed.

It is with personal pleasure that I welcome you as a prospective member
of the Northwestern Medical community.

Sincerely,

James E. Eckenhoff

James E. Eckenhoff, M.D.
Dean

JEE/caw

THE McGAW MEDICAL CENTER OF NORTHWESTERN UNIVERSITY

Charles Modlin's acceptance letter to
Northwestern University Medical School

The Daily Northwestern tuition article

Dr. Charles Modlin, Cleveland Greater Partnership MLK
Community Service Award at Severance Hall, Pictured
with Cleveland Mayor Honorable Frank Jackson

In Memorium (2015), special thanks to my friend and research
associate Carlumandarlo Zaramo, PhD
"Secrets of My Success" article 5662
"Role Models" article about CSM

"Heroes Are Everywhere" article about Dr. Modlin's Father
Dr. Charles Modlin, Cleveland Black Professional
Charitable Foundation, Black Professional of
the Year Award Recognition (2015)

Plain Dealer articles
Validated National Stress, Depression, and Anxiety Survey

Appendix B

Special and Meaningful Photos

Father Charles Modlin, Sr. Pictured with National
Senior Games Association Athletic Victor Medals

Dr. Charles Modlin pictured as Chief Urology
Resident at New York University

Dr. Charles Modllin pictured in State of Ohio Covid-19 Minority
Strike Force More Than A Mask Public Service Announcement

Father Charles Modlin Sr. and Dr. Modlin pictured with
Former United States Congressman Honorable Louis Stokes

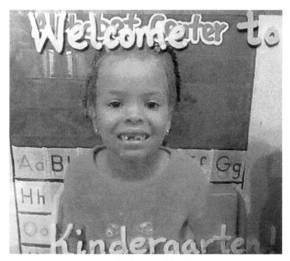

Daughter, Meredith Modlin, kindergarten,
Orientation Day Picture

Meredith, first day of kindergarten

Meredith with Dad,
Shaker Heights High
School Graduation

Meredith playing
euphonium in Shaker
Heights High School
Marching Band

Daughter, Meredith Modlin, freshman, drop-
off day, Northwestern University (2018)

Meredith, freshman, Northwestern, move-in
day with Mother and Father

Sarah Modlin, graduation (May 2018),
College of William & Mary

Sarah, freshman, move-in day, College of William & Mary

Sarah in College of William & Mary, Biology Lab,
where she performed research and taught

Sarah playing clarinet with College of
William & Mary Wind Ensemble

Modlin children with their grandfather, Charles Modlin
Sr., at Senior Games event in Canton, Ohio

In Rome, Italy, with Meredith on High School Latin trip (2017)

Hannah Grace Modlin

With Hannah and Meredith

Hannah in Miami University (2017) Fashion Show

Hannah singing in Shaker Heights High
School Musical Production

Hannah, research student at Cleveland Clinic,
Office of Civic Education Initiatives

Hannah Modlin, Shaker Heights High School Graduation

Hannah's first day of kindergarten. Meredith
happy thinking she is starting school too.

With Sarah and Hannah

Hannah and Meredith at Lake Erie Beach

As urology resident with son Trey (Charles Modlin III)

Shaker Heights' Trey Modlin gets chess scholarship from Texas Tech

Posted Jul 20, 2011

181
shares

By Brian Lavrich, Sun News

Trey Modlin gets chess scholarship to Texas Tech University

Son Trey Modlin, National Chess Champion,
president Texas Tech Chess Team

Trey sporting cowboy hat in Texas

Trey Modlin graduates from Texas Tech University

Congratulating son Trey upon his graduation from
Texas Tech University in Lubbock, Texas

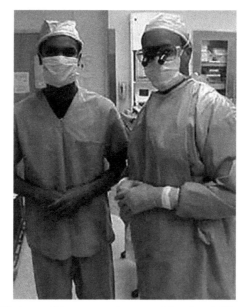

With son Trey researching at Cleveland Clinic

Hannah and Meredith at Summer Day Camp

Modlin family

With sisters Deborah Modlin Edmunds and Rebecca Modlin

Sister Deborah Edmunds, Master's Degree
in Clinical Psychology Graduation

Sister Rebecca Modlin with Daddy

Mentor, Stuart Flechner, MD

Dr. Anthony Shaffer, Former Chairman Urology
Northwestern Med School and Mentor to Dr. Modlin

Dr. James Holland, my Urology Mentor
at Northwestern Medical School

Dr. John T Grayhack, Northwestern University Urology
Chairman and my mentor in medical school

Dr. Charles Modlin delivers commencement address
to John Hay High School (May 2014).

Dr. Charles Modlin, commencement speaker, with
2014 John Hay High School Graduating Class

2010 Annual Cleveland Clinic Minority
Men's Health Fair participants

Dr. Charles Modlin, Cleveland Clinic First Annual
Minority Men's Health Fair Flyer (2003)

Dr. Charles Modlin pictured with United Pastors in Mission

Rev. Dr. E. Theophilus Caviness with Dr. Charles Modlin

Dr. Charles Modlin, pictured with former US
congressman Hon. Louis Stokes (2006)

Charles Modlin, Northwestern University, senior photo

Charles Modlin, freshman, Medical Student Food Service photo

Charles Modlin, MD, chief urological surgery resident
(1993), New York University Medical Center

Morning Spark in partnership with Tropicana. "7
Things Successful People Do Every Morning That
Help Them Become Their Best Selves All Day Long."
They just happen to be seven things you can totally do
too. Presented by Tropicana (January 10, 2017)

Dr. Charles Modlin with Ohio Commission
on Minority Health Leadership Award

Back Visiting my first apartment in New York
City when I was a surgery intern

Sunrise in Shaker Heights over Horseshoe Lake,
photograph by Dr. Charles Modlin

Dr. Charles Modlin, success tips summary and additional thank-you recognitions

With childhood and lifelong friend Mr. Jeffrey Ayers

With NU classmate and friend Henry Pak

Friend and Minority Men's Health Center
volunteer Mr. Robert Allen

With friend and fellow NYU urology resident Dr. Yan Wolfson

At Chicago DuSable Museum of African
American History, remembering the sacrifices
of those who helped pave the way for me

Honored to have been invited to play my trumpet on the
College of William & Mary United Kingdom Tour, 2018
(Thank you, Sarah, for asking the conductor and thank you,
Conductor Dr. Richard Marcus and Wind Ensemble students)

Charles Modlin (pictured in last row trumpet
section) in eighth grade jazz band, Parkview Junior
High School, Director, Mr. Larry Ash

My mother taught me one of my favorite past
times, growing bountiful tomatoes

Dr. Andrew C. Novick, chairman, Department
Urology, Cleveland Clinic

With friend and Hollywood actor Bill Cobbs

Charles Modlin, receiving undergraduate college
diploma from Northwestern University, June 1983

First Childhood Home of Dr. Charles Modlin,
South 23rd Street, New Castle, Indiana

Robert Fairchild, Ph.D. Cleveland Clinic
Lerner Research Institute, Mentor

Cleveland Clinic 17th Annual Minority Men's Health Fair,
April 2019. Pictured with Cleveland Clinic CEO Dr. Tom
Mihaljevic and hundreds of health fair volunteers who come
together to make the health fair successful year after year

Photograph at Cleveland Clinic Minority Men's Health Fair

Comedian Mr. George Wallace at Minority Men's Health Center

Dr. Charles Modlin with Mr. Stedman
Graham and son Trey Modlin

Dr. Modlin with TV Personality & News
Anchor Mr. Geraldo Rivera

Dr. Modlin mentoring medical students

Pictured with Mr. Robert Allen, Minority
Men's Health Center Advocate

Health Fair Photo, Nurse with "Arms Around" Patient

Men attending the Cleveland Clinic Minority Men's Health Fair

Men attending Cleveland Clinic Minority Men's Health Fair

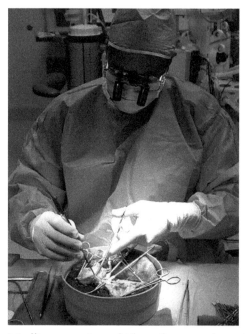

Dr. Modlin preparing a kidney for transplantation

After a long day of surgery

After another successful Minority Men's Health Fair

Dr. Modlin receiving Dr. Martin Luther King, Jr. Community Service Award from Cleveland Mayor Frank Jackson at MLK Concert with Cleveland Orchestra at Severance Hall

Beautiful Flowers at Northwestern University, Evanston, Illinois

At beautiful Lake Michigan beach

At my 30th Birthday Party with Dr. Bert Fichman, who was my first intern partner at NYU Medical Center. I am grateful to him_

At my 30th Birthday Party with fellow Urology
Residents Drs. Richard Maggio and David Cohen

Aunt Mildred Faye with mother Grace
Modlin, both were school teachers

Charles & Sheryl Modlin 1992

Daughter Sarah Modlin with Uncle Buddy

Dr. Modlin with Father, Charles Sr., Charles III (Trey), Sarah and Dr. Sheryl Modlin at Heights Ed-Care Daycare Center Thanksgiving Celebration

Dr. Paul Caldron & Family, Northwestern University Medical School Clinical Medicine Rotation Mentor

In New York City with fellow Urology Resident Dr. Steven Yu

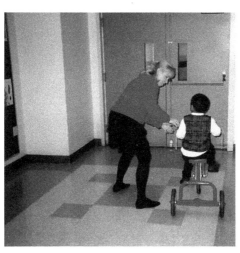

Son, Trey Modlin, with Preschool Teacher, Mrs. Lynn Hutter

With Nephrew Ryan William

With sister Beverly Williams

With sisters Beverely Williams and Rebecca Modlin,
Niece Jeniece Edwards and others at Thanksgiving

With sisters Beverly Williams, Rebecca Modlin, Nehew
Randall Williams, Niece Jeniece Edwards and others

Appendix C

Some Important Internet Links

- Trey Modlin speech. Google "Trey Modlin Woodbury Scholars" or at the following link: https://youtu.be/2xrlPYw8jVw
- Hear an inspirational interview of eighty-year-old Charles Modlin Sr., National Senior Games Association Track and Field Champion on Growing Bolder Radio Show (https://www.growingbolder.com/charles-modlin-3365/)
- "7 Things Successful People Do Every Morning That Help Them Become Their Best Selves All Day Long": https://aplus.com/a/successful-people-share-inspirational-morning-tips
- Dr. Charles Modlin tribute video: https://www.youtube.com/watch?v=ZGg0wGVnVpw
- Dr. Charles Modlin Cleveland Clinic professional short biography: https://www.youtube.com/watch?v=EZZck8QOjOg
- Cleveland Clinic Minority Men's Health Fair video: https://www.youtube.com/watch?v=SCwPYxzd4cA
- Dr. Charles Modlin, Northwestern University Alumnus Feature Article: https://www.weinberg.northwestern.edu/after-graduation/weinberg-magazine/fall-winter-2013/paths-fall-winter-2013/degree-paths-charles-modlin-83.html
- Dr. Charles Modlin at Cleveland Cavaliers discusses organ donation: https://www.youtube.com/watch?v=Hh_BV6GuzzU

- Dr. Charles Modlin *MD Magazine* article: https://www.mdmag.com/sap-partner/cleveland-clinic/charles-modlin-md-the-man-working-to-make-healthcare-care-about-black-men
- Up close National Kidney Foundation Highlight of Dr. Charles Modlin: https://www.kidney.org/newsletter/board-to-board/July2016/close-section-dr-charles-modlin
- Dr. Charles Modlin WKYC TV Minority Men's Health Fair Video: https://www.wkyc.com/video/home/dr-charles-modlin-the-cleveland-clinics-16th-annual-minority-mens-health-fair-41618/95-8097735

Dr. Modlin's additional important demonstrated inspirational leadership links to view:

- https://www.youtube.com/watch?v=Ak4ng4_uiu8
- https://www.youtube.com/watch?v=324d1_XKHWY
- http://www.crainscleveland.com/article/20150516/HEROES15/305179995/dr-charles-modlin-founder-and-director-minority-mens-health
- http://wviz.ideastream.org/programs/city-club-forum/unsung-heroes-behind-the-scenes-of-organ-eye-and-tissue-donation
- http://btn.com/2014/08/31/btn-livebigdr-modlin-leading-minority-doctors/
- http://www.cleveland.com/healthfit/index.ssf/2011/03/cleveland_clinic_doctor_expand.html
- http://fox8.com/tag/dr-charles-modlin/
- http://wtam.iheart.com/onair/mike-trivisonno-2339/triv-today-dr-charles-modlin-on-14621865/
- http://www.neighborhoodgrants.org/events/black-professionals-association-salute-dr-charles-modlin/
- http://www.diversityjournal.com/10510-the-cleveland-clinics-modlin-tackles-minority-health-disparities/

Appendix D

List of books, videos, and music that I myself found helpful and inspirational growing up and on my journey and/or I used to inspire my kids growing up. You and your parents may find some of these sources beneficial in your own ways.

- *Bringing Up Boys: Practical Advice and Encouragement for Those Shaping the Next Generation of Men* (James C. Dobson)
- *The Wealth Choice: Success Secrets of Black Millionaires* (Paperback) (Dennis Kimbro, June 3, 2014)
- *Paying for College Without Going Broke, 2018 Edition: How to Pay Less for College (College Admissions Guides)* (Paperback) (Kalman Chany, Princeton Review, September 19, 2017)
- *Filing the FAFSA, 2015–2016 Edition: The Edvisors Guide to Completing the Free Application for Federal Student Aid* (Mark Kantrowitz and David Levy, December 16, 2014)
- *Madame C. J. Walker (Life Skills Biographies)* (Katie Marsico, August 1, 2007)
- *The 100 Steps Necessary for Survival in America for People of Color* (Sam Chekwas)
- *Robert's Rules of Order in Action: How to Participate in Meetings with Confidence* (Randi Minetor, July 25, 2015)
- *Robert's Rules: QuickStart Guide—The Simplified Beginner's Guide to Robert's Rules of Order (Running Meetings, Corporate Governance)* (ClydeBank Business, March 5, 2016)

- *Reader's Digest Parenting Guide: What to Do when Kids Are Mean to Your (What to Do Parenting Guides)* (Paperback) (Elin McCoy, August 4, 1997)
- *How to Handle Bullies, Teasers and Other Meanies: A Book That Takes the Nuisance Out of Name Calling and Other Nonsense* (Paperback) (Kate Cohen-Posey, MS, LMHC, LMFT, November 1, 1995)
- *Dads and Daughters: How to Inspire, Understand, and Support Your Daughter* (Hardcover) (Joe Kelly, May 14, 2002)
- *How to Be a Ballerina* (VHS): Ziggie Bergman (director)
- *The Cricket in Times Square* Paperback (George Selden, September 15, 1970)
- *Raising a Thinking Child Workbook* (Myrna B. Shure and Theresa Foy Digeronimo)
- *Raising a Thinking Preteen: The "I Can Problem Solve" Program for 8- to 12-Year-Olds* (Myrna B. Shure)
- *Bridge to Terabithia* (Katherine Paterson [author] and Donna Diamond [illustrator])
- *The Making of a Woman Surgeon* (Elizabeth Morgan)
- *The Negro in Indiana before 1900: A Study of a Minority* (Emma Lou Thornbrough)
- *Rich Dad, Poor Dad: What the Rich Teach Their Kids About Money That the Poor and Middle Class Do Not!* (Robert T. Kiyosaki and Sharon L. Lechter)
- *Maurice Ashley Teaches Chess [CD]*
- *The 7 Habits of Highly Effective Teens* (Sean Covey)
- *The Traveler's Gift: Seven Decisions that Determine Personal Success* (Andy Andrews)
- *Chicken Soup for the African American Soul: Celebrating and Sharing Our Culture, One Story at a Time (Chicken Soup for the Soul)* Paperback (Jack Canfield, Mark Victor Hansen, Lisa Nichols, and Tom Joyner, September 14, 2004)
- *Sesame Street: Platinum All-Time Favorites* (audio CD)
- *Reallionaire: Nine Steps to Becoming Rich from the Inside Out* (Farrah Gray and Fran Harris)

- *Fleeing for Freedom: Stories of the Underground Railroad as Told by Levi Coffin and William Still George Hendrick*
- *Crucial Confrontations* (Paperback) (Kerry Patterson and Joseph Grenny)
- *The Secret: What Great Leaders Know and Do* (Hardcover) (Kenneth Blanchard and Mark E. Miller)
- *The One Minute Manager* (Ken Blanchard and Spencer Johnson)
- *Fierce Conversations: Achieving Success at Work and in Life One Conversation at a Time* (Susan Scott)
- *1001 Things Everyone Should Know About African American History* (Jeffrey C. Stewart)
- *Black Enterprise Guide to Starting Your Own Business (Black Enterprise Series)* (Wendy Beech)
- *From Brotherhood to Manhood: How Black Men Rescue Their Relationships and Dreams from the Invisibility Syndrome* (Hardcover) (Anderson J. Franklin, October 25, 2002)
- *Mastering the Art of War (Shambhala Dragon Editions)* (Hardcover) (Liang Zhuge et al.)
- *The Book of Leadership and Strategy: Lessons of the Chinese Masters* (Paperback) (Thomas Cleary)
- *The Art of War* (Sun Tzu)
- *The American Heritage Student Dictionary* [Hardcover] (American Heritage)
- *Then Darkness Fled: The Liberating Wisdom of Booker T. Washington (Leaders in Action)* (Stephen Mansfield)
- *Book of Virtues* [Hardcover] (William J. Bennett)
- *The Children's Book of Home and Family* (William J. Bennett, editor, and Michael Hague, illustrator)
- *Merriam-Webster's Spanish-English Dictionary* [Paperback] (Merriam-Webster, editor, and Eileen M. Haraty, preface)
- *Climbing Jacob's Ladder: The Enduring Legacies of African-American Families* (Andrew Billingsley)
- *Masters of Networking: Building Relationships for Your Pocketbook and Soul* (Ivan Misner)

- *Gifted Hands: The Ben Carson Story* (Paperback) (Ben Carson and Cecil Murphey)
- *The Big Picture* (Paperback) (Ben Carson and Gregg Lewis)
- *Think Big* (Hardcover) (Ben Carson and Cecil Murphey)
- *Community Organizing* (Meredith Minkler)
- *A Testament of Hope: The Essential Writings and Speeches of Martin Luther King Jr.* (Martin Luther King Jr.)
- *The Millionaire Next Door* (Thomas J. Stanley and William D. Danko)
- *Ten Commandments of Working in a Hostile Environment* (T. D. Jakes)
- *Blackonomic$: The Way to Psychological and Economic Freedom for African Americans* (James Clingman)
- *Losing the Race: Self-Sabotage in Black America* (Paperback) (John McWhorter)
- *Live Your Dreams* [Paperback] (Les Brown)
- *It's Not Over Until You Win: How to Become the Person You Always Wanted to Be No Matter What the Obstacle* (Les Brown)
- *Feed Your Kids Well: How to Help Your Child Lose Weight and Get Healthy* (Fred Pescatore, MD)
- *Podium Humor* (James C. Humes)
- *Public Speaking for Dummies* (Malcolm Kushner)
- *What Should I Do With My Life?: The True Story of People Who Answered the Ultimate Question* (Hardcover) (Po Bronson, December 24, 2002)
- *The Complete Idiot's Guide to Public Speaking* (2nd edition) (Laurie E. Rozakis)
- *Leadership for Dummies* (Marshall Loeb and Stephen Kindel)
- *Communicating Effectively for Dummies* (Marty Brounstein)
- *Eat, Drink, and Be Healthy: The Harvard Medical School Guide to Healthy Eating* (Walter C. Willett and P. J. Skerrett, contributor)

- *Helping Someone with Mental Illness: A Compassionate Guide for Family, Friends, and Caregivers* (first edition) (Rosalynn Carter and Susan Golant, MA)
- *There Is a Spiritual Solution to Every Problem* (Wayne W. Dyer)
- *Schoolhouse Rock!* (Grammar Rock), Jack Sheldon (actor)
- *Exiting Nirvana: A Daughter's Life with Autism* (Clara Claiborne Park and Oliver W. Sacks)
- *Raising Cain: Protecting the Emotional Life of Boys* (Ballantine Reader's Circle) (Daniel J. Kindlon et al.)
- *Helping the Child Who Doesn't Fit in* (Stephen Nowicki and Marshall P. Duke)
- *What Does It Mean to Me?* (Catherine Faherty et al.)
- *High-Functioning Individuals With Autism (Current Issues in Autism)* (Eric Schopler and Gary B. Mesibov, editors)
- *How to Defend Yourself in 3 Seconds (or Less!): Self-Defence Secrets You NEED to Know!* (Phil Pierce, April 12, 2013)
- *Roots* (Giftset) (Burton [primary contributor] et al.)
- Mozart, Beethoven, Brahms, and others
- Franz Joseph Haydn (composer)
- *Field of Dreams* (Phil Alden Robinson, director)
- "100 Masterpieces Vol 10: Top 10 of Classical Music 1894–1928" (Richard Strauss, composer)
- *Essentials of Wado-Ryu Karate* (Chris Thompson, primary contributor)
- Karate and Self-Defense
- "The Best of Andrew Lloyd Webber"
- The Starlite Orchestra
- *Mr. Magoo: The Collector's Edition* (Jim Backus, primary contributor)
- *Our Solar System* (Simon Seymour)
- *The 48 Laws of Power* (Robert Greene)
- *Black Pioneers of Science and Invention* (Louis Haber)
- *Secrets to Winning at Office Politics: How to Achieve Your Goals and Increase Your Influence at Work* (Marie G. McIntyre)

- *1001 Things Everyone Should Know About African American History* (Jeffrey C. Stewart)
- *Heroes, Gods and Monsters of the Greek Myths* (Bernard Evslin)
- *100 African Americans Who Shaped American History (100 Series)* (Chrisanne Beckner)
- *Hanging by a Thread: Survival Guide for Blacks in Corporate America* (Paperback) (Lisa Brown)
- *Talks to Teachers on Psychology and to Students on Some of Life's Ideals* (William James, Dodo Press)
- *How to Live on 24 Hours a Day: with The Human Machine (Dover Empower Your Life Series)* (Arnold Bennett)
- *Ultraprevention: The 6-Week Plan That Will Make You Healthy for Life* (Mark Hyman and Mark Liponis)
- *Social Determinants of Health: The Solid Facts* (Michael Marmot and Richard G. Wilkinson)
- *Steel Drivin' Man: John Henry, the Untold Story of an American Legend* (Scott Reynolds Nelson)
- *Influence: Science and Practice (5th Edition)* (Robert B. Cialdini)
- *Yes!: 50 Scientifically Proven Ways to Be Persuasive* (Noah J. Goldstein et al.)
- *Save the Males: Why Men Matter Why Women Should Care* (Kathleen Parker)
- *How to Choose a College Major, revised and updated edition* (Linda Landis Andrews)
- *The Sports Scholarships Insider's Guide* (Dion Wheeler)
- *The Real ACT Prep Guide: The Only Official Prep Guide from the Makers of the ACT (Real Act Prep Guide)* (ACT Inc. [author] and Wallie W. Hammond [editor])
- *Will Work for Fun: Three Simple Steps for Turning Any Hobby or Interest into Cash* (Alan R. Bechtold)
- *Fiske Guide to Colleges* (Paperback) (Edward B. Fiske)
- *100 Successful College Application Essays (Second Edition)* (Paperback) (Harvard Independent)

- *50 Successful Harvard Application Essays, Second Edition: What Worked for Them* (Staff of the Harvard Crimson, compiler)
- *Untangling the Ivy League (College Prowler)* (College Prowler [editor] and Marc Zawel [author])
- *How To Say It (R) to Boys* (Richard Heyman)
- *Athletic Scholarships for Dummies* (Paperback) (Pat Britz and Alexandra Powe Allred)
- *The New Dictionary of Thoughts: A Cyclopedia of Quotations* (Tryon Edwards)
- *Student Athlete Handbook for the 21st Century: A Guide to Recruiting, Scholarships, and Prepping for College* (Christine Grimes)
- *The Tipping Point: How Little Things Can Make a Big Difference* (Paperback) (Malcolm Gladwell)
- *The Emotional Intelligence Quick Book* [Hardcover] (Jean Travis Bradberry et al.)
- *Influence Without Authority (2nd Edition)* (Allan R. Cohen and David L. Bradford)
- *Influencer: The Power to Change Anything* (Kerry Patterson et al.)
- *2 of the 4-Hour Workweek: Escape 9-5, Live Anywhere, and Join the New Rich* (Timothy Ferriss)
- *The Power of Body Language* (Tonya Reiman)
- *Kaplan SAT Critical Reading Workbook* (Kaplan)
- *The 100+ Series Vocabulary in Context: 1500 Words Every Middle School Student Should Know* (Margaret Brinton)
- *The Middle School Survival Guide: How to Survive from the Day Elementary School Ends until the Second High School Begins* (Arlene Erlbach and Helen Flook)
- *Dream Real: A Top Sports Agent's Tips for Teens Serious About "Going Pro"* (Eugene W. Napoleon and Michael J D'Amato)
- *Ultimate High School Survival Guide (Peterson's Ultimate Guides)* (Peterson's)
- *1000 Most Important Words* (Norman W. Schur)

- *Becoming a Professional Life Coach: Lessons from the Institute of Life Coach Training* (Patrick Williams and Diane S. Menendez)
- *240 Vocabulary Words 6th Grade Kids Need to Know* (Linda Ward Beech)
- *I Read It, but I Don't Get It: Comprehension Strategies for Adolescent Readers* (Cris Tovani)
- *Read for Your Life: 11 Ways to Better Yourself Through Books* (Pat Williams and Peggy Matthews Rose)
- *Macbeth* (William Shakespeare)
- *Hamlet* (William Shakespeare)
- *The College Application Essay: Revised edition* (Sarah Myers McGinty)
- *Outlines & Highlights for The Earth and Its Peoples: A Global History, Brief Edition, Volume II: Since 1500* (Richard Bulliet, ISBN: 9780618992409)
- *Colleges That Change Lives: 40 Schools That Will Change the Way You Think About Colleges* (Loren Pope)
- *Power Ambition Glory: The Stunning Parallels between Great Leaders of the Ancient World and Today…and the Lessons You Can Learn* (Steve Forbes et al.)
- *Guns, Germs, and Steel: The Fates of Human Societies* (Jared Diamond)
- *The Art of Sacrifice in Chess* (Rudolf Spielmann)
- *Snakes in Suits: When Psychopaths Go to Work* (Paul Babiak and Robert D. Hare)
- *Accounting for Dummies* (John A. Tracy, CPA)
- *Complete MBA for Dummies* (Dr. Kathleen Allen and Peter Economy)
- *Reading Financial Reports for Dummies* (Lita Epstein)
- *Economics for Dummies* (Sean Masaki Flynn)
- *The Simple Solution to Rubik's Cube* (James G. Nourse)
- *Three Moves Ahead: What Chess Can Teach You About Business* (Bob Rice)
- *The Heart of Change: Real-Life Stories of How People Change Their Organizations* (John P. Kotter and Dan S. Cohen)

- *Our Iceberg Is Melting: Changing and Succeeding Under Any Conditions* (John Kotter et al.)
- *The Little Guide to Your Well-Read Life* (Steve Leveen)
- *Marketing Management: A Strategic Decision-Making Approach* (John Mullins et al.)
- *The Magic of Dialogue: Transforming Conflict into Cooperation* (Daniel Yankelovich)
- *Organizational Behavior: Key Concepts, Skills And Best Practices* (Angelo Kinicki and Robert Kreitner)
- *Freakonomics: A Rogue Economist Explores the Hidden Side of Everything (P. S.)* Steven D. Levitt and Stephen J. Dubner
- *Questions or My Father: Finding The Man Behind Your Dad* (Vincent Staniforth)
- *Plan to Win Bill Glass* (James E. McEachern)
- *How to Be Like Walt: Capturing the Disney Magic Every Day of Your Life* (Pat Williams and Jim Denney)
- *Making Peace with Your Parents* (Harold Bloomfield, MD, and Leonard Felder, PhD)
- *"Always Wear Clean Underwear!": And Other Ways Parents Say "I Love You"* (Marc Gellman and Debbie Tilley)
- *Ask Your Father: Fifty Things Your Father Should Have Told You But Probably Didn't* (Michael Powell)
- *Head First: The Biology of Hope and the Healing Power of the Human Spirit* (Norman Cousins)
- *Man's Search for Meaning* (Viktor E. Frankl)
- *Acing the College Application: How to Maximize Your Chances for Admission to the College of Your Choice* (Michele Hernandez)
- *What to Say When You Talk to Yourself* (Shad Helmstetter)
- *The Power of Focus: What the World's Greatest Achievers Know about The Secret of Financial Freedom and Success* (Jack Canfield et al.)
- *Turn Boring Orations Into Standing Ovations* (Pat Williams et al.)
- *Speed Reading for Professionals (Barron's Business Success Guides)* (H. Bernard Wechsler and Arthur Bell)

- *The Road Less Traveled, 25th Anniversary Edition: A New Psychology of Love, Traditional Values and Spiritual Growth* (M. Scott Peck)
- *How Life Imitates Chess: Making the Right Moves, from the Board to the Boardroom* (Garry Kasparov)
- *The Self-Improvement of Chess* (Mark Borders)
- *The Courage to Be* (Paul Tillich)
- *You've GOT to Read This Book!: 55 People Tell the Story of the Book That Changed Their Life* (Jack Canfield and Gay Hendricks)
- *How to Read People Like a Book: 50 Uncommon Tips You Need to Know (Succesful Living)* (Murray Oxman)
- *Letters to Young Black Men: Advice and Encouragement for a Difficult Journey* (Daniel Whyte III)
- *Northwestern University: The Campus Guide* (Jay Pridmore)
- *Life's Greatest Lessons: 20 Things That Matter* (Hal Urban)
- *We Proudly Hail: A Collection of Biographies of Famous Citizens of Shaker Heights* (Richard D. Klyver)
- *Cracking the AP World History Exam (College Test Preparation)* (the Princeton Review)
- *Every Day a Friday: How to Be Happier 7 Days a Week* (Joel Osteen)
- *Slideology: The Art and Science of Creating Great Presentations* (Nancy Duarte)
- *How to Think Like a Ceo: The 22 Vital Traits You Need to Be the Person at the Top* (D. A. Benton)
- *Condoleezza Rice: An American Life: A Biography* (Elisabeth Bumiller)
- CEO Priorities: Master the Art of Surviving at the Top Neil Giarratana
- *How to Think Like a CEO: The 22 Vital Traits You Need to Be the Person at the Top* (D. A. Benton)
- *Executive Presence: The Art of Commanding Respect Like a CEO* (Harrison Monarth)
- *Trump: The Art of the Deal* (Donald J. Trump and Tony Schwartz)

- *How to Drive Like a Maniac (Self-Hurt)* (Knock Knock)
- *What I Didn't Learn in Business School: How Strategy Works in the Real World* (Jay Barney and Trish Gorman Clifford)
- *Buy-In: Saving Your Good Idea from Getting Shot Down* (John P. Kotter)
- *Leading Change* (John P. Kotter)
- *Our Iceberg Is Melting: Changing and Succeeding Under Any Conditions* (John Kotter et al.)
- *The Unfinished Nation: A Concise History of the American People, Volume 1* (Alan Brinkley)
- *Barron's AP United States History* (Resnick M. A. and Eugene V.)
- *Ignite Your Creative Spark: 20 Ways to Fire up Your Imagination (The Power of One)* (Jordan Ayan)
- *The Best 167 Medical Schools, 2015 Edition (Graduate School Admissions Guides)* (Princeton Review)
- *Northwestern University* (Jack Mellott)
- *How to Be Pre-Med: A Harvard MD's Medical School Preparation Guide for Students and Parents* (Suzanne M. Miller)
- *The Art of Asking* (Amanda Palmer)
- *I Can See Clearly Now* (Dr. Wayne W)
- *Master Getting Things Done the David Allen Way with Evernote: Your 7-Day GTD Immediate Action Plan* (Dominic Wolff)
- *John T. Molloy's New Dress for Success* (Paperback, January 1, 1988)
- *New Women's Dress For Success* (John T. Molloy, December 1, 1996)
- *The Tycoons: How Andrew Carnegie, John D. Rockefeller, Jay Gould, and J. P. Morgan Invented the American Supereconomy* (Charles R. Morris)
- *Who Moved My Cheese?: An Amazing Way to Deal with Change in Your Work and in Your Life* (Spencer Johnson)
- *Race for Success: The Ten Best Business Opportunities for Blacks in America* (George C. Fraser)

- *Success Runs in Our Race: The Complete Guide to Effective Networking in the Black Community* (George C. Fraser)
- *The $100 Startup: Reinvent the Way You Make a Living, Do What You Love, and Create a New Future* (Chris Guillebeau)
- *5 of Daily Rituals* (Mason Currey)
- *Coach Wooden's Pyramid of Success* (Jay Carty)
- *The Leadership Secrets of Colin Powell* (Oren Harari)
- *It Worked for Me: In Life and Leadership* (Colin Powell)
- *The War of the Worlds* (H. G. Wells)
- *Surgery, Subspecialization & Science: a History of Urology at the Cleveland Clinic 1921–2008* (Dawson Bowles)
- *My Girl* (Anna Chlumsky, actress)
- *Grit: The Power of Passion and Perseverance* (Angela Duckworth)
- *The Pocket Stylist: Behind-the-Scenes Expertise from a Fashion Pro on Creating Your Own Look* (Kendall Farr)
- *The Healthy Habit Revolution: Create Better Habits In 5 Minutes A Day* (Derek Doepker)
- *Crossing the Thinnest Line: How Embracing Diversity—from the Office to the Oscars—Makes America Stronger* (Lauren Leader-Chivee)
- *Why You're Stuck: Your Guide To Finding Freedom From Any Of Life's Challenges* (Derek Doepker)
- *Magic of Impromptu Speaking: Create a Speech That Will Be Remembered for Years in Under 30 Seconds* (Andrii Sedniev)
- *How to Write an Impressive CV & Cover Letter: Includes a Cd With CV and Cover Letter Templates Plus Real-life Examples* (Tracey Whitmore)
- *The Complete Conversations with God* (Neale Donald Walsch)
- *MCAT Complete 7-Book Subject Review: Online + Book* (Kaplan Test Prep)
- *Into the Boardroom: How to Get Your First Seat on a Corporate Board* (D. K. Light)
- *The Checklist Manifesto: How to Get Things Right* (Atul Gawande)

- *SAT Premier 2017 with 5 Practice Tests: Online + Book* (Kaplan Test Prep)
- *Surviving the Freshman Year and Beyond: A College Academic Survival Kit* (Dr. Olutunde A. Ogunsunlade)
- ACT Premier 2016–2017 with 8 Practice Tests: Online + DVD + Book (Kaplan Test Prep)
- *Women's Health: Your Body, Your Hormones, Your Choices (Cleveland Clinic Guides)* (Holly L. Thacker, MD)
- *The Presentation Secrets of Steve Jobs: How to Be Insanely Great in Front of Any Audience* (Carmine Gallo)
- *Conversationally Speaking: Tested New Ways to Increase Your Personal and Social Effectiveness* (Alan Garner)
- *The Charisma Myth: How Anyone Can Master the Art and Science of Personal Magnetism* (Olivia Fox Cabane)
- *Lincoln on Leadership: Executive Strategies for Tough Times* (Donald T. Phillips)
- *Expect to Win: 10 Proven Strategies for Thriving in the Workplace* (Paperback) (Carla Harris, 2010)
- *Talk Like TED: The 9 Public-Speaking Secrets of the World's Top Minds* (Carmine Gallo)
- *TED Talks Storytelling: 23 Storytelling Techniques from the Best TED Talks* (Akash Karia)
- *The Battle for Room 314: My Year of Hope and Despair in a New York City High School* (Ed Boland)
- *The 5-Ingredient College Cookbook: Easy, Healthy Recipes for the Next Four Years & Beyond* (Pamela Ellgen)
- *1001 Things Every College Student Needs to Know: Like Buying Your Books Before Exams Start* (Harry H. Harrison Jr.)
- *If I Could Keep You Little* (Marianne Richmond)
- *1984 (Signet Classics)* (George Orwell)
- *The Wonderful Things You Will Be Martin* (Emily Winfield)
- *I Wish You More* (Amy Krouse Rosenthal)
- *The Things You Can See Only When You Slow Down: How to Be Calm and Mindful in a Fast-Paced World* (Haemin Sunim)

- *Summary—StrengthsFinder 2.0: By Tom Rath—A Chapter by Chapter Summary*
- *When Doctors Don't Listen: How to Avoid Misdiagnoses and Unnecessary Tests* (Leana Wen)
- *Make Your Bed: Little Things That Can Change Your Life And Maybe the World* (William H. McRaven)
- *Laugh Tactics: Master Conversational Humor and Be Funny On Command—Think Quick* (Patrick King)
- *Connect Instantly: 60 Seconds to Likability, Meaningful Connections, and Hitting* (Patrick King)
- *The Social Skills Guidebook: Manage Shyness, Improve Your Conversations, and Make Friends, Without Giving Up Who You Are* (Chris MacLeod MSW)
- *How to Talk to Anyone: 92 Little Tricks for Big Success in Relationships* (Leil Lowndes)
- *Conversation Tactics: Strategies to Command Social Situations (Book 3)* (Patrick Wittines King)
- *How to Be Successful by Being Yourself: The Surprising Truth About Turning Fear and Doubt into Confidence and Success* (David Taylor)
- *Remember It!: The Names of People You Meet, All of Your Passwords, Where You Left Your Keys, and Everything Else You Tend to Forget* (Nelson Dellis)
- *Team of Teams: New Rules of Engagement for a Complex World* (General Stanley McChrystal)
- *Oh, the Places You'll Go!* (Dr. Seuss)
- *8 to Great: How to Take Charge of Your Life and Make Positive Changes Using an 8-Step Breakthrough Process* (MK Mueller)
- *Eight Great Comedies: The Complete Texts of the World's Great Comedies from Ancient Times to the Twentieth Century* (Sylvan Barnet)
- *How to Tie a Tie: A Gentleman's Guide to Getting Dressed (How To Series) Flexibound* (Potter Gift, April 21, 2015)
- *Dress Casually for Success…For Men* (Paperback) (Mark Weber, September 1, 1996)

- *Emily Post's Etiquette, 19th Edition: Manners for Today* (Hardcover) (Lizzie Post and Daniel Post Senning, April 25, 2017)
- *You Can Win: A step by step tool for top achievers* (Paperback) (Shiv Khera, May 22, 2014)
- Webster's New World Dictionary, Fifth Edition (editors of Webster's New World College Dictionaries)
- *Essays That Worked for College Applications: 50 Essays that Helped Students Get into the Nation's Top Colleges* (Paperback) (Boykin Curry, Emily Angel Baer, and Brian Kasbar, July 29, 2003)
- *Best Colleges 2018: Find the Best Colleges for You!* (US News and World Report [author], Anne McGrath [editor], Brian Kelly [foreword], Robert J. Morse [contributor], Ned Johnson [contributor], Beth Howard [contributor], Arlene Weintraub [contributor], Elizabeth Gardner [contributor], Margaret Loftus [contributor], and Courtney Rubin [contributor])
- *Fiske Guide to Colleges 2019* (35th Edition) (Edward Fiske)
- *The Best 384 Colleges, 2019 Edition: In-Depth Profiles & Ranking Lists to Help Find the Right College For You (College Admissions Guides)* Kindle Edition (Robert Franek)

Items

- Large wooden dual-foot massager roller, relieves plantar fasciitis and foot/heel pain and reduces stress
- Acupressure and reflexology tool
- Sock ring holders

Additional Items for Students to Purchase

- Texas Instruments TI-89 Titanium Graphing Calculator Texas Instruments
- MayBron Gear Bike Cover: Waterproof Outdoor Bicycle Storage (Extra Heavy Duty 210D Oxford Fabric, Size L)

- BIKEHAND Bike Bicycle Floor Parking Rack Storage Stand
- Red LED Emergency Roadside Flares, Magnetic Base and Upright Stand: These Magnatek Red LED Beacons May Save Your Life
- 2 of AT-A-GLANCE DayMinder Weekly Pocket Planner, January–December (3 1/2" x 6–3/16", Black) (SK4800)
- InterUS Key Caps Tags (80 Pcs ID label tags with split ring, assorted colors with 10 round flat metal key ring)

Movie and Videos

- *Beaches* (Bette Midler)
- *The Dream Team* (Michael Keaton)
- "Put One Foot in Front of the Other" from 1970 Rankin/ Bass Christmas Special, "Santa Claus is Coming To Town"
- *Born Free* (James Hill, director)
- *Willy Wonka and the Chocolate Factory* (Julie Dawn Cole, actor)
- *Fed Up* (film documentary, 2014) by producer Stephanie Soechtig

Music that I Have Found Enjoyable and Stimulating for Myself and later for My Children Growing Up

I completely realize that your tastes in music will likely vary considerably from my tastes, given that I grew up in a different era than your students. However, classical music does transcend generations. Nevertheless, I include this partial list as an illustration as to the importance of music in helping me focus and relax and in contrast to stimulate and energize me during my success journey and to this day. I am sure you too have favorite music either to help you wind down or to invigorate you. I remind you to please refrain from listening to loud music either with or without headphones to avoid ear damage.

The following is only a partial listing:

- 1970s music
- 1980s music
- Michael Jackson
- Jackson 5
- Motown
- Stylistics
- Aerosmith
- Kiss
- The Beatles
- Paul McCartney and Wings
- James Brown
- Diana Ross
- Whitney Houston
- Natalie Cole
- Anita Baker
- Miles Davis
- Van Halen
- The Who
- Rocky Theme
- Led Zeppelin
- Journey
- Genesis
- Electric Light Orchestra (ELO)
- Styx
- The Police
- Elton John
- Amazing Grace Mahalia Jackson
- Ultimate Broadway Original Casts
- Piano by Candlelight
- The Carpenters
- Barry Manilow
- Christopher Cross
- Lionel Richie
- The Commodores

Music that stimulated and motivated my young kids:

- "So Big—Activity Songs for Little Ones" (Hap Palmer)
- "Rise and Shine" (Raffi)
- "Early Childhood Classics: Old Favorites with a New Twist" (Hap Palmer)

About the Author

Charles S. Modlin Jr., MD, MBA, son of the late Charles and Grace Modlin who inspired him to write this book, is Cleveland Clinic's first ever and only African American staff kidney transplant surgeon and is Cleveland Clinic's first ever African American staff urologist. At last count, he was recognized as being one of only approximately twenty or fewer black transplant surgeons in the entire country and the only one who is also a urologist. Dr. Modlin is also a nationally renowned innovative leader in addressing the elimination of health disparities in African Americans and is founder and director of Cleveland Clinic's Minority Men's Health Center and Health Fair that addresses the elimination of health disparities in men of color and has saved and improved the lives of thousands of men.

As a kidney transplant surgeon, Dr. Modlin is most proud of having participated with the team in the care of thousands of kidney transplant patients and is proud of personally having enhanced the lives of approximately five hundred patients for whom he has personally performed kidney transplants. Dr. Modlin is the first and only African American at Cleveland Clinic to date to serve as president of Cleveland Clinic's medical staff and is a proud and active member of Cleveland Clinic's board of governors, trustees, and board of directors.

He routinely mentors high school, college, graduate, medical, and nursing students to guide them on their career paths and also serves as a mentor to other Cleveland Clinic professional staff.

In 2011, Dr. Modlin was named by *the Atlanta Post* as one of the Top 21 Black Doctors in America. He proudly has been featured in *MD Magazine*, *Jet Magazine*, and *WebMD*.

Dr. Modlin has delivered commencement addresses and academic achievement speeches for high schools and colleges. He is now also authoring *the History of the Cleveland Clinic's Minority Men's Health Fair* book. He has been featured in the *Cleveland Plain Dealer* newspaper and was featured in the *Plain Dealer's* section of "the Secret of My Success." Dr. Modlin has been featured in *Who's Who in Black Cleveland* and was among a select few of Cleveland high-profile leaders featured in its inaugural issue as one of "Cleveland's Most Interesting Personalities."

Dr. Modlin graduated from Northwestern University in 1983 and from Northwestern University Feinberg School of Medical School in 1987 and was inducted into the AOA Honor Medical Society by Northwestern University Medical School. He is a very active alumnus.

Dr. Modlin's honors and recognitions are numerous and include several appointments to the Ohio Commission on Minority Health, the Northwestern University Presidential Alumni Medal in 2003, the highly prestigious Greater Cleveland Partnership Cleveland Orchestra MLK Community Service Award in 2007, the Northwestern University Medical School Inaugural Humanitarianism in Medicine Award, the Cleveland Clinic Bruce Hubbard Stewart Humanitarianism Award, and the highly prestigious Black Professional Association Professional of the Year recognition in 2015, becoming the first physician to receive this award in the more than thirty-five-year BPA existence.

Dr. Modlin welcomes your comments and communications.

Dr. Modlin is also available to book for speaking engagements, mentorships, board appointments, community activities, Diversity, Equity, Inclusion, Health Equity, Organizational Development, Process Improvement Consultations and More.

EMail: Contact@DrModlinMD.com
Twitter: @CharlesModlinMD
Website: DrModlinMD.com
Facebook: https://www.facebook.com/DrCharlesModlinBooks

Please be on the lookout for my upcoming future inspiring and informational books

CPSIA information can be obtained
at www.ICGtesting.com
Printed in the USA
BVHW021408010322
630322BV00011B/234